Pg. 9
* pg. 22 + 23

Kawaida and Questions of Life and Struggle
African American, Pan-African and Global Issues

(Kawaida)
Kah-wah-e-da

Also By the Author

Maat, The Moral Ideal in Ancient Egypt:
A Study in Classical African Ethics

Odu Ifa:
The Ethical Teachings

Introduction to Black Studies

Kwanzaa:
A Celebration of Family, Community and Culture

Handbook of Black Studies
(co-authored with Molefi Asante)

Selections from the Husia:
Sacred Wisdom of Ancient Egypt

The Book of Coming Forth By Day:
The Ethics of the Declarations of Innocence

Kawaida:
A Communitarian African Philosophy

The Million Man March/Day of Absence:
Mission Statement

The Ethics of Sharing:
Towards A New Collective Vocation and Public Philosophy

Essays on Struggle:
Position and Analysis

Maulana Karenga

Kawaida and Questions of Life and Struggle

African American, Pan-African and Global Issues

Sankore

University of Sankore Press
Los Angeles
2008

Sankore

University of Sankore Press
Los Angeles
2008

Kawaida and Questions of Life & Struggle:
African American, Pan-African and Global Issues

© 2008 by Maulana Karenga

Cover Design: Images & Illuminations
Cover Photo: Tiamoyo Karenga
Designed by: University of Sankore Press Collaborative

International Standard Book Number: 978-0-943412-29-0

Library of Congress Cataloguing-in-Publication Data

Karenga, Maulana.
  Kawaida and questions of life and struggle : African American, Pan-African, and Global Issues / Maulana Karenga.
     p. cm.
  Includes index.
  ISBN 978-0-943412-29-0 (alk. Paper)
  1. African Americans—Social conditions—1975- 2. African Americans—Ethnic identity. 3. African Americans—History. 4. African Americans—Biography. 5. African American leadership. 6. African American philosophy. 7. Pan-Africanism. 8. Black nationalism. 9. United States—Relations—Africa. 10. Africa—Relations—United States. I. Title.
  E185.615.K29 2007
  305.896'073—dc22

To

Us

that is to say,

Our people

and

Our organization

In memory of
our ancestors
always, who
paved the way

Asali
Cynthia
Rashidi
Ridley
Nalo
Nicole
2012

Nguzo Saba

The Seven Principles

Umoja

Kujichagulia

Ujima

Ujamaa

Nia

Kuumba

Imani

Umoja ▲ Unity
To strive for and maintain unity in the family, community, nation and race.

Kujichagulia ▲ Self-Determination
To define ourselves, name ourselves, create for ourselves
and speak for ourselves.

Ujima ▲ Collective Work and Responsibility
To build and maintain our community together and make our brother's
and sister's problems our problems and to solve them together.

Ujamaa ▲ Cooperative Economics
To build and maintain our own stores, shops and other businesses
and to profit from them together.

Nia ▲ Purpose
To make our collective vocation the building and developing of
our community in order to restore our people to their traditional greatness.

Kuumba ▲ Creativity
To do always as much as we can, in the way we can, in order to leave
our community more beautiful and beneficial than we inherited it.

Imani ▲ Faith
To believe with all our heart in our people, our parents, our teachers,
our leaders and the righteousness and victory of our struggle.

Dr. Maulana Karenga
Creator of Kwanzaa
©1965

University of Sankore Press, 3018 West 48th Street, Los Angeles, CA 90043 • (323) 295-9799

Table of Contents

Table of Contents

Table of Contents

Preface

Except for the introductory essay, the collection of articles in this book were written mainly over a period of two years, with some interruptions, for a weekly column in the *Los Angeles Sentinel*, the recent recipient of the National Newspaper Publishers' John B. Russworm Award for "Best Black Newspaper in America." This work approaches critical questions and issues from a Kawaida philosophical standpoint which is African-centered, rooted in tradition and reason, and framed and developed in a language and logic of liberation. It is a self-consciously accessible activist-intellectual approach which offers both critique and correctives in a tradition which reaches back to ancient Egypt with its stress on the pursuit, acquisition and use of knowledge in the interest of human good and the good of the world. The introductory article on Kawaida is designed to explain how it works as both foundation and framework for the social and ethical understanding and analyses brought forth in this book.

The insights and assertions which emerge in this book, are, above all, born out of decades of dialog within my organization, Us, about African people and the world and our shared experience in work and struggle since the 60's around issues on behalf of our people and in the interest of *cultural revolution, radical social change* and *bringing good in the world.* As reflected in these writings, these moral and social issues and struggles are world-encompassing and range from the local and national to the international. These writings include our discussions, reflection, work and struggle around issues of the Holocaust of enslavement, reparations and Katrina; work and a living wage; unionization; health and wholeness; immigration; war and peace; manhood, womanhood and male/female relations; environmental care and justice; police violence; the death penalty; the right of resistance; and active support for Africa and African people and oppressed and struggling peoples in Darfur, Haiti, Congo, Palestine, Venezuela, Cuba, Iraq, Afghanistan and around the world. The dialogs on these critical issues and our work and struggles around them are conducted especially in our weekly Black and World News Forum and Sunday Soul Sessions, but also in our special forums and the annual summer seminar in Social Theory and Practice at the Kawaida Institute of Pan-African Studies. These KIPAS seminars draw a national cross-section of participants from various professions, activists, students and lay persons who embrace Kawaida philosophy and values for their personal and social practice.

Always there is a long list of people to whom I owe thanks. Certainly, I am grateful to Danny Bakewell, Sr., Executive Publisher and CEO of the *Los Angeles Sentinel* for inviting me to write a weekly column and valuing my contribution to the paper, our people and the Movement. Asante sana (many thanks) goes also to all the advocates and supporters of Us for an expansive dialog and dedicated and instructive work together; especially: Sanifu Adetona, Sikivu Alston, Thabiti Ambata, Thanayi Karenga, Seba Tiamoyo Karenga, Mpinduzi Khuthaza, Mshujaa Komoyo, Sebati Mshinda Nyofu, Kojo Rikondja, Thema Rikondja, Hasani Soto, Aminisha Tambuzi, Robert Tambuzi, Sebati Wasifu Tangulifu, Malaika Msaidizi, Seba Chimbuko Tembo, Sebati Limbiko Tembo and Ujima Wema, and the advocates of the National Association of Kawaida Organizations (NAKO), especially Segun Shabaka, chair, New York; Maisha Ongoza, chair, Philadelphia; and Kamau Tyehimba, chair, Chicago; for ongoing exchange, support and our work together.

A special thanks to Seba Tulivu Jadi for his constant and valuable research assistance and to him and Seba Chimbuko Tembo for their roles as co-vice chairs of Us. I would like to thank also the participants in the 29 annual seminars in Social Theory and Practice at the Kawaida Institute of Pan-African studies for valuable intellectual exchange and creative challenge. Many thanks also go to my colleagues and friends Professors Molefi Asante and Amen Rahh for their insights and model of the activist-intellectual, teacher and long-distance soldier. Asante sana too, to Seba Chimbuko Tembo and Sebati Limbiko Tembo, my publisher and friends, for enduring support and assistance in varied and valuable ways. And as always, asante sana to my friend, house and wife, Seba Tiamoyo Karenga, for her rich record of dedication, assistance and partnership in this work and all I do.

MAULANA KARENGA
Professor of Black Studies
California State University, Long Beach

Executive Director
Kawaida Institute of Pan-African Studies
Los Angeles, 2007 June

xiv

I

Introduction

Kawaida is a communitarian African philosophy created in the context of the African American liberation struggle and developed as an ongoing synthesis of the best of African thought and practice in constant exchange with the world. Forged in the crucible of struggle in the 60's and continuously addressing both ongoing and new issues, Kawaida bears the tone and texture of an organization, Us, and a movement engaged in intense ideological and practical struggle to change society and the way we think about and approach it and the world. It is constantly concerned with the interrelated issues which pose and frame the task of an ethically grounded and empowered community, a just and good society and a peaceful, just and good world. Within this overarching framework, Kawaida can be understood in terms of seven basic dual emphases: (1) philosophy and practice; (2) culture and community; (3) tradition and reason; (4) dialog and recovery; (5) language and logic; (6) critique and corrective; and (7) synthesis and exchange with the world.

Kawaida Philosophy

Definition

Kawaida is a communitarian African philosophy created in the context of the African American liberation struggle and developed as an ongoing synthesis of the best of African thought and practice in constant exchange with the world. Forged in the crucible of struggle in the 60's and continuously addressing both ongoing and new issues, Kawaida bears the tone and texture of an organization, Us, and a movement engaged in intense ideological and practical struggle to change society and the way we think about and approach it and the world. It is constantly concerned with the interrelated issues which pose and frame the task of an *ethically grounded* and *empowered* community, a *just* and *good* society and a *peaceful, just* and *good* world. Within this overarching framework, Kawaida can be understood in terms of seven basic dual emphases: (1) philosophy and practice; (2) culture and community; (3) tradition and reason; (4) dialog and recovery; (5) language and logic; (6) critique and corrective; and (7) synthesis and exchange with the world.

Philosophy and Practice

Kawaida is both a *philosophy* and *practice.* The interrelatedness and close interaction of philosophy and practice in Kawaida can be seen in one way by defining Kawaida as both a *philosophy of practice* and a *practice of philosophy.* It is a philosophy of practice in that it is critical and systematic thought about engaging the world, acting in it and on it. And it is a practice of philosophy in that it is a practice rooted in and reflective of a certain philosophy, that is to say, a certain *worldview* and *value system.* It is also a practice of philosophy in that it is the practice of critical and systematic thinking about the world, both as it was and is and how it could become.

Kawaida is a *philosophy of life* in the fullest sense, a way both to think about the world and to approach it. This particular way of thought and practice is defined as Afrocentric. And by Afrocentricity or African-centeredness, we mean a *quality of thought and practice* or a *methodology* rooted in the *cultural image* and *human interest* of African people. Rootedness in the cultural image of African people means based in and on the cultural views, values, representations and practice of African people. This position assumes shared orientations of African cultures and peoples. Among these are: profound spiritual and ethical orientation; high levels of respect for tradition, the human person, elders and the environment; rootedness in community and communitarian values, etc. This does not mean all African persons share all of these in the same measure or number. It only suggests a generalized orientation in the same way one understands this when speaking of Native American, Latino, Asian or European cultures as wholes.

To say that an Afrocentric approach to the world is defined also by its rootedness in the human interests of African people is to say that it is based on common moral claims and grounding we share with other humans which represent the best of what it means to be both African and human in the fullest sense. This position assumes that the best of African culture is and must be reflective of its highest moral and spiritual views and values and that these views and values can be justified by the most stringent moral reasoning in the court and community of humanity.

Culture and Community

Kawaida is self-consciously a cultural and communitarian philosophy and practice, focusing on *culture* and *community* as the twin pillars of its intellectual and practical focus, framework and foundation. Its fundamental thrust is to inspire, inform and sustain cultural revolution and national or communal liberation and new paradigms of being human in the world. Culture is central to both *Kawaida* and community. We are, above all, a cultural community, a cultural nation. And the struggle for

4

liberation is first and at its foundation a struggle to free ourselves culturally in the fullest sense. By culture we mean the totality of thought and practice by which a people creates itself, celebrates, sustains and develops itself and introduces itself to history and humanity. This occurs in at least seven basic areas: spirituality and ethics (religion); history; social organization; economic organization; political organization; creative production (art, music, literature, dance); and ethos—the collective psychology shaped by activities in the other six areas.

Kawaida argues that the problem of unfreedom is first a problem of cultural hegemony by the dominant society. It rules not simply by gun and interest-protecting law, but also by an established definition of reality which even the oppressed often accept. A key challenge is to wage cultural revolution to break this hold and pose and pursue a new paradigm of society and what it means to be human and pursue human flourishing.

develop your own culture

Cultural revolution or struggle is key to the preparation and process of any other revolution or struggle. Until we break the monopoly the oppressor has on our minds, liberation is not only impossible, it's unthinkable. For what you can't conceive you can't achieve. Cultural revolution is the ideological and practical struggle to rescue and reconstruct our own culture, break the cultural hegemony of the oppressor over the people, transform persons so that they become self-conscious agents of their own liberation, and aid in the preparation and support of the larger struggle for liberation and a higher level of human life. Thus, the cultural revolution is tied to and part of all forms of struggle for liberation.

The problem of liberation of the community, then, is a problem of culture and the problem of culture is a problem of liberation. Without a cultural revolution, there can be no real liberation of the people. But without the struggle for total liberation, a dynamic, self-affirming, self-developing, *past-and-future-facing* culture cannot be created. The struggle for national existence as a people is a cultural struggle and the struggle to defend, maintain and develop our culture is in the final analysis a struggle for national existence, i.e., our right and responsibility to exist as a people, to speak our special truth to the world and make

Have to see it to do it

our own unique contribution to the forward flow of human history.

Tradition and Reason

Tradition, above all, is a *lived, living and transmitted history*. It is narrative, the story of a people's self-formation and at the same time core culture, i.e., thought and practice central to the survival and development of a people. In fact, the viability of a community of people is directly related to their rootedness in their own tradition and their ability to preserve and constantly enrich it.

Tradition also is *foundation*, the indispensable foundation upon which are raised other cultural constructions. As an African proverb says, "no matter how high a house is built it must stand on something." And that "something," that foundation, is tradition. Another way to put this is that tradition as foundation is a source of position. It gives a person or people a standpoint, a vantage point from which to discover and speak their own special truth to the world. Tradition, furthermore, is a *source and measure of authenticity*. One's genuineness, truthfulness to one's history and humanity is discovered and measured in the truthfulness to one's core culture or tradition.

Finally, tradition is a *form of authority*, i.e., a criterion for the correctness and authenticity of a position, concept, etc. This, of course, is one of the main criticisms of tradition and traditional life. For tradition as a form of authority is seen as opposed to reason and freedom. But there is no inherent opposition between tradition and reason or freedom. In fact, living tradition presupposes and requires differing and contending tendencies in the tradition or even rival traditions within an overall culture. These differing tendencies and rival traditions provide exchange and creative challenge so that a people may have choices and also discover the possibilities and limitations of each. The nationalist and civil rights traditions among African Americans are a case in point and it is out of these two rival traditions that much of our history as a people has been made. Substantive and meaningful

6

tradition, then, must and does bear within it both reason and context for developmental change.

Kawaida is not simply rooted in African tradition as foundation, narrative, grounds of authority and authenticity, but is also rooted in and very respectful of reason. Here reason is first a measure of the desirability and acceptability of a certain element in tradition and in *Kawaida* philosophy itself. One cannot, as Amilcar Cabral points out, accept *in toto* past thought and practice. One must, he says, make a *selective analysis* of past and current popular culture in order to contribute to the construction of a self-conscious national culture. Reason, then, is critical reflection on past and current thought and practice and judicial selection and application in terms of what we need and determine as best. This we do in accordance with our values, current knowledge and the liberational project before us as a people. In other words, reason becomes a source for evaluating the rightness, value and authenticity of thought and practice and its relevance to African liberation and a higher level of human life.

Dialog and Recovery

If Afrocentric, African centeredness and Afrocentricity are to have any meaning or groundedness in reality, *Kawaida* contends, one must constantly dialog with African culture. In fact, one of the central ways that *Kawaida* understands and defines itself is as an *ongoing dialog with African culture*. Again, constant dialog with African culture is indispensable for any serious claim to an Afrocentric approach. And it is also essential to resistance to being absorbed by the powerful presence of other cultures and the weakness or absence of the knowledge of one's own culture. To truly dialog with African culture means, first of all, using it as a resource rather than a mere reference. It means posing questions and seeking answers within African culture concerning central issues of life and the world. To simply use African culture as a reference is to name things considered important in the culture, but never use it to answer questions, solve problems or extract and shape paradigms of excellence in thought and practice. To

7

dialog with African culture, then, is to constantly engage its texts, oral, written and living practice texts, its paradigms, its worldview and values, its understanding of itself and the world, in an ongoing search for better answers and even better ways to pose our questions.

Key to the dialog with African culture is to reach back and recover its best thought and practice, its paradigms, possibilities, visions and values and to reconstruct them to enrich our present and frame and forge our future. Recovery, then, has three basic aspects: to reach back, to reconstruct, and to pose paradigms of human possibility and achievement. Reaching back is looking back and studying the past; reconstruction is rebuilding in light of new knowledge and moral reasoning and posing paradigms is putting forth models of excellence as ways to pursue the possible and the good.

Language and Logic

Key to understanding *Kawaida* is grasping its stress on logic, language and definition. It is Malcolm who taught that the logic of the oppressed cannot be the logic of the oppressor if liberation is to be achieved (Malcolm X, *Lectures at Harvard*). *Kawaida* reads Malcolm's concern as essentially a call for a liberational logic, but also for a liberational language. For thinking freely requires a language of freedom. The catechism of impossibilities of the established order can only be broken if we have a liberational language which opposes and overcomes it. Likewise, only with a liberation language and logic can we break thru the conceptual imprisonment that an inadequate or constraining language imposes on us. So again, Malcolm's call for a different logic requires at the same time a different language. For thinking always requires a language to initiate, inform and sustain it.

Kawaida is, of course, a language and logic of liberation. In this regard it makes two fundamental and continuing assertions. The first is that: until we break the monopoly that the oppressor has on our minds liberation is not only impossible but also unthinkable. And if it's unthinkable, it's at the same time unachievable, for what you can't conceive you can't achieve. In a word, if you can't imagine even reform, you can't make it, let alone revolution. Secondly, *Kawaida* contends in this regard that: one of the greatest powers in the world is the ability to define reality and cause others to accept it. This power is even increased although negatively when one can define reality and make others accept it even when it is to their disadvantage. Thus, the oppressor's power is not only that he defines reality and makes others accept it, but also that he makes the oppressed accept it even when it's to their disadvantage.

The logic of liberation must be both oppositional and affirmative. By oppositional, *Kawaida* means it is self-consciously *distinct from*, i.e., clearly different from the logic of the established order. Secondly, the liberational logic of *Kawaida* is oppositional in that it is in challenge of and resistant to established order logic and the established order itself. Inherent in *Kawaida* logic, then, is an internal concern for and commitment to liberation. It is, thus, constantly seeking liberational or emancipatory modes of thinking and acting. This is to say, it seeks to subvert the oppressive order of thinking by both critique and corrective, by both intellectual and practical opposition. But for *Kawaida*, the logic and language of liberation must be affirmative also. It cannot simply oppose the evil and oppressive, it must also affirm the good and the liberational. It must identify correctly the unnamed and misnamed, uncover the hidden truth, give voice to the voiceless, discover possibility in the face of the catechism of impossibilities and emancipatory keys in the midst of conceptual imprisonment, and negate the negative and posit the positive. And it must always reaffirm the power and potential of the people.

Given that language is the substance and material out of which logic is constructed, *Kawaida* is constantly concerned with discovering new and ancient ways of naming and defining the world. Thus, *Kawaida* pays strict attention to words, categories and definitions. For categories are not simply descriptions of reality, when embraced and acted on, they become forms of reality. Therefore, categories are also important in that they reflect forms of consciousness, levels of knowledge and also problems and possibilities of change.

Critique and Corrective

Kawaida evolving out of the liberational struggle of the 60's, linked intellectual emancipation with political emancipation in a joint project of struggle to overturn ourselves, recover our culture and return to our history, end domination and expand the realm of freedom in society and the world. The *Kawaida* critique is both of the established order of things and the internal community contradictions which mask, justify and facilitate the established order's dominance over us. It is an unrelenting battle against both *ignorance* and *illusion,* against the *poverty of knowledge* and the *perversion of truth.* It seeks to reach beyond and below the surface manifestations of society and the world, to break through the catechism of impossibilities taught by the established order, to penetrate and grasp the relations which give them their motion, meaning and character. *Kawaida,* as critique, focuses not only on the contradictions in society, especially race, class and gender ones, which identify the fundamental constraints on human freedom, dignity and flourishing, but also focuses on the liberational possibilities inherent in these very conditions. The critique, of course, is both framed and founded in the new language and logic of liberation.

Kawaida joins corrective to critique as both an indispensable and indivisible project. Corrective is posed as both politically and ethically compelling engagement with the problems and possibilities identified. It poses long term and short terms solutions, develops alternatives to break through the established order's cultural hegemony and political and economic dominance, expand the realm of freedom and pose a new African way of being human and of human flourishing in the world. And these correctives will occur, like the critiques, in at least seven areas of culture as listed above.

Synthesis and Exchange with the World

To characterize *Kawaida* as an *ongoing* synthesis is to emphasize its open texture, its unfinished and developing

10

character. Moreover, it is to suggest its capacity for self-critical and self-corrective thought and practice. It reaffirms the fact that *Kawaida* is a living philosophy and thus does not remain static and unchanged over time. Because it seeks to address the ongoing aims and interests of African people, it must and does engage the issues of the day and age in which it finds itself. Moreover, it is constantly engaged in an internal questioning of itself seeing its teaching in a new light as time and circumstance warrant. *Kawaida's* developed and developing positions on the importance of class and gender as analytical focuses and tools are reflective of this open-texturedness and currency.

To define *Kawaida* as an ongoing *synthesis* is also to indicate that it is a critical selection and joining into a system of thought and practice various elements, in this case the best of African thought and practice, i.e., that which meets the standards of the most rigorous moral reasoning concerned with thought and practice which protect and promote human life and development and good in the world. This joining into a system of the *selected best* of African culture is distinguished from eclecticism in that that which is selected is fitted into a system and adds to the quality and development of it. Thus, nothing is added to *Kawaida* that does not fit within it in a positive and developmental way. In fact, *Kawaida's* internal commitment to subject both tradition and modernity to stringent moral reasoning enhances and insures its capacity to be self-critical and self-corrective.

To stress *Kawaida's* involvement in and commitment to constant exchange with the world points to its concern with the relevance and reality of its understanding and assertion. It, of necessity, searches *in the world* for models and modes of human thought and practice which can enhance the African understanding of the world and our approach of it. We learn from the world while we teach it. But we absorb without being absorbed and never imagine that another culture or history is richer or more sacred than our own. *For again, the best of African culture is among the best of human culture.*

Also we test and temper ourselves in the exchange, measuring ourselves in an ongoing exchange that compels us to bring forth the best of what it means to be both African and

11

human in the fullest sense. Moreover, it is our obligation as persons and a people to speak our own special cultural truth in the world and to <u>make our own unique contribution to the forward flow of human history</u>. And we do this not simply for ourselves, but in the interest of the reciprocal solidarity of humanity in the shared goal of creating and sustaining a good world, a world of peace, justice, freedom and human flourishing.

via clothes,
jewery, conversation,
or anything else (art)
used to represent
represent who you are
and how you think with
regards to your love for Africa
people and culture.

II

Us, Kawaiòa anò Kwanzaa

It is no easy and everyday achievement to endure, develop and remain productive for 40 years, especially as an organization which continues to put African interests first in spite of changing times and constantly shifting attitudes and allegiances. We, as a people, are given so many easily assembled "reasons" to reject our Blackness and to turn to others for answers, models and meaning. There is, then, something to be said about and to be learned from the Organization Us which has endured and developed for 40 years, overcome government suppression and disinformation, political opposition, continued character assassination, and other obstacles, and yet has not been defeated, dispirited or diverted from its original commitment to Black liberation, cultural revolution, constant struggle and excellence on every level.

Kwanzaa comes each year as a special season of celebration, meditation and recommitment. It is a season which brings to mind and sets in motion the ancient and uplifting practices of our ancestors gathering together in joyous and thankful harvest celebrations of the good in the world: the good harvests of fields and forests, the good of family, friends and community, and the good of life and the living of it fully and the shared good we weave into patterns of possibility and achievement out of the beautiful, ancient and indestructible cloth we call African culture.

13

Cultural Grounding, Unbudging Blackness and Steadfastness in Struggle

It is no easy and everyday achievement to endure, develop and remain productive for 40 years, especially as an organization which continues to put African interests first in spite of changing times and constantly shifting attitudes and allegiances. We, as a people, are given so many easily assembled "reasons" to reject our Blackness and to turn to others for answers, models and meaning. There is, then, something to be said about and to be learned from the Organization Us which has endured and developed for 40 years, overcome government suppression and disinformation, political opposition, continued character assassination, and other obstacles, and yet has not been defeated, dispirited or diverted from its original commitment to Black liberation, cultural revolution, constant struggle and excellence on every level.

In spite of these challenges and White preference and promotion of only one Black radical organization in the 60's, Us has played a unique and vanguard role in Black intellectual, creative and political culture since the 60's. Emerging September 7, 1965, Us put forth a project of cultural revolution to recover the best of African culture—ancient and modern, to emulate its models of human excellence and achievement, and put in practice its liberating and life-enhancing values. In this context *Kawaida* philosophy, *Kwanzaa* and the *Nguzo Saba* were created and Us initiated its program of work, service, struggle and institutional building, which included its co-founding the Brotherhood Crusade, the Black Congress, Mafundi Institute, the Community Alert Patrol, and the Operational Unity Committee, co-planning Kedren Community Health Center, the Watts Health Foundation, and the Ujima Housing project.

On the national level, Us played a vanguard role in virtually every national African-centered movement: Black Arts, Black Power, Black Studies, Black student unions, independent schools, rites of passage, Afrocentricity, ancient Egyptian studies, Black United Fronts, and the Million Person Marches. Currently, Us continues to maintain several ongoing programs and institutions: the African American Cultural Center, Kawaida School of African American Culture, Rites of Passage programs, Kawaida Institute of Pan-African

15

Studies, Mateka (Captive) support program, Senu Brotherhood and Senut Sisterhood Societies, Timbuktu Book Circle, International Black Coalition for Peace and Justice, Coalition in Solidarity with Haiti, and the Coalition for Equitable and Sustainable Development in Africa. In addition, Us participates in various organizations on the local and national level in progressive work and struggle.

Us' uniqueness begins with its commitment to African culture, to the ongoing task of recovering and reconstructing from this culture the best of what it means to be African and human and using it to inform, enrich and expand our lives. We dared to dialog constantly with African culture, asking it questions and seeking from it answers to the fundamental concerns of humankind. It has been the accepted custom to turn to other cultures for such critical answers, but Us dared to ask Africa and discovered valuable and enduring answers.

A central part of Us' uniqueness and importance clearly lies in its role as the founding organization of Kwanzaa, celebrated by over 28 million persons throughout the world African community and which reaffirms us in our Africanness and binds us together in ways like no other institution or celebration. Moreover, at the heart of Kwanzaa is the Nguzo Saba, the Seven Principles, which are not only central to its practice, but also serve as philosophical grounding and a guide to daily living for millions of people and thousands of organizations representing a wide range of educational, political, social, economic, and cultural formations. No other group or philosophy from the 60's has had such widespread programmatic and philosophical impact on African organizational, family and personal life.

Us also has had a unique and tremendous impact on spiritual and ethical discourse since the 60's beginning with its contribution to conversations in the development of Black Liberation Theology. Here Us insisted on a God in our own image and interests, the sacredness of our own history, the chosenness of our own people, the presence and priority of our own prophets and the anteriority, originality, richness and ongoing relevance of our own sacred texts. In this regard, Us translated and published the *Husia*, the sacred text of ancient Egypt and the *Odu Ifa: The Ethical Teachings*, the sacred text of ancient Yorubaland and created an international discourse around ancient African ethics, reaffirming their value as a rich resource in addressing modern moral issues.

Us' uniqueness lies also in its <u>ability and determination to endure in spite of challenges</u> that destroyed other less durable contemporary groups. Of all the challenges mentioned above, none was more difficult to deal with than the decline of the Movement and with it, the decline of the deep, defiant and unapologetic commitment to things Black which was so evident and essential in the 60's. Nevertheless, in the midst of those who turned their back on their Blackness, Us reaffirmed Marcus Garvey's call to put our people first and to work tirelessly to free and empower them.

In the Sixties, we had stood up seeing ourselves as descendents of Malcolm with an awesome obligation to wage the revolution he had conceived and called for. We thus saw ourselves as servants and soldiers of the people always on post and on point wherever called and needed. Indeed, our motto was/is "anywhere we are Us is." We declared revolution the answer and ourselves the agents of this radical change. As Simba Wachanga—the Young Lions, we self-confidently declared, "we are the last revolutionaries in America. <u>If we fail to leave a legacy of revolution for our children, we have failed our mission and should be dismissed</u> as unimportant." Even older, the message retains its original meaning and urgency, and we remain ever grounded in our culture, unbudging in our Blackness and steadfast in our struggle to create a just, good and sustainable world and help rebuild the Movement to achieve this. For, as we say, if not this then what and if we don't do it who will?

2005 September 22

40th Anniversary Reflections on Us: Harnessing the Hurricane of Righteous Anger and Activism

Last week the Organization Us hosted the 40th Anniversary of Us and the Nguzo Saba 2005 Conference to celebrate its 40 years of work, service, struggle and institution-building, and to recognize and honor those present, who came from all over the country and who, like thousands of other organizations and institutions and millions of persons throughout the world African community, use the Nguzo Saba, the Seven Principles, to ground their work and guide their daily lives. The conference was also called to share best practices and ideas, strengthen organizational and personal ties, and recommit ourselves to continuing struggle. Below are excerpts from my Chair's Message for the occasion.

We meet on this our 40th anniversary in the shadow of the shattered lives of our people caused by the combined natural destructiveness of Hurricane Katrina and the man-made disaster in its wake. We likewise meet under the compelling obligation to insure the dead are treated with the dignity due them, to care for the survivors with compassion and loving kindness and to continue to struggle to end the conditions which caused this awesome tragedy and injustice.

At this critical and tragic moment in our history, I can offer you no good news which is not tied to and dependent on struggle. For we know there is no real and lasting relief except in continuing resistance, no freedom from oppression except that forged in the furnace and field of constant struggle, and no justice, peace or possibility of liberation except that achieved and secured on the battlefield for a new and better world. In a word, we can only heal and repair ourselves by reordering and repairing the world.

In this context of continuous struggle, this is our charge and challenge then: to know the past and honor it, to engage the present and improve it, and to imagine the future and forge it. And we can only forge that future in the most expansive interests of our people and humankind by prefiguring in our daily lives the good world we want and deserve to live in and bringing forth from the past the best of what it means to be African and human and using it to improve our present and to forge our future. And this means for us, constantly reflecting on, practicing and promoting the Nguzo Saba and the philosophy of Kawaida.

18

For in a world wracked by division, alienation, hostility and hatred, the principle of *Umoja* (Unity) teaches the oneness of our people, the common ground of our humanity, and our shared human status as bearers of dignity and divinity. In a world where there are repeated denials and violations of persons and peoples' rights to freedom and self-rule, the principle of *Kujichagulia* (Self-determination) upholds the right and responsibility of every people to speak their own special cultural truth, control their destiny and daily lives and make their own unique contribution to the forward flow of human history, whether in Haiti, Africa, Palestine, Iraq, Afghanistan or anywhere else in the world.

In contrast, to the vulgar individualism that envelopes this country and preaches self-promotion at the expense of others, the principle of *Ujima* (Collective Work and Responsibility) teaches the constant search for common ground and cooperation for common good. In a world where corporations export their wares and waste all over the world and appropriate other people's wealth and future under the destructive practices and deceptive name of globalization, the principle of *Ujamaa* (Cooperative Economics) upholds the values of shared work and wealth, and the right of all to an equitable and just share of the goods of and in the world. In a world where purposelessness is pervasive and the response "whatever" is a cover for controlled confusion, the principle of *Nia* (Purpose) teaches us the collective vocation of constantly building and developing community and the overarching ethical obligation to constantly bring good into the world.

In a world where lives and lands are regularly destroyed and persons, whole peoples and the environment are relentlessly degraded, the principle of *Kuumba* (Creativity) puts forth the ancestral ethical teaching of *serudj ta*—the obligation to constantly heal and repair the world making it more beautiful and beneficial than we inherited it. And in a world where faith is funded and religion is an obsequious servant of racism and of the outrageous claims of the right to rule and ruin the lives and lands of the vulnerable, *Imani* (Faith) teaches us to believe in the Good, the Right and the possible and to join our faith with work and struggle to bring into being the good world we all want and deserve to live in.

There is a great work to be done, brothers and sisters, a hard and heroic struggle to be waged and won and a new, just and good society

19

and world to bring into being and secure. Let's get up, then, get organized, intensify the struggle and get it all done, my people. Let's harness the hurricane of righteous anger and activism of our people in the face of this tragedy and injustice, repair our devastated and depressed communities and rebuild our Movement in the process.

Let's pick ourselves up, wipe the blood and dirt of our oppression from our faces and our future, empty our minds and hearts of the toxic residue of racism, restore our historical memory, and regain the historical initiative in determining our destiny and daily lives. For only with such an uninfected, healthy and wholesome self-understanding and self-assertion in the world can we truly know our past and honor it, engage our present and improve it, imagine our future and forge it in the dignity-affirming and life-enhancing ways worthy of the name and history African.

2005 September

Us in the Tradition of Our Ancestors:
Decades of Daring Distinction

No matter how many times I am to write or speak at length on the Sixties and its significance for Us as an organization and a people, and on our role in this decisive decade, I do not take it lightly. Nor do I let my first-hand active knowledge of this period of fierce passage and fundamental turning diminish my sense of obligation to always give it the careful and considered attention it deserves. And so I sit down in solemn meditation like a Maatian or Ifa priest before prayer, and I read and study the sacred words of the women and men who made me, our organization and the Movement possible. These include men and women like Malcolm X, Marcus Garvey and Sekou Toure; Anna Julia Cooper, Mary McLeod Bethune and Julius Nyerere; Messenger Elijah Muhammad, Fannie Lou Hamer and Frantz Fanon; Maria Stewart, Ida B. Wells, Frederick Douglass and countless others, as well as the writers and teachers of our sacred texts, the *Husia* and the *Odu Ifa*.

Thus, on this, the 41st anniversary of our organization Us, we pause to pay due and depthful homage to our ancestors whose teachings and lives have informed, inspired and guided us thru good and terrible times and whose awesome legacy we've tried our best to honor thru the steadfast and worthy ways we understand and assert ourselves in the world. We have, since the 60's, self-consciously walked and talked daily with our ancestors, reverently researched their thought and practice and used these findings as a foundation and framework for the intellectual and practical work we do. For we understand and appreciate in a profound and productive way their legacy of dignity-affirming and life-enhancing teachings about the awesome obligation and meaning of being African and human in the world.

The Sixties remains for us a fundamental time of turmoil and turning, vital re-Africanization, essential cultural rootedness, righteous revolt and revolutionary struggle. And we dare to continue this unfinished struggle for freedom, justice, power for the masses of people, and peace in and for the world. To have truly savored and been seasoned and strengthened by the Sixties, to have grown and grasped the deeper meanings of the ethics and essentiality of struggle, and to have stood steadfast and righteously resisted the hard and heavy winds of calls to cop out, confess the futility of struggle and concede the unblessedness of being Black, is a record few can claim and a report not many can make. And we are always modestly, but unquestionably aware of this and other differences that distinguish Us. Indeed, it's a necessary distinction, especially from those who have turned to what they or at least the Movement once criticized and cringed from, i.e., vulgar materialism, self-deforming defense of the established order, and addiction to various fantasies of "in house" transactions, post-struggle collaboration and self-mutilating mergers with the established order or its speak-no-race racist representatives of its deceptive pledges and pretensions of reform.

Yes, we are the self-conscious and profoundly committed keepers of the tradition, the oldest tradition of history and humankind, the African tradition, the tradition of our ancestors. And if we were asked in the traditional collective way in Zulu, "ninjani nina?—how are you all?", in spite of modern alternative ways to respond, we would answer in the traditional way saying, "cha, sisabelandela—indeed, we are still following them," i.e., the ancestors.

Since its founding on 1965 September 7, Us has seen and embraced as its central mission the recovery, reconstruction, practice and promotion of the best of African culture and the use of it to improve, enrich and expand our lives. We have been and remain, of necessity, engaged in progressive practical activities of varied kinds. These have ranged from the cooperative building of the major movements of our time—from Black Arts, Black Studies and Black Power to Reparations and the Million More Initiatives, as well as numerous institutions—from health care facilities to affordable housing, and from Black United Fronts to leadership institutes, alternative schools and cultural centers. And, of course, we of necessity have engaged in demonstrations and struggles around union-building, draft resistance, opposition to war and police violence, and quality education and equal opportunity everywhere.

But all of these efforts and others would have less meaning and would lack focus and a coherent intellectual foundation if they were not informed and undergirded by the philosophy of *Kawaida*. This is the defining difference for Us. For in Kawaida, is contained an ongoing synthesis of the best African thought and practice and it provides us with a coherent system of views and values which gives us a moral, material and meaningful interpretation of life and demands our allegiance and a corresponding practice of good in the world.

Our distinctiveness, then, lies essentially in the way we understand, value and approach our culture and people, the way we constantly dialog with African culture and see Africa in its best thought and practice as a moral and spiritual ideal. It's also how we actually use our culture in our daily lives to ask and answer simple and complex questions, generate paradigms and solve problems. Moreover, it is how we believe and know there is no culture richer or more ancient than ours, no history more sacred, no people more chosen and no one more worthy of respect or possessing greater rights to the shared good and goods of the world than we. And it is how we have created a culturally-grounded language and logic of liberation and a corresponding literature, and how we cultivate conversations around these and the way Africans ought to understand and assert themselves in the world throughout the world African community.

At the center of all our efforts and any achievement we've made, then, is this stress on culture and its indispensability in our living improved and enhanced lives and waging and winning our unfinished struggle for liberation. Our culture, we teach, gives us identity, purpose and direction. It is a defense against coercive and seductive envelopment by the vulgar values of the established order. It is our shield against the shallow consumerist attachment this society has to life and good in the world. And it is the foundation for knowing and honoring our past, engaging and improving our present, and imagining and forging our future in more moral and human ways.

2006 September 7

Kawaida
Kah-wah-e-da

Choosing to Be African: A Lifetime Resolution

In the 60's when we first collectively declared that we are an African people, we did not do so simply to reaffirm our historical source of origin. We did it also as an act of self-determination, a reaffirmation of our right as the *Nguzo Saba*, the Seven Principles, say, "to define ourselves, name ourselves, create for ourselves and speak for ourselves." Moreover, we did this to make a definite cultural claim and cultural commitment, a claim of uniqueness, distinctiveness and difference from our oppressor, and a commitment to extract and emulate the models of excellence and achievement rooted in our culture.

We made this claim of distinctiveness while reluctantly conceding some similarities in our thought and behavior due to the cultural dominance of the ruling race/class and its powers of coercion and enticement. After all, we had been here so long and the dominant society had done its best and worst to insure we lost our historical memory and cultural grounding. That is to say—outlawing our languages and access to education, killing off our cultural leaders, erasing and rewriting our history, undermining our family formation, splitting our families apart with the devastating axe of the auction block, brutally imposing their nonsense names on us, "giving" us a god in their own racial and racist image and irrationally claiming they had saved us from ourselves, freed us by enslaving us and were "civilizing" us by the savagery they served as daily bread.

But where there is oppression, there is also resistance. And thus in the midst of the Holocaust of enslavement and subsequent forms of savage oppression, we held to core values of what it means to be African, even though we forgot in many, perhaps most, cases the original source of our understanding and assertion in the world. Hidden behind a thick veil of forced historical amnesia and ongoing oppression, our Africanness became invisible to us on one hand and inaccessible on the other. It is here in the 1960's that we joined our claim of cultural distinctiveness worthy of recognition and respect to a commitment to constantly study and learn from our culture and to hold fast to those core values that teach us to seek and speak truth, practice and promote justice and always pursue and do the Good.

24

That is why Us took up the challenge to initiate and sustain a cultural revolution, an ongoing struggle to recover, reaffirm and reconstruct the best of our culture and use it to repair and transform ourselves in the process of repairing and transforming our consciousness and the conditions of our lives in society and the world. This is the meaning of Us' position that we must constantly dialog with African culture, asking it questions and seeking from it answers to the fundamental issues and challenges of African and human life and then daring to add an African imagination and initiative to the ongoing historical struggle for human freedom and human flourishing in the world.

It's important to note that this cultural core of what it means to be African has both continental and diasporan, historical and current sources. For our identity is not a fossilized product, but an ongoing living project in which we all take part. This is the meaning of the Kawaida contention that Blackness, Africanness, is not a static identity, but a constantly renewed result of the struggle we wage daily to defend our dignity as persons and a people, to hold fast to those values which define our identity and gives us purpose and direction in our lives, and to avoid any proposition or practice that undermines our effort and obligation to bring forth in ever expansive ways the best of what it means to be African and human in the world.

We have said that as African Americans, we are American by habit and African by choice. By this is meant that most of what we do and think has its roots in the social process that surrounds and seduces us. And we do what we do often out of habit, i.e., in an unconscious and unexamined way. The mindless consumerism, vulgar individualism, the divisive and destructive competitiveness, and the embrace of the racist catechism of impossibilities and inferiority directed toward us and other peoples of color, all grow out of and find fertile ground in U.S. society. And each day we mindlessly and routinely follow these and similar values and practices or self-consciously choose to be and bring forth the best of what it means to be African in the world.

It is not easy to be African or Black in a White-dominated world. As Fanon taught, the intense levels of oppression can and do make some of us doubt ourselves, deny ourselves, condemn and even mutilate ourselves, psychologically and physically. And so it is important to pause, pay homage and say asante, thanks, to those who

we are in the west but NOT of the west

25

do not doubt or deny the dignity and divinity of our personhood nor the sacredness of our narrative we know as our history, and who go forth daily with the underestroyed dignity and values inherited from our ancestors, cherishing their identity and duty as Africans to bring good into the world. Asante also to those who understand and appreciate the category African as a synonym and metaphor for excellence and the best of our culture as a moral and spiritual ideal we all must embrace in order to realize and reaffirm the best in ourselves as persons and a people.

And finally, asante to the brothers and sisters who will not stop loving and believing in each other, who openly admit we need each other like the next breath, and who hold fast to the tradition of our ancestors who taught us that *together in love and struggle*, we can do it right, keep it real and make it good in every way and sense of the word. *Hotep. Ase. Heri.*

2006 January 12

- Each one teach one -

Asante

In Search of the Sacred Within Ourselves: Ancient Africa as an Ethical Ideal

We live in a time of unmatched material wealth and yet of unequalled material and spiritual poverty; a time of unparalleled U.S. military power and yet an increased sense of vulnerability, insecurity and fear; a time of an almost unlimited access to information and yet a decreased possession of real knowledge about self, society and the world; and a time of ever-expanding means of communications and yet a parallel increase in alienation and disengagement. Indeed, we live in a world where conquest, competition and control over others are praised and promoted as personal and national goals; where care and concern for others are considered weak, wasteful, self-deceptive and ultimately self-destructive; and where wars are packaged as peace-making, occupation as self-defense for aggressors, and high-tech-terror bombing as a brutal but necessary lesson to teach the oppressed the futility of their resistance. And in the midst of such social madness, the environment is steadily being plundered, polluted, depleted and destroyed in the name of a marketplace mentality where buying, selling, consuming and wasting have reached the level of religious practice and only prayers are offered for future generations.

In this context we must ask ourselves, how do we understand ourselves and the world, and engage in practices which do honor to our people and the highest ideals of our culture? And if we are to be true to ourselves, we must ask first and foremost what does Africa, i.e., African culture and African people, have to say about this and other critical issues and concerns that confront us as a people, society and vital members of the human community? It is within this framework that the Organization Us holds its 29th Annual Seminar in Social Theory and Practice, July 23-29, 2006, at the African American Cultural Center, 3018 West 48th Street, Los Angeles, (323) 299-6124.

At the center of the ideas, aspirations, interests and efforts of the Organization Us over the last 40 years has been this profound, pervasive and enduring concept of Africa as a moral and spiritual ideal, a most rich and ancient source of some of humanity's highest ideals and in its most expansive concept, a metaphor for an ancient and ongoing moral and spiritual tradition, constantly reaffirmed, enriched and expanded by the sacred people who are its creators and preservers. Whether we are given credit for *Kwanzaa*, the *Nguzo Saba*, or *Kawaida* philosophy, from which they come, they are all rooted in and rise out of the sacred conception we have of African people and African culture. Likewise, the unique, varied and vanguard role we've played in African intellectual and political culture since the 60's and in the major movements of our time from Black Power, Black Studies, and Black Arts to Afrocentricity, the Million Person Marches, ancient Egyptian and Ifa studies and reparations, is rooted in our understanding and embrace of the transcendent message and meaning of Africa as a sacred people and a culture.

Clearly, when we say Africa is a moral and spiritual ideal, we are not talking about modern Africa in its current condition of undermined magnificence, forgotten grandeur, falsified history, imposed poverty and vulnerability to the various predators who prey on it. Similarly, no one seriously talks about modern Israel, a U.S. favored and funded military goliath and occupying power in Palestine and a society of religious and racial limitations for those called goyim or gentiles as a moral ideal. Indeed, it is biblical Israel, not current Israel that serves as the Jewish and Christian moral and spiritual model. Likewise, no serious Muslim sees modern Arabia with its problems of oppression, injustice and unequal wealth distribution as the moral and spiritual ideal of Islam, but rather ancient Arabia under the rule and righteous teachings of the Prophet Muhammad.

Surely, we stand on solid and unshakeable ground, for ancient Africa, especially thru its classical civilization Egypt, Kemet, gave humanity some of its highest ethical and spiritual ideals. These include the concepts of humans as the image of God and human dignity which is derived from it, the interrelated concepts of resurrection, judgment after death and immortality thru righteousness, preference and care for the poor and vulnerable, care and responsibility toward the environment, the moral essentiality of service, and the ethical obligation to constantly heal, repair and transform the world, making it more beautiful and beneficial than we inherited it.

Here, we will use my new book, *Maat, The Moral Ideal in Ancient Egypt: A Study in Classical African Ethics* (University of Sankore Press 2006) as the central text for this dialogue with African culture. For the governing interest of this text and the seminar is to present a critical explanation of *Maat*, a world-encompassing moral

28

ideal, and to use it to engage in moral reflection and discussion of critical issues facing us and the world.

The Kawaida seminar is about cultivating leadership as a moral vocation, teaching Afrocentric critical thinking and reinforcing and refining moral sensitivity to enduring and urgent issues and providing a cultural and ethical foundation and framework for a mutually beneficial challenge and exchange to achieve this. It is about raising and dealing with critical issues of our time such as Katrina, government criminal negligence and communal responsibility in the struggle to rebuild and secure justice, about the ethics and efforts of reparations, immigration, war and peace, male/female relations, the funding and transformation of faith communities, environmental care and justice, shared wealth and the right and responsibility of resistance in New Orleans, Sudan, Haiti, Palestine, Iraq, Afghanistan and everywhere.

Finally, the seminar is about bringing our own ideas, imagination, aspirations, and experiences to bear on the critical concerns of our times daring to imagine a whole 'nother world in which people actually seek and speak truth, do and defend justice, overcome alienation and disengagement and self-consciously struggle to repair, renew and transform themselves and the world, and bring into being a whole 'nother way of being and becoming African and human in the world.

2006 July 13

Reconceiving Our New Year Resolutions:
Remembering Our Work in the World

This New Year is now the year 6246 on our oldest calendar, the ancient Egyptian calendar, the oldest calendar in the world. And we are the oldest people in the world, the elders of humanity. Therefore, before we get caught up in the established order ritual of new-year-lite resolution-making on everything from loss of weight to giving less to the lotto, we might want to make resolutions worthy of our weight and work in the history of the world. And this requires that in the midst of the diminished and distorted portrait of ourselves painted by the dominant society, we remember and rightly conceive of ourselves in more truthful, dignity-affirming and expansive ways. Having done this we can then recommit ourselves to a vision and values that evolve from the ancient and ever-present richness of our culture and thus self-consciously recommit and assert ourselves as Africans in the world.

Indeed, each year on the last day of Kwanzaa, January 1, called *Siku ya Taamuli*, the Day of Meditation, we are to sit down and meditate on the meaning, motion and direction of our lives and the awesome responsibility of being African in the world. And we do this by remembering and measuring ourselves in the mirror of the best of our culture and history, and determining where we stand in terms of our own principles and practice and the models of human excellence and achievement left by our ancestors. It is within this process that we ask ourselves and answer three questions: who am I; am I really who I am; and am I all I ought to be? And it is then that we are to make recommitments which reaffirm our identity as Africans, our central purpose of bringing good in the world, and our time-tested direction of knowing our past and honoring it, engaging our present and improving it, and imagining our future and forging it in the interest of our people and the well-being of the world.

So in answering these questions, let's remember and teach our children the good, beauty, meaning and the responsibility of being African in the world. We are, I repeat, elders of humanity, the ones who stood up first, most likely in Ethiopia, spoke the first human truth, imagined the infinite and the possible, began to form families and community and put forth principles that shaped the dawn of

30

human consciousness and conscience. And we are the fathers and mothers of human civilization, the ones who introduced some of the basic disciplines of human knowledge in the Nile Valley and who first taught some of humanity's most essential spiritual and ethical principles: the oneness of being, the sacredness of life, the dignity and divinity of human beings, and profound respect for the awesome wonder and web of interdependence we call the world.

We taught first also that the moral measure of any society is how it treats its most vulnerable members. And thus the *Husia* teaches we must give bread to the hungry, water to the thirsty, clothes to the naked and a boat to crossover for those without one. Moreover, we are to be a servant of the needy, a sustainer of the poor, a parent for the orphan, a shelter for the battered, a caretaker of the ill, a supporter of the aged, an ally of the oppressed, a raft for the drowning, a ladder for those in the pit of despair and an outreached hand for those on the road to ruin.

We are also the sons and daughters of the Holocaust of enslavement. It is in this white-hot human-made hell that we demonstrated a human durability, adaptive vitality and resistance to genocidal destruction unsurpassed in the annals of human history. We held on to our humanity in the most inhuman of situations, refashioned our faith so we could retain its spiritual and ethical essence while appearing not to threaten the established order. And we did this so well, we tended to forget what we had before we came here. We also formed families in our hearts in spite of the devastating effect of the auction block and the raptors that raided our lives and ravished our loved ones. And after the Holocaust we went to find the lost, sold and traded ones.

Also even in the face of laws that prohibited it and the promise of mutilation if caught, we struggled in secret to learn to read and write and master knowledge of the world. And we waged a long, hard and heroic struggle for freedom, resisting in numerous ways, from day-to-day and cultural resistance to armed resistance in revolt and alliances with Native Americans and Mexicans. And when the Civil War came, Frederick Douglass, Harriet Tubman and other leaders called us to arms, teaching us that we are our own liberators, and that no matter how numerous or supportive allies are, those who want freedom must achieve it in the heat and hardship of struggle.

31

And finally, we are the authors and heirs of the Reaffirmation of the 60's, a time when we were determined to reaffirm our Africanness and our social justice tradition in and through our liberation struggle. As Amilcar Cabral taught, the liberation struggle is in fact a struggle to return to our own history, to determine our destiny and daily lives, and open pathways onward and upward in the interest of freedom, justice, peace and other good in the world. Thus, we fought and won with our allies struggles that challenged the claims and changed the course of this country, expanded the realm of human freedom, and inspired the liberation movements of other oppressed and struggling peoples of the world.

And so, given this ancient and ongoing commitment of our people to human excellence and achievement and to the constant struggle to bring good in the world, be it therefore resolved in this the year 6246 that whatever else we commit ourselves to, we will uphold and advance this awesome legacy.

2006 January 5

Doing Good in the World:
Reaffirming the Ethics of Service

There is a great and ever-growing need to reaffirm the indispensability of recovering and reinforcing the principle and practice of service among our people. Indeed, an ethics of service is not only essential to effectively address the ongoing needs and aspirations of our people, but also to our spiritual grounding and ethical understanding of ourselves as persons and a people. And it is also essential to creating the moral community of mutual caring and active concern we all want and deserve to live in. And so, at our recent assessment and planning meeting for the Millions More Movement, when we began to discuss the concept of ministries for the Movement advanced by Min. Farrakhan at the MMM March, I thought of how this was rooted in the ancient African concept of service as an ongoing ethical obligation.

At the gathering I suggested that we understand "ministry" in three basic ways—as: 1) a transcendent ideal; 2) an ethical practice; and 3) an institutional initiative. The concept of *ministry* must be first of all understood and embraced as a transcendent ideal. By transcendent I mean an ideal that is spiritual, ethical, overarching, and attached to the ultimate. In a word, it is that which serves as an anchor and essential explanation for the way we understand and assert ourselves in the world. The transcendent ideal that anchors and explains ministry is a divine and fundamental social mission which speaks to a sense of purpose, calling, chosenness, assignment, special task, and destiny. In ancient Egypt in the Maatian tradition, the pharaoh as righteous ruler and priest, the civil servants as servants of the people, the Seba Maat as moral teachers, and the people in general were all infused with the idea that they had been divinely assigned to do and preserve Maat (rightness, truth, justice, good) in the world.

Therefore, Pharaoh Hatshepsut says of her divine assignment to rule in righteousness in the world: "I am an effective image of the Lord of the Universe . . . , whom he chose as guardian of Egypt, as protector of the nobles and the masses, one whom Ra, God, begot so as to have a service-minded offspring on earth for the well-being and flourishing of humankind." And Pharaoh Amenhotep III says of his divine assignment: "It was my father who commanded me to do it

(Maat), Amen Ra, the Creator of Good. He appointed me as guardian (shepherd) of this land, because he knew I would administer it (in Maat) for him. He has assigned to me (all) that which is under him," i.e., responsibility for the world—natural and social.

This conception clearly finds parallels in the Christian concept of ministry which sees ministers, priests, preachers and persons acting as agents of the Divine, carrying out an assignment to preach the good news, and work for and live a good life in the world. This is the meaning of the statement by Rev. Dr. Dennis Proctor, (pastor, Pennsylvania Avenue A.M.E. Zion Church, Baltimore) in our Issues Committee that ministry to him "is living out my divine assignment," a calling by God to serve in righteous and useful ways in the world.

The concept of ministry or assignment falls also well within the Islamic concept of humans as servants and vice-regents of Allah, God in the world. As servants of Allah, the Quran teaches, they must worship and serve God and as vice-regents and agents of Allah they must "give good news and do good deeds in the world." And finally, the *Odu Ifa*, the sacred text of the Ifa spiritual/ethical tradition says, "Let's do things with joy...For surely humans have been divinely chosen to bring good in the world." And it teaches, this is the fundamental meaning and mission of human life.

Secondly, ministry is an ethical practice of service. Indeed, the ancestors taught in the *Husia* that service reflects our identity not only as images of God in a spiritual essence, but also images of God in emulative action—co-creators and doers of Good in the world. Indeed, the fundamental way we must understand and assert ourselves in the world is in doing service for others and the world, especially the most vulnerable. Thus, the *Husia* says, "Serve God that he may protect (and provide for) you; serve your brothers and sisters that you may be respected for it; serve a wise person that s/he may teach you wisdom. Serve one who serves you; serve anyone so you may benefit from it; and serve your father and mother so you may go forward and prosper." And the *Odu Ifa* teaches "when it becomes your turn to take responsibility for the world, do good for the world." Indeed, "speak truth, do justice, be kind, do not do evil."

Thirdly, ministry is and must be an institutionalized initiative, the building and maintaining of structures that effectively address our needs, house and advance our aspirations as a people and aid us in our efforts to build the good world we all want, work for and deserve. To build institutions is also to establish a permanent, organized and structured frameworks of principles, policies and practices which insure continuity throughout the history of a people or nation. And again at the heart of this institutionalized initiative is the concept and practice of service, especially to the poor, less powerful, the ill, the aged, the disabled and those disadvantaged by systems of oppression in the world.

So regardless of our particular spiritual and ethical traditions, our sacred texts teach us and our ongoing struggles reassure us, we are chosen by heaven and history to bring, sustain and increase good into the world. Thus, we must willingly accept this personal and collective assignment and vocation of service as mission and ministry. And as Mary McLeod Bethune teaches us, we must so live our lives that at the end of them, we're able to stand tall on the platform of service.

2005 December 8

Kwanzaa: A Season of Celebration, Meditation and Recommitment

(Annual Founder's Kwanzaa Message, 1966—39th Anniversary—2005)

Kwanzaa comes each year as a special season of celebration, meditation and recommitment. It is a season which brings to mind and sets in motion the ancient and uplifting practices of our ancestors gathering together in joyous and thankful harvest celebrations of the good in the world: the good harvests of fields and forests, the good of family, friends and community, and the good of life and the living of it fully and the shared good we weave into patterns of possibility and achievement out of the beautiful, ancient and indestructible cloth we call African culture. And always and everywhere we celebrate the good of life and the joy it brings, the rich diversity of all living creatures; and the enduring links of life that shape, build and bind us together in the world. Kwanzaa is also a season of meditation, a time to pay special homage to our ancestors, to give rightful care and consideration to the important issues in our lives and the world and to think deeply and continuously about the meaning and responsibility of being African in the world.

Moreover, in this season of meditation, we are taught to give rightful and sustained attention to the important issues that affect and shape the way we live and die in the world: issues of ending wars and pursuing peace, the unfinished struggles for freedom; human rights and civil liberties; poverty; health care and human services; rightful relations with the environment, and standing in steadfast solidarity with the oppressed and struggling peoples of the world.

Certainly, during this special time of meditation, we must pause and pay homage to the victims of Hurricane Katrina, the deceased and the living. We must think deeply about this awesome tragedy and its meaning to them and us as a people, praise the survivors for their strength, courage and cooperation in crisis and continue to aid them in their efforts to rebuild their lives and communities and to obtain justice for the great injury done to them.

Kwanzaa is also a season of recommitment, a special time to recommit ourselves to our highest values and thus to living an African way of life in the world. It is thru these values and others practiced in the overarching framework of the *Nguzo Saba*, the Seven Principles, that we define our identity and thus the way we understand and assert ourselves as Africans in the world.

The principle of *Umoja* (unity) teaches us the oneness of life, the kinship and common interests of humanity, our interrelatedness and interdependence as persons and peoples, the needful foundation of family and community, the equal and indispensable partnership of men and women in life, love and struggle and the rightfulness and good of gathering together in mutual respect and harmony.

The principle of *Kujichagulia* (self-determination) teaches us to uphold the right and responsibility to live free and dignity-affirming lives, to bear witness to the beauty and goodness of being African in the world; to hold fast to the culture that call us into being and sustains us, to reaffirm the sacredness of our lives and the narrative we know as our history, and to embrace it as a moral and spiritual ideal, to study it, learn it, self-consciously live it and leave it as an eternal legacy for those who come after us.

The principle of *Ujima* (collective work and responsibility) teaches us our shared responsibility for the work and struggle for good in the world and calls on us to be actively concerned about the well-being of the world as well as each other and to seek always common ground in the midst of our many differences, constantly cooperate for the common good, and know and feel the joy and justice of creating and sharing the good world we all want and deserve.

The principle of *Ujamaa* (cooperative economics) teaches us an ethics of shared work and shared wealth and calls on us to uphold the right of all people to the good and wealth of the world; to reaffirm the ethical urgency then for a just equitable distribution, and policies and practices that are just, and genuinely respectful of the needs and aspirations of the poor, vulnerable and less powerful, the integrity and value of the environment, and the right and need of all people for a life of dignity and decency.

The principle of *Nia* (purpose) teaches us to understand and assert ourselves as the *Odu Ifa* says, as those chosen to bring good in the world; to see this as the fundamental mission and meaning of African and human life, to embrace sacrifice, service, work and struggle as indispensable to this mission; and to fit firmly within this overarching assignment our collective vocation of rebuilding and developing our people so that we can strengthen ourselves and increase our capacity to serve the interests of our people and do greater good in and for the world.

The principle of *Kuumba* (creativity) teaches us the ethical obligation to do always as much as we can in the way we can in order to leave our community and world more beautiful and beneficial than we inherited it; to strive ceaselessly to create new good in the world, to emulate that divine initiative of making place out of no place that brought the world into being and practicing the ancient ethical instruction found in the *Husia*, to recognize, repair and undo the damage we do to each other and the world and build the good world we all work and long for.

Finally, the principle of *Imani* (faith) teaches us to hold fast to the faith of our ancestors who taught us to believe in the sacred and Transcendent, and in the good, the right and the possible; to know ourselves as bearers of dignity and divinity, divinely chosen to bring good in the world; to believe we can and must be an informed, active and powerful presence for good in the world; to hold on to hope when others think it's hopeless; and to refuse to be defeated, dispirited or diverted from the steadfast and rightful way we understand and assert ourselves in the world as those divinely chosen and who self-consciously choose to bring good in the world.

2005 December 29

Nguzo Saba:
The Principles and Practice of Bringing Good into the World

(Annual Founder's Kwanzaa Message, 1966—40th Anniversary—2006)

The season of Kwanzaa has come again, this celebration and season of joyous harvesting and sharing of good in the world. This year marks the 40th anniversary of the recovery and reconstruction of this ancient celebration which has found a valuable and enduring place in the hearts, homes and daily lives of over 28 million people throughout the world African community. This year's theme is, of necessity, focused on the *Nguzo Saba* as a vital source of principles and practices to bring, increase and sustain good in the world. Indeed, they represent values and vital teachings of our ancestors about how we are to live good lives, rightfully relate to each other and the world, and teach our children by word and deed what it means to be an African man and woman in the world.

The Nguzo Saba begins with the principle and practice of *Umoja* (Unity). This speaks to the ancient African ethical understanding that we come into being and flourish in relationship and that *being of and with each other*, logically and morally leads us to *being for each other* in real and mutually rewarding ways. Thus, the principle and practice of unity cultivates in us a sense of oneness with each other and a responsibility to each other, our people, humanity and the world. It is also this principle which calls on us to stand in solidarity with the suffering, oppressed and struggling peoples of the world in their rightful resistance to oppression and their just quest for the good life we all want and deserve. And it is this principle that makes us ever conscious of our obligation to care for the environment as sacred space and to preserve and promote its health, wholeness and flourishing.

The Second Principle of the Nguzo Saba, *Kujichagulia* (Self-determination), obligates us to respect our own cultural way of being human in the world and to avoid self-deforming and dignity-denying imitations of others. Moreover, it urges us to define ourselves by the life-and-dignity affirming ways we walk and work in the world, and to name ourselves in deep-rooted respect for our identity as bearers of dignity and divinity. And it calls on us to create for ourselves in the good-producing and world-preserving ways of our ancestors, and to speak for ourselves in ways that reveal our rootedness in our own culture and our commitment to the uniqueness and goodness of being African in the world.

The Third Principle of the Nguzo Saba, *Ujima* (Collective Work and Responsibility) encourages us to commit ourselves to work and struggle to build the caring family, the moral community, the just society and the good world we all want and deserve to live in. It teaches us to constantly search for and sustain common ground in the best of our moral values, to engage in cooperative projects for the common good. Thus, we are called on to increase our efforts in the struggle to confront and solve the persistent and pervasive human problems of poverty, homelessness, hunger, disease and needless deaths, and war which disfigures the face and future of humanity.

The Fourth Principle of the Nguzo Saba is *Ujamaa* (Cooperative Economics). It is a principle and practice of shared work and shared wealth of the world. It calls for and cultivates economic practices which demonstrate due respect for the dignity and life-affirming necessity of work, the right to a life of dignity and decency and thus a right to an equitable share of the good and goods of the world. Moreover, as a project of cooperative creation and sharing of good, Ujamaa seeks care and support of the vulnerable and a rightful relationship with the environment that protects it from the evils of plunder, pollution and depletion.

Nia (Purpose) is the Fifth Principle of the Nguzo Saba and it speaks to us of our collective vocation to do good in and for the world, and to restore our people to their traditional greatness defined by this ongoing creation and pursuit of the good. For in this practice, we follow the path of service like the great ones before us who gave their lives so we could live fuller, freer and more meaningful ones. This is the essential lesson of Dr. Martin Luther King's teaching on service as the substance of greatness, Min. Malcolm X's teaching on offering one's life as a testimony of some social value, and Dr. Mary McLeod Bethune's teaching that we must so live our lives that at the end we are able to stand tall on the platform of service.

The Sixth Principle of the Nguzo Saba, *Kuumba* (Creativity), calls on us to always do as much as we can in the way we can in order to leave our community and the world more beautiful and beneficial than we inherited it. In this principle and practice, we reaffirm the ancient African ethical commitment to constantly heal, repair and

40

transform the world, called *serudj ta* in ancient Egyptian. It requires us to revere life and to apply the active arm and healing hand to end the social injustice and persistent suffering around us and throughout the world. And it challenges us to become and be examples of the new world we struggle to bring into being.

The Seventh and final Principle of the Nguzo Saba is *Imani* (Faith). It is a faith founded in the ancient ethical and spiritual teachings of our ancestors, forged in struggle, and reaffirmed in the reality of every day life directed toward doing good in the world. So against all sense of despair, cynicism and the enduring evidence of evil in the world, we believe in the eventual triumph of Good in the world. We dare to believe that eventually thru *hard work, long struggle and acts of deep and enduring loving-kindness,* Africa will come into its own again, and that the people of Darfur, the Congo and Haiti, and the survivors of Katrina and all other suffering and oppressed peoples will be liberated, recover and rebuild their lives and forge a future of expansive freedom, justice and forward movement.

Let us move forward, then, confident in our right and responsibility to challenge and expand the social and moral imagination of society and the world. And let us keep the good faith of our forefathers and mothers, steadfastly devoted to justice, self-consciously open to sharing and profoundly committed to that ancient and ongoing ethical mandate to constantly strive and struggle to make good ever more present and powerful in the world. *Heri za Kwanzaa* (Happy Kwanzaa).

2006 December 21

Maintaining the Miracle of Kwanzaa

The 40th anniversary of Kwanzaa marks another milestone, not only in the holiday's history, but also in the history of African people from whom it emerged and who made it a central pillar and permanent part of their cultural practice and daily lives. Kwanzaa came into being to provide cultural grounding, to teach vital principles, to raise self- and social consciousness, and to cultivate commitment to return to our history and culture and to wage the liberation struggle that opens the path to pursue and achieve this. Indeed, Kwanzaa also contains the ongoing call for us to constantly work and struggle to forge a future-in-freedom worthy of our identity as African people and bearers of dignity and divinity. Kwanzaa's essential activities are about that which stresses, strengthens and celebrates family, community and culture. It's about the ingathering and unity of the people, and reverent concern for the health and wholeness of the world. It's about rightful remembrance of our ancestors and our past, recommitment to our highest and most expansive values and visions, and celebration of the good in and of the world.

Kwanzaa came into being and assumed an international reach and relevance without petition for permission or recognition from the larger society. It was conceived, created and came into its own as an act of self-determination. It was and remains a way to speak our own special cultural truth, to celebrate ourselves and our awesome march thru human history and to raise up and recommit ourselves to principles and practices that represent and bring forth from us the best of what it means to be African and human in the world.

Over these 40 years of forward movement and flourishing, Kwanzaa has encountered numerous naysayers, character assassins, talkers of the wrong and unrighteous, falsifiers, faddists, and men and women of the marketplace in any way you want to take or tell it. And yet, Kwanzaa has not only survived, but developed and flourished. But Kwanzaa will be overwhelmed and undone if we do not continue to protect, promote and practice it in its most meaningful and rightful form. And this, of necessity, requires continuing struggle. For struggle is required not only to bring and increase good in the world as the *Odu Ifa* teaches, but also to sustain it. Goodness in the world, the ancestral sacred texts tell us, requires struggle on both a personal and collective level. But this also relates to Amilcar Cabral's teaching that the greatest struggle we must wage, regardless of the obstacles put in our path, is the struggle against ourselves. That is to say, that in us which is in contradiction to our best values and the choice we've made to be African, free, excellent and worthy in the world by our highest standards.

Thus, we say in Us, we are American by habit and African by choice. Indeed, we must make the choice for good over evil, right over wrong, and faithfulness over fad. So in spite of any attempts to undermine or erode it, we must choose to stand steadfast and struggle against convenient purchase and practices, co-mingling symbols and practices from other cultures and holidays, the crass commercialism of the consumer society and corporate world, and corruptive interpretation of the original values and vision, especially the Nguzo Saba in ways that violate and undermine the beauty, integrity and expansive meaning of this miracle we call Kwanzaa.

The problem of convenience is posed by our life in the U.S. where we learn to expect and seek it. Thus, if we are not careful, we will embrace convenient ways to celebrate Kwanzaa. Again, it's about choice of conveniences, like choosing artificial fruit and flowers instead of real ones and choosing to turn on an electric candle rather than light a real one as an essential part of the ritual of "lifting up the light that lasts." Commitment to convenience also leads to reading short booklets and pamphlets or web notes, or any available book rather than extending an effort to obtain and read the authoritative text on the subject, *Kwanzaa: A Celebration of Family, Community and Culture.*

Indeed, convenience also causes some to mindlessly use a Jewish menorah from the internet, the greeting card or conveniently-located store, instead of a Kwanzaa kinara which is clearly and definitively different and usually uses some form of an African symbol, i.e., Ashanti throne, Egyptian pyramid, Baluba couple, etc. On the other hand, the menorah is "U" shaped whether it's a round or a square "U". And to use it provides an illusion for some that Kwanzaa borrowed symbols from Hanukah.

The second challenge, co-mingling, is related to the first. Indeed, it is commitment to convenience which often leads to all the others. There is no need to mix Christmas or Hanukkah with Kwanzaa.

Kwanzaa has no mistletoe, trees, Santa Claus in Black face or other form, no stockings, nuts, bulbs, wreaths, holly or poinsettias, and no Kwanzaa carols with Christmas tunes. And there is no Kwanzaa menorah. Kwanzaa, like Christmas and Hanukkah, has its own symbols, songs, message and meaning, and to mix Christmas or Hanukkah items with it detracts from both the meaning and practice of them all.

Commercialism is a challenge also related to convenience. For those who seek convenience often buy out of convenience of price and place. To avoid this, we must first uphold the practice and principles of Kujichagulia (Self-determination) and Ujamaa (Cooperative Economics). Here we must make a distinction between normal Ujamaa or the cooperative economic practices of our artists, producers and vendors to provide Kwanzaa materials for our celebration and the corporate world's attempt to penetrate the community Kwanzaa market. Ujamaa is appropriate, but the corporate moves are exploitative and oppressive and should be resisted.

Finally, the problem of corruption of the original meaning and spirit of the holiday is also a major challenge. It seems harmless at first to change the order of the principles in their presentation or to add some personal approach to their interpretation, but it can be corrupting and erosive of the original meaning and purpose of the text. The key to this is to always present the principles first as they are, in their original order and language, and then give one's interpretation of them keeping in harmony and spirit with the original message and meaning.

The future of Kwanzaa is in the hands, hearts and minds of African people. It is they who are responsible for its rapid growth and wide-reaching impact. And thus, I am confident that Africans will protect this miracle they've created, be rightfully attentive to its integrity, well-being and wholeness, and insist on respect for it in every venue it's practiced and presented.

2006 December 28

III

Perspectives and Portraits of History

At the heart of the meaning, message and forward motion of history is the practice and promise of struggle. It is an ongoing struggle to be free and flourish as social and natural beings in the world, to know the world and to cooperatively create and enjoy the common good of it, and to always be responsible and responsive in our approach to life and living with others. Thus, to honor our sacred heritage, to bear the burden and glory of our history, we must self-consciously resume our vanguard role in the midst of the liberation struggles of the world.

It is written in the sacred text of our Yoruba ancestors, the Odu Ifa, that we are all, every human being, divinely chosen to bring good into the world and that this is the fundamental mission and meaning of human life. Likewise, there are critical junctures in history when we, as persons and a people, already chosen by heaven are also chosen by history. That is to say, we are given an invitation and opportunity to do great things and in cooperation with others achieve a great good in the world. But even as we are chosen, we must also choose, choose to accept the invitation and seize the opportunity to do good in the world.

Historical Perspectives

Black History:
Its Meaning, Message and Forward Motion

As we move into the celebration of Black History Month, we must ask ourselves how do we pay proper homage to this sacred narrative we know as Black History? How do we think and talk about this, the oldest of human histories and about the fathers and mothers of humanity and human civilization who made it? And how do we honor the lives given and the legacy left in and on this long march and movement through African and human history?

The answer to these questions lies in our understanding our history and history itself, its essential meaning, message and forward motion. Achieving this, we approach its celebration not simply as an episodic engagement, but rather as an ongoing process of remembering, studying and practice which aids and grounds our self-understanding and self-assertion in the world and honors the legacy left by those who worked, struggled and made the sacrifices we see as miracles and mighty wonders in our history.

At the heart of the meaning, message and forward motion of history is the practice and promise of struggle. It is an ongoing struggle to be free and flourish as social and natural beings in the world, to know the world and to cooperatively create and enjoy the common good of it, and to always be responsible and responsive in our approach to life and living with others. Thus, to honor our sacred heritage, to bear the burden and glory of our history, we must self-consciously resume our vanguard role in the midst of the liberation struggles of the world.

It is here that the sacred teachings of our ancestors found in the *Odu Ifa* become so clear and compelling. For the *Odu* teaches us that we are divinely chosen to bring good in the world and that this is the fundamental mission and meaning in human life. Thus, we must self-consciously become and be fathers, mothers, midwives and mentors who constantly give birth to good in the world and who sustain and increase it in the interest of the people and well-being of the world.

So let us continue and expand our struggle and put an end to the oppressors' illusion about the end of history, the final dispiriting and pacification of the people and Borg-inspired contentions that all resistance is futile. Indeed, we must always find ourselves in the ranks of resistance, alongside the peoples of the world—in Haiti, Africa, Palestine, Iraq, Cuba, Venezuela, Bolivia, Afghanistan and other sites of struggles and paths which open on a new history of humankind.

To achieve this urgent objective, we must first reaffirm our social justice tradition by reviving and expanding its ethical discourse on such issues as freedom, justice, power of the masses, and peace in the world. And as Malcolm taught, we must craft a logic and language of liberation that not only reaffirms our social justice tradition, but also draws a clear line of distinction between us and our oppressor. Moreover, it must disassociate us from those Africans and others in service and support of the rulers of this country and the oppressors of the world. This means reaffirming the right of resistance of oppressed people everywhere and rejecting any attempts to give an oppressor equal or greater status than the oppressed or call on the oppressed to justify their relentless and rightful resistance to occupation, conquest or any other form of oppression.

Secondly, we must stand in steadfast and defiant solidarity with the oppressed, suffering and struggling peoples of the world. This is central, even indispensable, to our social justice and liberation tradition and thus to our self-understanding and self-assertion in the world. Our oppressor cannot be our teacher, or advisor, or the selector of our friends and enemies. This is the meaning of President Nelson Mandela's defiant embrace of President Yasser Arafat and the Palestinian people who supported the South African struggles and other African liberation struggles when others called them and the Palestinians terrorists.

It is also the meaning of Congresswoman Maxine Waters' rejection of the U.S. overthrow of the legitimate and democratically-elected government of Haiti, and her retrieval and return of President Jean Bertrand Aristide to the Caribbean from a U.S. forced exile in the Central African Republic. And it is also a lesson of Harry Belafonte's criticism in Venezuela of the U.S.' terrorism and banditry around the world. In standing in active solidarity with the oppressed and struggling peoples of the world we can, in the tradition of Fanon, pose and pursue a new paradigm of how humans ought to live and relate in the world.

Finally, we not only must rebuild the movement, indeed, we must rebuild simultaneously three movements that transform into one movement for a new history of humankind. The first movement is the Black liberation movement, local in grounding and pan-African in scope and ultimate practice. Secondly, we must build a Third World movement which constantly searches for and builds on common ground with the peoples of color of the world. And finally, we must build a progressive movement of committed peoples in this country and the world in the ongoing and common struggle to secure and expand the realm of human freedom and human flourishing in the world.

This month, moment and each day, we are always and ever-standing at the crossroads of history with our foremother Harriet Tubman. We are there when she chooses freedom over enslavement, defense of our dignity over daily degradation, active resistance to oppression over passive acceptance of it. And we are there too with her each day as she self-consciously chooses to understand and approach freedom, not as individual escape or personal license, but as collective liberation, as a practice of self-determination in and for community. It's these choices and the struggles they inspire and sustain that are the hub and hinge on which African and human history turn. And likewise, they are the root and reason of the celebrations and commemorations we engage in this month and all year.

2006 February 2

Black Women's History:
Celebrating Miracles, Wonders and Struggle

This is the month for celebrating the miracles and wonders we call Black women, that other half of our community which makes us, as a people, whole, these equal and most worthy partners in love and struggle to bring good in the world. Certainly, this does not mean we don't celebrate Black women any other time or all the time in the varied ways we do. It simply means this is a special month of marking, intentionally set aside to remind us and them of the great and indispensable good they have brought and bring in the world. It is a special time to reinforce the rightful attentiveness we owe them, to reaffirm the great value we find in them, and to express in countless ways the profound love and appreciation we have for them. In a word, it is a time to think deeply about and appreciate the meaning and responsibility, the glory and burden, the joy and stress, and the wonder and work of being African women in the world.

In the larger society, March is called Women's History Month, but we in Us call March, Black History Month II—Women Focus, and call February, Black History Month I—General Focus. We do this first to reaffirm the fact that Black women's history takes place within Black history itself—not as a separate practice and product, but as a cooperative project within the context of a people, African people, as well as in the context of humanity as a whole. Moreover, the seamless move from February to March from general Black history to focus on Black women's history within it rightfully stresses continuity rather than rupture, and unity in diversity rather than separateness and antagonism.

Such centering of Black women in the midst of their own history and culture as African people gives the celebration both realness and relevance. For it talks of women as concrete cultural beings, living, loving, suffering, rejoicing, working, struggling and achieving in the context of a definite cultural community. It focuses on the lives they live and make for themselves within the families, communities and historical narrative that makes their lives meaningful. And thus, it respects the diversity of their lives, needs and aspirations as African women, while recognizing common ground for cooperative and mutually beneficial exchange with other women.

50

Moreover, Black History Month II—Woman Focus reminds us and them that our first and continuing focus must be on Black women, African women, in order to give authenticity and accuracy to the celebration. This shows proper respect to the original women who stood up first with the original men, African men, and together spoke the first human truth and began the long struggle and record of humans overcoming the obstacles and oppositions of nature, society, others, and self to establish and constantly expand the realm of human freedom and human flourishing. For, indeed, not only are African women the beginning of women's history in the world, they are also the mothers of humanity and human civilization itself.

Thirdly, understanding and celebrating Black women in the context of Black history as a whole represents an act of self-determination. It is a choosing of oneself and thus one's culture as an instructive source and an empowering model of what it means to be women in the world. And it is a rightful insistence on the dignity-affirming, depthful engagement with African women's history as a central paradigm of woman, African and human excellence, possibility and achievement. This position avoids the tendency to lose or lessen the importance of African women's history in the history of women of the dominant society who might, even unintentionally, put forth their ancestors and contemporaries as the central source for understanding the history of women.

It is this spirit of self-determination that animated and informed the origin and development of womanism. For in the evolving discourse on the equal rights and dignity of women as a whole, Black women reasoned that neither White feminists nor feminism spoke to their unique identity, history and culture as African women. On the contrary, and as a matter of agency, they felt compelled to speak their own special cultural and experiential truth and create a unique discourse and discussion around the current and historical context and contours of their own lives and the future they were forging in love, work and struggle within their community and the world.

Finally, to celebrate Black women's history within the context of Black history, the most ancient of all human history, is to be able to draw on an ancient and ongoing tradition of womanhood. It is to open space for discussion from the earliest sources on what it means to be both woman and man in the world. In the *Husia*, the sacred text of ancient Egypt, we read the sacred teaching that all humans, women and men, are bearers of divinity and dignity in equal measure. In the *Odu Ifa* we read the sacred teaching that all humans—men and women, are divinely chosen to bring good in the world. And they are chosen not over and against each other but *chosen* with each other to bring, increase and sustain good in the world in love and struggle. Indeed, in our sacred texts and our experience, we have discovered the indispensability of the voice, visions and equal partnership of women in the success and meaningfulness of anything of weight or worth we as men aspire or attempt to do.

Moving thru history we not only have sacred texts that represent the highest form of spiritual and ethical understanding of women and men as humans as a whole, but we also have countless numbers of women whose lives are rich and indispensable lessons in how to walk as African women in the world. And in their strength and dignity, dedication, discipline and achievement, they become models of excellence, achievement and possibility, not only for women, but also for humanity as a whole. And thus, to really celebrate the history of Black women is to live lives worthy of the best of what it means to be African, woman and human in the world.

2006 March 2

De-Africanizing King Tut: A Forensic Fantasy

King Tut is back in the house and with him comes a new controversy concerning his depiction by the promoters of his exhibition as a reborn White man, reconstructed out of a pseudo-science reminiscent of early European theories of superior races and differing human brain sizes and thus different capacities for culture and civilization. As a part of the ongoing attempt at the racial remaking of ancient Egypt, this new initiative can easily be called a forensic fantasy born of the continuing need to de-Africanize ancient Egypt, counter Afrocentric contentions regarding the Africanness of Egypt and reverse the gains Afrocentric scholars have made in correcting the historical record and creating a new discourse about ancient Egypt and Africa as a whole. It also speaks to the collaboration of the Egyptian government and Egyptian scholars with this falsification of King Tutankhamen's image and ancient Egyptian history, given their modern split identity as a nation of ancient Africans and of descendents of Arabs who arrived in Egypt in the seventh century.

The controversy raises two interrelated issues. The first is how to respond effectively to the latest efforts to de-Africanize and Europeanize King Tutankhamen and by extension ancient Egypt, its people and its culture. The second issue is how to avoid over focusing on this problem and missing the opportunity to deepen our understanding and appreciation of the awesome legacy of this Africa's greatest civilization and the world's greatest civilization of antiquity.

But regardless of the problematic character of the exhibition, it serves several basic functions. First, it reaffirms the splendor, glory and high level of achievement of ancient Egypt, and thus ancient Africa and African people. Second, it offers us an excellent opportunity not only to deepen and expand our own understanding and appreciation of ancient Egypt's achievements, but also to initiate a discourse vital to the recovery and accurate reconceptualization of this legacy.

Finally, the exhibition serves as a reminder of our responsibility to recover, reconstruct and engage ancient Egyptian culture for the purposes set out by that Imhotepian scholar and Egyptologist, Dr. Cheikh Anta Diop. He stated that a recovered and reconstructed legacy of ancient Egypt will aid us in achieving three basic goals: (1) to reconcile African and human history; (2) to build a new body of human

53

sciences; and (3) to renew African culture. To reconcile African and human history, we must struggle constantly against Europe's falsification of African and human history, especially its attempt to de-Africanize Egypt. To do this, it seeks to take Africans out of Egypt; Egypt out of Africa, and then Africa out of human history. To take Africans out of Egypt is to deny their presence except as captives or enslaved Nubians, to present a "racial" distinction between Egyptians and Nubians rather than a national one and to selectively present only those images which lean toward mixtures or variation from what is considered prototypical African.

The promoters of the exhibit note in the exhibition catalog that a whitened image of King Tutankhamen represents a "miracle of forensics." However, it is not a miracle of forensics, but a miasma of falsified and fossilized racist thinking that has produced this whitened caricature of King Tut. It is a fantasy forensics which sees Whites when there is none, overrides the evidence of history and objective observance and manipulates science in the image and interests of white supremacy. Seeking to keep a scientific veneer to this whitening process, the promoters also note that a CT-scan, an x-ray process that produces a cross-sectional image of the thing under study, was made of King Tut's mummy. But the CT-scan only yielded data on the health, age, height, weight and condition of the skeleton. It did not inform and corroborate the decision to make King Tut White. That decision is derived from a deeper source and longer history. It has its origins in white supremacist ideology which willfully distorts facts and history and only allows things and people white to be right, beautiful, creative and brilliant.

The pursuit and presentation of this forensic fantasy by Europeans has a long and tortured history. It began with the early pseudo-scientific contention that White Semitic invaders taught the Africans of ancient Egypt the arts and ideals of civilization. Then, there were the occultist Whites who conjured up White space beings who descended in "chariots of the gods" to enlighten us. Also, there were those who argued a minor role for Africans in a multicultural mix and those, who unable to prove either of the above, declared the "racial" identity of the ancient Egyptians irrelevant.

The latter two arguments were a counteroffensive to Afrocentric discourse which was rooted in the works of Cheikh Anta Diop and defiantly claimed ancient Egypt as an African heritage and refused to concede or share it. The latest initiative of forensic fantasy is a rearguard action, representing failure on the other fronts and an undignified and embarrassing retreat to familiar grounds of white supremacist claims of having created all things of value and relevance in the world.

Diop has given us adequate, indeed, extensive proof of the Blackness of ancient Egypt. This includes various forms of evidence including melanin, bone and blood tests; ancient Egyptians' self-definition as Kemetiu, Black people; and eyewitness reports by Greek, Roman and Hebrew contemporaries of the ancient Egyptians. Also, there is the evidence of cultural similarities with other African cultures; the artistic self-presentation of the ancient Egyptians; linguistic affinity of ancient Egyptian with other African languages; and finally, the evidence of geography. Indeed, ancient Egypt is the only country in history that has to justify its geography, that is to say, explain why it's in Africa when it should not be there, if racists are right about the absence of real or significant history in Africa.

Thus, we need only to reaffirm and expand on these arguments. But we should not spend so much time on defending our heritage from racist claims that we miss the opportunity to recover its rich and ancient insights and use them to engage modern moral and social issues of our time. Indeed, the contribution of ancient Egypt to human civilization in the major disciplines of human knowledge is immense, enduring and well-documented. However, no legacy left by ancient Egypt is more significant and enduring than its ethical and spiritual legacy, *Maat* which obligates us to constantly struggle to repair and rebuild the world making it more beautiful and beneficial than we inherited it.

It is *Kemet*, ancient Egypt, which gave humankind the concepts of humans as the image of God and the concept of human dignity which is derived from it, resurrection and judgment after death, preference and care for the poor and vulnerable, care and responsibility toward the environment, the moral essentiality of service and the ethical obligation "to bear witness to truth and set the scales of justice in their proper place, (especially) among those who have no voice." It is concepts like these which should inform our approach to and embrace of ancient Egypt. For it is these world-encompassing and life-enhancing concepts that form the hub and hinge on which the real and expansive meaning of ancient Egypt to us and the world turns. 2005 June 23

Freeing Morgan Freeman:
Reaffirming Black History

Somehow, I can never get used to White people asking Black actors, athletes and entertainers what they think on issues beyond the range and reality of their intellectual competence. They do not ask Barbra Streisand to explain Israel's occupation of Palestine or Richard Dreyfuss to explain the Jewish concept of "chosenness" in a multicultural world which stresses the equal dignity and divinity of every person and people. They ask the appropriate persons who are grounded in the topic or area. Surely, anybody can say anything within the framework of respect for others' rights; but one does develop a healthy suspicion of White motives when Blacks are trotted out to condemn people and things Black, distort or deny their own history and humanity and display an embarrassing degree of ignorance, insensitivity and willingness to be used.

So, when 60 Minutes touted last Sunday's edition with the academy award winning actor Morgan Freeman by airing his contrived controversial position on Black History Month, some of us braced for the song and sound of "racial"/ethnic suicide which Whites religiously request and urge from those whom they advertise and give the opportunity. Thus, the hype and feigned horror around Freeman's statement of no race and no Black History Month, should be seen not only as an attempt to increase their Black audience, but also, as is the custom, a move to strike an ever-ready blow against Afrocentric thinking, to promote an idea while pretending to question it and to put the attack on Black History Month in the mouth of a Black celebrity. This unavoidably calls to mind how the established order pays young Black men and women millions to self-mutilate in public, to sing and say degrading things about themselves and their people which Whites could not say without being condemned and opposed as racists.

Let me rush to say I see no conspiracy in this. My assumptions are more concretely focused. What I see is a system of racism which set in motion in 1776 in this country and even before, continues to operate unless and until it is stopped. It is a system which denies and deforms peoples' history and humanity and assigns them a level of human worth and social status based on how close they look or act like White folks. Thus, you have self-mutilation by peoples of color, i.e., the yellowing of hair, blue contacts, chopped-off cheeks, narrowed noses and the relining of lips, in order to look like and please the people who cause the pathology of self-hate in them in the first place.

Indeed, the denial of one's identity and one's history is a part of the toxic and terrible effect of racism. Thus, I wondered if Freeman's statement that he was against the Mississippi flag and its confederate logo because "it excludes Jews, N--- and homosexuals" and then, for no apparent reason, walking toward Mike Wallace mocking a flamboyant homosexual, wasn't in part an attempt to hide or minimize Blackness and Black maleness which are so threatening to Whites. His inclusion of other excluded groups—though not others of color, his use of the "N" word to refer to us and not the "K" word for Jews or the "F" word for homosexuals and his mockery of homosexual flamboyance, all speak to a pattern well-established in the White media. For the initiative was not to present one of the most accomplished and skillful actors of our time in dignity-affirming ways. Rather it was, as racial protocol demands, to present him as a problematic personality, a denier of the value of Black, and a defector from the people who brought him into being and informs the artful way he acts on screen. It was said that Freeman took this stand because his money has moved him beyond race. But even money—ask Oprah who has more—may improve social status, but not racial status, and it won't until we eliminate racism.

However, regardless of 60 Minutes' motives and Freeman's conscious or unconscious collaboration in them, this provides us with an opportunity to critique the media's racial (racist) protocol in presentation of Africans and other peoples of color. And it also provides an opening to revisit and reaffirm the meaning and message of Black History Month and Black history as a whole. Black History Month is a special time of focus, but Black history is everyday. And since, as our ancestors in Egypt taught us, we are not just in history, we are history, we already discuss ourselves, our thoughts and actions, everyday and all year.

No one seriously complains about only one day for Christmas, eight days for Hanukkah, or one month for Ramadan. For they know there is a need for a special time to mark messages and meanings that should enrich and guide our daily lives. It is the same with King Day,

Malcolm Day, Fannie Lou Hamer Day, Kwanzaa week and Black History Month.

So we have a special time when we, as a national and world community of African people, focus on the ancient and ongoing record and struggle of our people in their awesome march through human history. We pause and pay homage to those who paved the paths down which we now walk, absorb their spirit of struggle and possibility, extract and emulate their models of human excellence and achievement, and study the lessons of our history that lie as a rich resource for our self-understanding and self-assertion in the world.

Yes, Morgan, we are African Americans and thus an indispensable and central part of American or rather U.S. history, like Native Americans, Latino Americans, Asian Americans and Euro-Americans. But each of us has our own history and it is this combination of histories that make U.S. history, just like the combination of peoples make up the country. Thus, to deny and eliminate these histories, intertwined as they are, is in a real sense, to deny and eliminate the existence of the peoples who make and are these histories.

2005 December 22

Message From Watts:
Liberation is Coming From A Black Thing

The year 1965 began on an ominous and unsettling note—the assassination and martyrdom of Malcolm X, the Fire Prophet. Even in the white and winter cold of February, it was a sign of the coming fire. Indeed, it pointed toward the fiery fulfillment of prophecy which Malcolm, himself, had predicted. It was there, too, in the title of James Baldwin's classic, *The Fire Next Time.* And it was the topic of countless conversations around the country. Baldwin had taken his title from a line in a Black gospel song which says: "God gave Noah the rainbow sign, no more water the fire next time."

Malcolm, following Messenger Elijah Muhammad, had talked about God's judgment of and on America and linked it to the rising tide of resistance to White supremacy around the world and to the coming revolt of the oppressed masses of Black people in this country. It was, he taught, only a matter of time before Black people engaged in a rightful and defensive response to the racist and violent oppression by White people. As a Muslim, Malcolm stressed divine fire, but those of us who were less religiously inclined read his prophecy as the coming fires of freedom rising from red-hot battles we would wage for a better world. And so we worked, watched and waited for the spark that would ignite the prairie fire and usher in the era of Marcus Garvey's promised return in the whirlwind.

Forty years ago on August 11, the people of Watts rose up in resistance to oppression, especially police abuse and brutality. It began with the arrest of Marquette Frye, the intervention and arrest of his mother, Rita Frye, and his brother, Ronald Frye. It was for the people a final unbearable act by the police, seen as an occupying army. And they rose up, and for six days fought running battles with the police who, unable to suppress them, called in the National Guard. They burned down and often emptied before hand stores and shops which they saw as sites and symbols of their exploitation and humiliation. They took over streets abandoned by fleeing police and began to police themselves, conducting traffic and calling for respect for businesses with window signs saying "Black owned." For a brief moment in history, the people had risen up to say "no" to police brutality, merchant exploitation, and systemic oppression, and "yes" to the right to rebel against oppression and injustice.

After the six days of righteous rage, upraised fists and fiery resistance, the revolt was over, exhausted in its spontaneity and overwhelmed by the force and violence of the established order. But on the seventh day, the community did not rest. After counting the casualties (34 dead, 1100 wounded), binding and bandaging the wounds and burying the dead, the people continued to struggle in honor of the fallen and for the future of the living, fighting for changes in other ways.

They demanded, first, new police practices and began a systematic monitoring of police in the streets and for a while came to an uneasy informal agreement of mutual respect. They demanded jobs and development monies, early education programs, teen programs and greater respect and representation in the political arena. And there was the constant threat of another revolt if the demands were not met. Also in this period, institutions were built to facilitate and expand this process including Us, the African American Cultural Center, *Kwanzaa* and the *Nguzo Saba*, Ujima Village, Mafundi Institute, Watts Health Foundation, Kedren Community Mental Health Center, King/Drew Hospital and Medical School, the Black Congress and the Brotherhood Crusade. The people now walked with a new sense of dignity, identity, purpose and direction. And they defiantly declared their determination to free themselves and perhaps the world, raising the battle cry, "Liberation is coming from a Black thing."

Meanwhile all over the country, revolts were being waged on the model of Watts. Watts had become an inspiration and symbol, a point in history where the Black Power phase of the Black Liberation Movement begins. To understand the meaning of this historical moment, learn its lessons and honor its legacy, we must, first, reject attempts to delegitimize the revolt by calling it a riot, i.e., an unrestrained outbreak without political aims or motivations. For it was a *revolt, a collective and open act of resistance to the established order, motivated by political aims and ideas.* We of Us defined the aims of Black revolt in Watts and elsewhere as a collective act of struggle to achieve and secure three things: *self-determination* (community control), *self-respect* (affirmation of dignity), *and self-defense* (protection against systemic violence). Indeed, we saw revolt as a fundamental and defining practice of Black Power and thus defined the Black Power Movement in the same way.

Also, we must understand the Watts Revolt was not an isolated historical event, but part of a long and continuous history of Black revolts in this country, from revolts during the Holocaust of enslavement to 1992. All were great sacrifices to secure a foothold of freedom for us to build on and expand in the wilderness of White oppression. Another lesson to learn from the Revolt is that there are strengths and weaknesses in spontaneous revolt and that for a revolt to turn into a thrust towards revolution, toward radical and far-reaching change, there must be a well-thought out philosophy and well-structured, disciplined and adaptable organization.

Finally, there is no more important lesson or legacy from the Watts Revolt than the lesson and legacy of the indispensability, unavoidability and incomparable benefit of struggle. Indeed, there is no relief or remedy except in resistance; no hope or future worthy of the name except that which is forged and founded in ongoing struggle.

Thus, we in Us rise everyday and say, "it's a good day to struggle," well aware of the ancestors' teaching that "everyday is a donation to eternity and even one hour is a contribution to the future." The struggle, then, continues for the good of Watts, our people and the world. And we are obligated to engage and sustain it. For again, as we say in Us, "If not this, then what; and if we don't do it, who will?"

2005 August 11

Six Days in August:
Freedom Fire, Summer Festival and Steadfast Struggle

The fortieth anniversary of the Watts Summer Festival offers us another important opportunity to pause and pay rightful homage to the struggling men and women, the way-makers and martyrs who for six days in August, 1965, compelled this country and the world to understand and approach African Americans in a whole 'nother way. But proper appreciation of a past event is not automatic or inevitable. It depends on a people's understanding of and commitment to their own history. And it depends on their resistance to the established order's continuous attempts to reinterpret and tame that event, to lift it from its legacy and history of struggle and make the celebration simply another consumer site for forgetful fun and deadening diversion.

Some wish to detach the Festival from its roots and deny the centrality and relevance of the Watts Revolt and its place in the long history of African resistance. And others want to reduce the Festival to a harmless gathering in the remembrance of days gone by or a multicultural mix devoid of focus on the particular people, culture and struggle that produced it. Certainly, others can participate in it, but like Cinco de Mayo, Chinese New Year, Ramadan, Hanukkah and St. Patrick's Day, the holiday must focus on the culture and people who brought it into being and in whose history it finds its deepest and most enduring meaning. Thus, to hold the Watts Summer Festival and attempt to detach it from the Watts Revolt, which is its foundation and fundamental focus, and from the larger history of African American struggle in which they both are located and lifted up, is to dishonor the legacy and give artificial life to a gross and grotesque lie. Indeed, it would make the celebration little more than a cold, formal ritual of official remembrance, tailored to the safe, sanitized and senseless speeches most politicians make, even on good days. And instead of focusing on the lessons and labors of history, the lost, injured and interrupted lives, the unfinished struggle and the hard and heavy work still to be done, it would lead to a drunken forgetfulness thru fun and games and an official interpretation empty of truth, life and worthy legacy.

No one has fought to preserve the integrity of the Festival and its fundamental meaning and message of struggle as consistently and commitedly as Tommy Jacquette-Halifu, the executive director of the Watts Summer Festival. It is he who has rescued the Festival from numerous premature pronouncements of its death and countless proposals to dilute, distort and deform it beyond recognition and respect. A student of Malcolm X and an early advocate of the organization, Us, he knows the value and meaning of a people's history, and remembers well Marcus Garvey's teaching that "Our history is too important to leave in alien hands."

And so the Watts Summer Festival is about commemoration, celebration and recommitment to struggle. For there is no real honoring the dead or uplifting the living except thru continuing the unfinished struggle and completing the heavy work of history in the African and human quest to expand the realm of freedom, justice and other good in the world. Certainly, the ongoing issues raised by the Watts Revolt and the Black Freedom Movement of which it was a part remain with us—issues of self-determination, self-respect and self-defense.

There is still the need for self-determination—to control the space we occupy, represent ourselves in critical social space, and participate effectively in every decision that affects our destiny and daily lives. There is also the need for self-respect, to understand and assert ourselves self-consciously as bearers of dignity and divinity, to struggle for economic, political and cultural conditions of life which support and sustain this conception and reality, and to insist on the same undeniably due respect from others. And we still need self-defense—from the structured violence of a race-and-class society that savages the body and mind of the oppressed in and thru its various institutions, denies lives of dignity and decency, and uses its police to suppress rather than serve, and to profile and prey on the people rather than protect them.

Indeed, the extraordinary importance of a people's history cannot be denied. There are laws that compel us to learn the history of the ruling race/class from grade school thru college under various functional names and false necessities. Moreover, there are signs and celebrations of themselves and their history throughout the country and year. Even when we turn on the TV and radio or go to the

63

movies, they are the subject and center of all that is done or is worthy of being noted or made into news.

Furthermore, there are those who see their histories as sacred narratives and themselves as an elect, chosen and holy people set above and apart racially and religiously from all the other peoples of the world. And they tell their narratives in schools, colleges and other critical sites as if they were the origin, end and owners of the world. Then, there are those without knowledge of their history who see themselves as children of a less accommodating God, as people cursed and confined to the outer limits of life and history, hoping to be included in the exclusive club of the elect of the world in some meaningful, though admittedly minor way.

And then, there are those like us, who are an ancient, resourceful and resilient people, the elders of humanity, who know their history is sacred, their people holy and the awesome responsibility history and heaven have placed on them. And yet they find no moral or rational reason to deny others the same sacredness of their history or the holiness of their persons. For it is in the sacred teachings of our ancestors in the *Odu Ifa* that all humans are chosen, sacred and elect in the world. And they are chosen, not over and against anyone, but chosen with everyone to do one main thing—to bring good in the world and not let any good be lost. It is thru love, memory, work and struggle that we strive to accomplish this. The Watts Summer Festival and similar celebrations of struggle pay due homage to our ancestors, way-openers and martyrs and reinforce our rightful attentiveness to the awesome task they've left us.

2006 August 10

Sankofa:
Seasons of Struggle and Change

As we close out February, Black History Month I—General Focus, we move to March, Black History Month II—Women's Focus, as naturally and necessarily as men and women meet and merge for joy and life, and seasons change and bring some new and needed good into the world. Our history is a self-conscious and sustained struggle for transition, transformation and transcendence to ever higher levels of human life in ever-expanding realms of human freedom and human flourishing. And it is important always to reaffirm the reasons and relevance of our celebrating it these months and as a life practice every day.

First, we celebrate history to learn its lessons, for as Malcolm X taught, "Of all our studies history is best prepared to reward our research." Secondly, we celebrate history to absorb its spirit of human possibility. For as Marcus Garvey taught, "What humans have done humans can do." Thirdly, we celebrate history to extract and emulate its models of human excellence and achievement, for as Mary McLeod Bethune taught "we are heirs and custodians of a great legacy" and must bear the burden and glory of that legacy with strength, dignity and determination. And finally, we, as an African people, celebrate history in order to honor the moral obligation to remember those who opened the way and created place for us to walk and live in dignity in the world. For as Fannie Lou Hamer taught us, there are two things we all "must care about: never to forget where we came from and always praise the bridges that carried us over."

It is out of this understanding of history that we constantly ask ourselves, how can we use our past to inform and improve our present and lay the foundation for a more expansive future? The Akan word for the historical quest which is inspired and informed by these questions is *sankofa* which means "to return and retrieve it." In a word, we must reach into the past, recover its richest lessons, most instructive models and best practices, and put them in the service of the present and future. In the midst of this sacred narrative we know as Black history, there are three modal or defining periods which offer us memories, lessons, models and a sense of human possibility which are most instructive, although there are other periods of similar instructiveness.

The first period is the classical period of African history in the Nile Valley Civilizations, c. 3900 BCE to 300 BCE. Here we become fathers and mothers of human civilization, introducing some of the basic disciplines of human knowledge, earning the name among surrounding nations as the navel and light of the world. We do wonders in and for the world, not just the awesome pyramids and exquisite temples, but also the science, math, geometry, physics and astronomy which made them possible. We teach the love of learning and its unbreakable link with life, calling humans "*rekhit*," knowing beings, and calling our schools and libraries, houses of life, thus linking the quality of life with the quality of learning.

But equally important and impressive is our ancestors' spiritual and ethical teachings which served as an original source for so many of our essential concepts in human moral development. Among these are: humans as bearers of dignity and divinity; the concept of judgment and justification after death; the essentiality of service; the obligation to heal and repair the world (*serudj ta*); and the obligation to care for the vulnerable. The lessons here are clear: knowledge, creativity and social and moral excellence are indispensable to what it means to be African and human in the world.

The second period is the Holocaust of enslavement. By holocaust is meant an act of genocide so morally monstrous it is not only against the people themselves but also a crime against humanity. Far from being a case of trade or business gone bad with collateral damage, it is a unique event of horrific and morally monstrous destruction of human life (tens of millions), human culture (cities, towns, villages, great works of art and literature) and human possibility (extraction from our own history and denial of our humanity). But as horrendous as our Holocaust was, it nevertheless seared into our consciousness lessons and challenges of continuing and compelling importance. They are: 1) to remember and bear constant and uncompromising witness to the horribleness of our Holocaust 2) to raise up and honor the legacy of those whose struggles and lives are our lessons; 3) to hold the oppressors and enslavers accountable thru the struggle of reparations; and 4) to continue the struggle against all forms of enslavement and oppression on the personal and collective levels—in our lives, society and the world.

The third modal period of Black History is the Reaffirmation of the 60's. It is a time of reaffirming both our Africanness and our social justice tradition in speaking truth to power and the people, seeking justice for the vulnerable, and struggling for the liberation of the oppressed everywhere. We also expanded the realm of freedom in this country and like our ancestors in ancient Egypt, we linked life with learning and demanded a relevant education which joined campus and community and aided the struggle for a just society and good world. In this overall process we launched and won with our allies, struggles that reshaped U.S. society and posed a paradigm of liberation for people in this country and the world. Indeed, in this country and around the world, people in struggle borrowed from and built on our moral vocabulary and moral vision and posed our struggle as a model to emulate.

Our lessons and challenges here, then, are: to continue the struggles of the 60's to end racism, classism, and sexism; to create a free and empowered community, a just and good society and a good and sustainable world and to pose in practice a new paradigm of human life and human flourishing. Thus, in meeting these ancient and ongoing obligations of our history, we truly honor our past, improve our present and forge a future worthy of the life-affirming ways and teachings of our ancestors.

2006 February 23

Historical Portraits

The Legacies of Mary M. Bethune: Knowledge, Sacrifice, Service and Struggle

We cannot pass the month of July without paying homage to our foremother, Dr. Mary McLeod Bethune, born July 10, 1875, laying down in peace and rising up in radiance May 18, 1955. Let us pour libation for her, then, and raise her righteous name in remembrance and honor for the great work and service she performed in the world and for the legacy she self-consciously left us. For it is written in the sacred *Husia* "To do that which is of value is forever, a person called forth by her work does not die, for her name is raised and remembered because of it." So in the tradition of the ancestors, we raise and praise the name and work of this our foremother, Dr. Mary McLeod Bethune, born to Mr. and Mrs. Sam and Patsy McLeod, who taught her to cherish freedom, to love learning, and to always do good.

Let us raise up her five royal and righteous names as done by our ancestors in ancient Egypt which speaks to the great woman she was and will, for us and the world, always be. *Master teacher* who taught us the good, dignity-affirming, and divine way to walk in the world. *Honored mother*, great one among the many who nurtured and sustained us in our early history as a new African people, emerging from the Holocaust of enslavement and reconstructing ourselves. *Institution-builder* who raised above the earth pyramids of possibilities, structures which housed our aspirations and advanced our interests as a people. *Freedom fighter* who fought to clear away the forests of oppression and injustice and secure and defend the rights, self-determination and dignity of Africans and other peoples of color of the world. *Peacemaker*, who challenged the peoples of the world to put down their weapons and join minds, hands and hearts to build a fellowship of freedom, mutual respect, equality and peace thru justice everywhere.

Nearing the end of her life, Dr. Bethune, like our ancestors of ancient Africa, set down in writing lessons garnered from a life of learning, service, sacrifice and struggle. She left us nine legacies or challenges which if embraced, would change our lives and serve us well in meeting the awesome challenge she posed to reconceive and "remake the world." First, Dr. Bethune leaves us the legacy and challenge of *love*. She challenges us to love ourselves, to cultivate brotherhood and sisterhood with each other and other peoples of the world, to be "interracial, inter-religious and international." She rightly wants us to resist that virulent strain of racist and religious hate the oppressor tries to infect us with, making his enemies ours and claiming us as allies in his color-coded rampages against freedom, justice and peace in the world. It is our task, she teaches, to pose a new model of how humans ought to relate and act together in the world.

But the stress is always on placing love at the center of our lives in our families and communities and especially, between men and women whose relationships will shape and affect all others. Therefore, in family and community, in every house and down every street, we must suppress the hatred and hostility, end the injuries and violence, and instead practice healing and peace, and cultivate the love we all long for and seek in private and public places.

She left us too *hope*, born of the historical record of our people's rising out of the Holocaust of enslavement, retaining their dignity and humanity in spite of the most dehumanizing of conditions, enduring and prevailing against all odds, and leaving a legacy of "ceaseless striving and struggle" on and upward, and thus, a better world for future generations. Also, she left us *the thirst for education*. "Knowledge," she said, "is the prime need of the hour." But she cautioned it must be a knowledge and education, not for enslavement but for freedom, not for collaboration in our own oppression, but to serve our people. We must, she says, "discover the dawn and then share it with our children and the masses who need it most."

Her next legacy is *the challenge of developing confidence in one another*, not only for defense against our oppression, but for the development and flourishing of our lives and the indispensable planning and cooperating for common good. She leaves us too, *respect for the use of power*, power directed toward freedom, human justice and the serving of our people. And in the pursuit of power she asks us to "select leaders who are wise, courageous and of great moral stature and ability" and "who will work not for themselves but for others."

Her next legacy is *faith*, faith in God, in ourselves and especially in our people. She was sure we loved and served the Creator, but she was concerned about our will to love and serve our people in spite of racism and class considerations. Thus, she asks us to challenge ourselves and our leaders to believe in and serve the people. For she says, "The measure of our progress as a race is in precise relation to the depth of faith in our people held by our leaders."

Bethune leaves us also *racial dignity*, the challenge for Blacks "to maintain our human dignity at all cost." She reminds us that "we are custodians and heirs of a great civilization," and that we must bear the burden and glory of our history with strength, dignity and determination. Furthermore, she leaves us the *"desire to live harmoniously with (our) fellow man."* She wants us to recognize that the "problem of color is world-wide," but she wants our people to "conduct themselves naturally in all relationships," with dignity, responsibility and respect for our own heritage and to constantly search for and build on common ground with others.

Finally, Dr. Bethune leaves us the legacy and *the charge of responsibility to our young people.* She urges us to prepare them for the future, to inspire and preserve "their zeal for building a better world," to insure they "not be discouraged from aspiring toward greatness," and to not let them forget their obligations to free and serve the masses in our "ceaseless strivings and struggle" as a people, to bring, increase and sustain good in our lives and the world.

2005 August 4

For Her People and History:
The Mission of Mayme Clayton

Perhaps, we had all imagined her there forever, serenely sitting, talking and teaching among the multitude of books and materials on her people which she had put at the center of her life. Indeed, we could not see her otherwise than constantly collecting, sorting and assembling, patiently putting together the pieces and pages of our history and sharing the wealth and wisdom she had painstakingly acquired and possessed. But the word came last week that Dr. Mayme Clayton, the honored and beloved librarian, the relentless researcher, the tireless teacher, the truth-seeker and the self-declared preserver of our heritage and history had made her transition to the other world.

Surely, we, personally and as a people, share this great loss with her family and loved ones. And in prayerful homage we say: *May the good she left last forever. May her family and all her loved ones be blessed with consolation, courage and peace. May her name be forever blessed, her work be always honored, and her legacy endure for eternity. May she rise in radiance and be received in the sacred circle of the ancestors, among the doers of good, the righteous and rightfully rewarded. And may her people praise her thru practice, by continuing the important and awesome work she has left for us to pursue and pass on to future generations. Hotep.*

In and thru her work, she had become a modern pillar and part of an ancient and ongoing tradition that cherished books, linked learning and life, and understood our history as sacred. Indeed, the sacred text of ancient Egypt, the *Husia*, taught that "better is a book than a well-built house. Better is a book than a memorial plaque in the temple." Moreover, this ancient African civilization of Egypt called human beings *rekhyt*, knowing beings, and its sites of learning "houses of life." This love of learning and its linkage to life extends forward thru the Holocaust of enslavement in which our people risked their lives to learn to read and write in defiance of the existing laws that made it a crime for us.

Born in Arkansas before the Black Freedom Movement, she had come early to the conclusion that the history of her people had been deformed, denied and distorted by the oppressor. Thus, like her predecessor and counterpart in the East, the famed bibliophile and institution-builder, Arthur Schomburg, she dedicated herself to

71

correcting the historical record and assembling facts to undermine the falsification of history. Dr. Clayton had begun her search for the missing pieces and pages of Black history in a quest to know more about the great educator and human rights activist, Dr. Mary McLeod Bethune. Indeed, Dr. Bethune inspired her with her timeless teaching on the meaning and obligation of our history saying, "we are custodians and heirs of a great legacy" and we must bear the burden and glory of that history with strength, dignity and determination. In fact, Dr. Clayton says of Bethune, "her strength and dedication gave me strength (and) inspired me." She goes on to say "that's what is important about Black History, it gives us direction and meaning."

Dr. Clayton wanted to recover and be a conscientious custodian of this history to which she and we are heirs. But she could not readily find it and thus made her life's work, the meticulous looking for the life history of our people, poking and peering thru piles of dusty and discarded materials in bookstores and basements, closets and closing libraries, garages and garden shacks, attics and everywhere else clues, calls, conversations and letters led her. Over the years she collected over 30,000 items, a rich cultural treasure of books, films and photos, records and other audio recordings, manuscripts, magazines and sheet music, artwork, journals, playbills, pamphlets, prints, posters, correspondence and memorabilia of various kinds.

She went forth with a joy in her work, a love for her people and a faith in the rightness and relevance of what she was doing. And she identified the grounds and joy of her work saying, "I love to read and I wanted to do something for my people." So she began collecting and amassing materials which not only revealed the rich, ancient and varied character of Black life, history and culture, but also countered the racist reduction of this history to uneducated athletes in and on court, gangstas in the street, gunstlers in the house, women and children in deep trouble, and men missing for all kinds of irresponsible reasons.

She noted frequently that her work had been a challenging project, first finding deficiencies and distortions in what was present and a great and ever-growing need for what was absent. She went to college to enhance her skills as a collector and librarian, and afterwards tried to bring new direction and definitive collections to USC and UCLA, but found insufficient administrative will and blocked ways in her efforts. And so she decided to build the educational center she looked and longed for, a library and research center that respected, recovered and reconstructed the history of African people and put it where it belonged at the beginning and center of U.S. and human history. It is to be rightfully called the Mayme A. Clayton Library and Cultural Center within the Western States Black Research and Educational Center she founded.

Dr. Clayton had shared her dream and project with me, as she had so many others. For she loved sharing her collection, reading from rare manuscripts, reciting early poems, and revealing facts that offered added evidence to the grand conception she held of Black history and Black people. W.E.B. DuBois, she said, had rightly revealed how the veil of racism had blocked and distorted the world's correct perception of us and our rightful understanding of ourselves. Completion of her project, she said, "will give reality its true dimensions and that truth will break through the veil and let us all see and let's us all know . . . ."

Given all she gave us, we owe it to her to contribute to the building of the center and to continue her work. As for her, she has built for eternity and will live for eternity. For surely it is written in the *Husia*, that those who bring good in the world, "they shall be counted among the ancestors. Their name shall endure as a monument and what they've done on earth, shall never perish or pass away."

2006 October 26

Garvey in the Whirlwind:
The Lesson and Legacy of Struggle

As we move towards the 40th anniversary of the Nguzo Saba 2005 Conference of the Organization Us on September 8-11 and the Millions More Movement March on October 15, let us pause and pay homage to the Hon. Marcus Garvey, who taught us so well the dignity, meaning and obligation of being African in the world. Blessed is his name; honored is his work and enduring is his legacy. Surely, as we seek to identify and exchange our best practices over the years at the Nguzo Saba 2005 Conference and prepare to transform the Millions More March into a movement, there are lessons to learn and remember from him.

In the tradition of our ancestors, let us understand and remember his legacy by raising up and remembering his work in five royal names. Indeed, it is he who inspires the Kawaida concept that there is no royalty except in righteousness, no one worthy of respect more than the doer-of-good in the world. Let us remember and praise Marcus Garvey in his name first as *righteous servant of the masses* who said "the only aristocracy is that acquired through service and loyalty to the people." He also taught us the meaning and morality of service saying, "The ends you serve that are selfish will take you no further than yourself, but the ends you serve that are for all, in common, will take you even into eternity."

Let us remember Garvey also as *unifier and organizer of the people*, builder of the largest movement of Africans in history, the Universal Negro Improvement Association, and the millions more who supported it. As unifier, Garvey stressed the unity, common interests and common struggle of African peoples throughout the world. And he urged us and worked to unite us as one people with one aim and one destiny—the redemption and liberation of Africa and African peoples and contribute to the freedom and flourishing of humankind. As a builder of a world-wide movement, he taught us the importance of unity and power and the earnest and ongoing organization it requires. The "emancipation of the race," he says and "the redemption of Africa" will come only thru organized struggle. Thus, he said, "show me a well-organized nation and I will show you a people and a nation respected by the world." On the other hand, he says "point to me a weak nation and I will show you a people oppressed, abused and taken advantaged of by others." Indeed, "race without power and authority is a race without respect." Thus, Garvey concludes, "Whether in industry, society, politics or war, it is the force of organization that tells; hence I can advise no better step toward racial salvation than organization among us."

Let us also raise the royal name of Marcus Garvey as *uncompromising advocate of self-determination*, as a political, economic and cultural practice. He stated that the UNIA advocated "self-help and self-reliance, not only in one essential, but in all those things that contribute to human happiness and well-being." If we are to develop, be free or even survive, he teaches, "it must be done through our own efforts." Garvey placed great emphasis on economic and political self-determination as interlocking goals and needs of a people, saying, "a race that is solely dependent upon others for its economic existence sooner or later dies" and "take away industry from a race, take away political freedom from a race and you have a group of slaves."

Garvey also taught that the key battle we are waging is to win the hearts and minds of our people, for he said, "propaganda has done more to defeat the good intentions of races and nations than even open warfare." Indeed, our oppressor seeks to convert us against our will and "to destroy our hopes, our ambitions and our confidence. In such a context we need our best minds, original thinkers, intellectuals and others who know "there is (no pride or) progress in aping white people" and seek to bring forth the best in our people. For "the best in the race is not reflected through or by the action of its apes, but by its ability to create of and by itself." As matter of dignity and self-determination, then, he urges us, "Let us not try to be the best or worst of others, but let us make the effort to be the best of ourselves."

Let us finally remember Marcus Garvey as a timeless *freedom fighter*, promiser of the whirlwind, who linked freedom, justice and peace and the necessity of struggle for both and promised that even in death he would return in the whirlwind to continue the struggle. He declared "so long as there is within me the breath of life and the spirit of God, I shall struggle and urge others of our race to struggle on to see justice done for Black peoples of the world." Moreover, he stated "there can be no peace among me and nations, so long as the strong continue to oppress the weak, so long as injustice is done to other people...."

If there is no peace without justice, there can be no justice without freedom. For as Garvey says, "we were created to be free" and to realize our highest aspirations for good in the world. Thus, he urges us all to struggle on regardless of the odds against us. He calls for men and women of faith, courage and character. To have faith, he says, is "to serve without regret or disgust, to obligate one's self to that which is promised and expected and to keep to our word and to do our duty well." And to be courageous and have character is to be men and women "who will never say die;...never give up, never depend on others to do for (them) what (they) can do for (themselves), ...who will not blame God ...nature ...(or) Fate for (their) condition but ...will go out and make conditions to suit (themselves)." *Hotep; Ase; Heri.*

2005 August 25

Garvey, God and Good in the World: Foundations for a Liberating Faith and Work

This is once again the month of the birth of our forefather, Marcus Garvey (1887 August 17), righteous servant of the masses, unifier and organizer, uncompromising advocate of self-determination, freedom fighter, producer of the storm and promiser of the whirlwind. To pay due and rightful homage to him, we are obligated to re-read his history, study and reflect on his lessons and measure ourselves in the mirror of the guidelines he left for our understanding and assertion as African people in the world. In this time of crisis, war, warmongering, mega churches, and minor concern for the poor and vulnerable, and in which faith is a funded project and the gospel of personal prosperity trumps and triumphs over the gospel of social justice, Garvey's concept of religion and spirituality is instructive and refreshing.

Marcus Garvey understood well the central role that religion plays in our lives as a people. Being ecumenical and dedicated to unifying African people under one spiritual banner, he preferred to use spirituality rather than religion and worked to unite Africans regardless of their faith or denomination. Garvey was a Christian in faith; a Catholic in confession and an African in everything he thought, hoped and did. And he reached out to Africans of every faith under the banner "One God, One Aim, One Destiny." Thus, he was rightfully concerned about a correct and appropriate interpretation of our relationship with God, our purpose and function on earth, and our obligation to live by moral and spiritual principles which aided us in the sacred work of African liberation and redemption to which he gave his life.

Faced with a form of religion infected with racism and acting as the handmaiden of imperial conquest, Garvey began to reformulate a spirituality more reflective of the God and Good he embraced. Rejecting any form of oppression-serving White Christianity, he said, Blacks want "no more of the White man's religion as it applies to his race, for it is a lie and a farce... propaganda pure and simple to make fools of a race and rob...the world." Certainly, the time has come when we must see God in our own image "canonize our own saints, create our own martyrs and elevate them to positions of fame and

77

honor..." For surely our history is sacred, our people holy, and our good work in the world sacred and righteous work, worthy of the highest respect and reward.

Garvey also insists that Black people have a God in their own image and interests. He stated that "If the White man has the idea of a White God, let him worship his God as he desires." And if others also have an idea of God in their own image, let them worship as they see fit. For "While our God has no color, yet it is human to see everything through one's own spectacles." Thus, "we believe in the God of Ethiopia the everlasting God...the one God of all Ages. That is the God in whom we believe, but we shall worship him through the spectacles of Ethiopia." Garvey and the UNIA were the first to Africanize images in the church and insist on it as a moral obligation and matter of dignity to recognize divinity in our own images and within our own selves.

He thus also held that we are in the image of God, a parallel and interrelated concept of God in our own image. And he stressed the meaning of this in terms of equal dignity, worth and status and equal rights to the goods of the world. He stated that "God created us free and...created each and every one of us for a place in the world." But only by self-confidence, conviction and constant action and struggle can we be free and carry out our divine assignment to do good in the world.

Marcus Garvey cautions us that in our struggle we must not imitate the cold, exploitative and oppressive detachment of our oppressor. Instead, he says "let us in shaping our own Destiny, set before us the quality of human justice, love, charity, mercy and equity. Upon such foundation, let us build a race, and I feel that the God who is Divine, the Almighty Creator of the world shall forever bless this race of ours, and who (is) to tell that we shall not teach men the way to life, liberty and true happiness."

Garvey wanted us to be morally sensitive to others and pursue peace with them, never using power "to oppress the human race, rather use our strength...to preserve humanity and civilization." Indeed, Garvey taught that abuse of power prevents peace and causes wars in the world. "There can be no peace among men and nations, so long as the strong continues to oppress the weak," he says; "so long as injustice is done to other peoples, just so long will we have cause for war and make a lasting peace an impossibility." Surely, these lessons are applicable to the liberation struggles of oppressed peoples around the world.

Marcus Garvey, like several African prophets and teachers before and after him—from Harriet Tubman, Sojourner Truth and Maria Stewart, to Messenger Muhammad, Malcolm X and Martin Luther King, saw us as a special and sacred people, chosen by heaven and history to bring good into the world, in spite of the radical evil around us. He said we are surrounded and confronted with "a civilization that is highly developed; a civilization that is competing with itself for its own destruction; a civilization that cannot last because it has no spiritual foundation; a civilization that is vicious, crafty, dishonest, immoral, irreligious and corrupt." He goes on to say that in spite of this, they find themselves happy in the midst of "the masses of the human race which (are) on the other hand dissatisfied and discontent...and are determined to destroy the systems that hold up such a society and prop up such a civilization." He concludes by saying, "the fall will come. A fall that will cause the universal wreck of the civilization we now see and in this civilization, the (African) is called upon to play his part. He is called upon to evolve a national ideal based on freedom, human liberty and true democracy," an ideal that offers a worthy and working model and message for the world.

2006 August 17

Mrs. Fannie Lou Hamer:
Womanist, Warrior and Way-Opener

Mrs. Fannie Lou Hamer is one of those awesome ancestors about whom it is said: They were so tall when they stood up, they were the height of mountains and when they lay down, they were the length of rivers. And so we raise our hands and bow our heads in homage to this wonder of an African woman, this womanist, warrior and way-opener in this month of her coming-into-being to bring a great good in the world. Indeed, it is she who taught us the morality of remembering saying, "there are two things we all should care about— never to forget where we came from and always praise the bridges that carried us over."

She was indeed a womanist in the fullest sense of the word, one deeply committed to the spiritual and ethical teachings and practices of her culture and faith which affirm, support and secure the dignity, rights, equality and indispensability of women in all things of importance in the world. She was a warrior woman, a freedom fighter who would not abandon the battlefield until the war was won. And she was a way-opener who prayed for a way and then opened it in practice, the practice of hard work and heroic struggle. Thus, she prayed, "O Lord, open a way for us. Please make a way for us . . . , where I can stand up and speak for my race and speak for my hungry children." And then she stood up and stepped forward to speak truth to power, serve and inspire the people, pursue justice, and uphold right everywhere.

Deeply spiritual, she strove daily to lift up what she called "this little light of mine," and worked tirelessly to drive away the long night of the evil, injustice and social savagery which surrounded and suppressed her people. At an early age, she made a vow to her mother saying, "When I get my chance, Mama, I'm sure going to do something to right this wrong." Later, she would reaffirm this commitment and call on us to embrace it also, telling us, "We must bring right and justice where there is wrong and injustice." And speaking especially to her sisters, she reiterated the call saying, "We have a job as Black women—to support whatever is right and to bring justice where we've had so much injustice."

For her, struggle was a way of life and living, a way to serve the people and open a way to freedom, justice and an expanded sense of our humanity. Indeed, she said "You've got to fight. Every step of the way you've got to fight." When asked why she did not just leave Mississippi and the murderous madness it represented, she replied: "Why should I leave . . . I got problems (here). I want to change Mississippi. You don't run away from problems. You just face them."

Mrs. Hamer clearly took a womanist position on the indispensability of partnership between Black women and men in life, love and struggle. She anticipated the growing rift between many Black men and women which began in the 70's. And she was deeply concerned about the damage it would do, not only to the struggle, but also to Black women and men themselves as well as the Black family. Therefore, she urged a group of Black middle class women not to separate themselves from each other, Black men or the struggle. For she said, "Whether you have a Ph.D., dd or no d, we're in this bag together." And the need is "not to fight to liberate ourselves from the men—this is another trick to get us fighting among ourselves—but to work together with Black men. And then we will have a better chance to act as human beings and to be treated as human beings in our sick society." Reaffirming this position, she stated "I'm not fighting to liberate myself from the Black man . . . because he's been stripped of being a citizen. I got a husband . . . that I don't' want to be liberated from. But we are here to work side by side with this Black man in trying to bring liberation to all people."

A way-opener for her people, she spoke of how she felt responsible for the lives and self-conception of so many, especially our children. She said, "I'm not actually living for myself. If I left, there'd be so many children who'd have no way of knowing that life doesn't have to be a tragedy because they're Black."

Moreover, she offered criticism of the Vietnam War that retains its relevance for the war in Iraq today. First, she criticized the racist hypocrites who talked about war as a way of "helping to have free elections in Vietnam and we can't even vote here at home." She said, "It's wrong to fight (in such a war). I don't just say this for the Black man. I just don't think anybody with any decency should go to a racist war like that," especially when they don't know what's really going on.

Strengthened by a faith that would never fail, she went forth fearless from the beginning. She said she first thought that maybe she should be afraid given the savagery she had seen and the brutality she knew awaited her and others in their quest for freedom. But then she thought "What's the point in being scared . . . the only thing they can do is kill me, and it seems like they had been trying to do that a little bit at a time ever since I could remember."

Since the summer of '62 when she first stood up to answer the call of civil rights workers to register and work to involve the masses of her people, she had stood steadfast and fearless. Even when she was beaten into bad health for the rest of her life, suffering from a damaged liver and diminished sight, she would not sit down. Mrs. Hamer, indeed, gave her life so that we could live freer and fuller ones. "One day I know the struggle will (bring) change," she said. "There's got to be change not only for Mississippi (and) for the people of the U.S., but (also for) people all over the world." And we, Black people, Native Americans, Latinos, Asians and Whites, she said, must struggle together to achieve it.

2006 October 12

Coretta Scott King:
Life Partner, Dream Keeper, Dawn Bringer

The ancestors taught that when the good and great leave this world, they lie down like a hill, still having height. Indeed, the *Husia* says, that the doers of good will be "a glorious spirit in heaven and a continuing power on earth. They shall be counted among the ancestors. Their name shall endure as a monument and what they've done on earth shall never perish or pass away." So it shall be with our Sister Coretta Scott King, this wife, widow, life partner and dream keeper of Dr. Martin Luther King, Jr.; this mother of Yolanda, Martin III, Dexter and Bernice, this dawn bringer who even before her partnership with Dr. King, began to imagine and work for a new and better world.

Mrs. King evolved, like and with her husband, in the midst of the Movement, that long, hard and heroic struggle of her people for freedom, justice, equality and power over their destiny and daily lives. She was his life partner in marriage and the Movement, at his side in support and assistance, and in complementary cooperation to create the just society and good world they and their people longed and worked for. And we know and honor her not only for what she meant and did for Dr. King, but also for how well she, in the womanist tradition of Black women, balanced and performed the varied roles which family, motherhood and Movement, husband and history had handed her and which she had chosen.

Still, it is as a capable and committed partner in their shared work for a good world and keeper of his dream after his martyrdom that we understand and appreciate her in the most deep and enduring ways. For in this all the other roles are included. And it is in this context, this crucible of struggle, tragedy, recovery and reassertion in the Movement and the world that Coretta Scott King comes into her own as a leader, builder, teacher and symbol in her own right.

She had entered the partnership of love and struggle with her own awareness, experience, and aspirations and became an indispensable source of her husband's defense and development. Indeed, he recalls that "on many points she educated me" and that their first discussion was around questions of "racial justice, economic justice and peace" and her active engagement with these issues. Thus, he said, "I must admit—I wish I could say—to satisfy my masculine ego, that I led her down this path; but I must say we went down together, because she was as actively involved and concerned when we met as she is now."

Thus, down every path he pursued, she was ever there beside him. On the first day when he accepted his assignment from heaven to be a minister and his invitation from history to be a Movement leader, she was there with him. She was always there counseling, comforting and encouraging him; accompanying and representing him at demonstrations, rallies, marches and meetings, and standing steadfast with him when Hoover, peeping thru a keyhole in the closet of his own tabloid life and self-covering, tried to undermine their marriage and Dr. King's status in the Movement. She was ever protective of his life and legacy building relationships with presidents, professionals, legislators, leaders and others to secure his release from political imprisonment, save him from harm and help him in his work of freedom, social justice and peace in the world.

They had traveled the world together, going to Africa in 1957 to celebrate with the people and president of Ghana, Kwame Nkrumah, their independence; to India in 1959 to pay homage to the memory of his philosophical mentor, Mahatma Gandhi, and to Norway to receive the Nobel Prize for Peace in 1964. She would afterwards stress our need for a world-encompassing approach, to "be concerned about others as well as ourselves . . . (to) study the cultures, languages and problems of the whole world," and to recognize the web of interdependence we share with others.

We know and honor Coretta Scott King also as the dream keeper, keeper of her husband's dream, no doubt shaped and clearly shared by both of them. It is a dream founded in faith and hope, secured in love and struggle and realized in an ever-expanding realm of freedom, justice, mutual respect and peace in the world. Only days after the assassination of her husband and even before burying him, she lifted herself up from the ground of grief on which she lay, and flew to the site of his martyrdom to lead the march he would have led in defense of the dignity and rights of Black workers. There she completed plans for his world-significant funeral and began working on plans for a living memorial for him called the Martin Luther King, Jr. Center for Non-Violent Social Change. Afterwards, she would work tirelessly for years to establish a national holiday for him and to build a protective wall around his work to secure it from exploitation, trivialization and distortion. "Martin was my soul mate," she said. "I believe that his spirit continues to live on and my spirit will live on and one day our spirits will be joined."

Finally, Coretta Scott King was a dawn bringer, a lifter up of the light that lasts in the best tradition of our people. In all Mrs. King did, from her college years of struggle thru her life partnership with Dr. King and her work as dream keeper, she was struggling to bring the dawn of a new world, a world without the evils of racism, oppression, poverty and war. Thus, she said "many despair at all the evil, unrest and disorder in the world today, but I see a new social order and I see the dawn of a new day." Our task, then, is to hold on to the good she and her husband gave us, remember the lessons of love and struggle they taught us, and continue their and our unfinished and ongoing work and struggle to bring and sustain good in the world.

2006 February 9

Living the Legacy of Dr. Martin Luther King, Jr.: A Sacred Narrative and Model

Within the sacred narrative we know as Black history, there is a long list of prophets, messengers, saints and holy men and women, who walked the world from its beginning trying to discern the Divine, who heard the call of heaven and history and stood up and went forth to seek and speak truth, promote and do justice and bring good in the world. The Most Reverend Dr. Martin Luther King, Jr. is such a person. Both his life and death offer us invaluable lessons about how we are to understand and assert ourselves in the world as both persons and a people. He taught us to value the sacredness of human life, arguing against capital punishment, war, police brutality and other forms of official violence as well as unofficial violence among human beings. He was especially opposed to wars of aggression and occupation like those against Vietnam, Haiti, Palestine, Iraq, and Afghanistan. And he taught us to love peace, cherish freedom, pursue justice and sacrifice for them.

Dr. King left us not only a world historical legacy of thought and practice, but defined us as a moral and social vanguard in this country and the world. Indeed, at the heart of his ethical philosophy is his recognition and reaffirmation of the rights, dignity, divine destiny and potentiality of Black people. He posed us as a people whose social situation, suffering and profound spirituality had prepared us for a divine historical mission. It was, he taught, not only a mission of liberating ourselves, but also of restructuring and spiritualizing U.S. society and offering a paradigm of human liberation to the world. Thus, he states that "first we must massively assert our dignity and worth; . . . stand up amidst a system that still oppresses us and develop an unassailable majestic sense of values, (and) no longer be ashamed of being Black." On the contrary, we must see in ourselves the image of the Divine and accept the divine mission to repair and free ourselves in the process of restructuring and freeing this country from the triple evils of "racism, materialism and militarism."

Dr. King rightly saw that unless we believe in ourselves, we could not believe in or successfully carry out our mission. And thus, he called for respect for the Divine in us and for what he called "a divine

86

dissatisfaction" with the wrongs and evils of the world—oppression, injustice, inequality and war. And he called on us to struggle in such a way that "when the history books are written in future generations, the historians will have to pause and say 'there lived a great people— a black people—who injected new meaning and dignity into the veins of civilization.' " Indeed, he said: "This is our challenge and our overwhelming responsibility."

Secondly, Dr. King argued that we had both the moral right and responsibility to resist evil, including disobeying the established order and its unjust laws. He maintained that our "highest loyalty is to God and not to the mores, or folkways, the state or the nation or any man-made institution." Thus, when a man-made law conflicts with moral law and reasoning, we have not only the right but the responsibility to resist it. Moreover, he said that justice for Black people will not come simply from court decisions or from legislation, but from a "radical restructuring of U.S. society."

Closely related to the above concept is Dr. King's contention that it is immoral and cowardly to collaborate in one's own oppression. One collaborates first when one accepts oppression. For he says, "to accept passively an unjust system is to cooperate with that system." One also collaborates when one turns a blind eye to injustice. For "to ignore evil is to become an accomplice to it." Thus, we must not ignore the grave injustice of government criminal neglect and negligence during and after Katrina, nor watch silently and passively as wars of aggression consume countless lives and resources and poison human relations in the world.

Fourthly, Dr. King, like all our great leaders, taught that religion must have a social role as well as a spiritual one. Indeed, he taught they are interrelated. A true religion, he states, is obligated to deal "with the whole man; not only with his soul but also with his body, not only with his spiritual well-being, but also with his social well-being." Thus, he asked us to develop a world perspective, respect the sacredness of life everywhere and struggle steadfast in our faith in the capacity for human good in the world.

Finally, Dr. King taught us the centrality of struggle, not only to free ourselves, but also to repair, transform and strengthen ourselves in the ongoing efforts to build and sustain the Beloved Community or good world. "Human progress is neither automatic nor inevitable," he stated. "Every step toward the goal of justice requires sacrifice, suffering and struggle." Moreover, he said, "freedom is never voluntarily given by the oppressor; it must be demanded by the oppressed." Indeed, he continues, "freedom has always been an expensive thing" and as history shows, "is rarely gained without sacrifice and self-denial."

It was Dr. King's hope that we could together build a good world, a beloved community of humanity based on mutual respect, non-violence, peace, justice and cooperation for common good. Here he linked peace and justice, stating that "peace is not simply the absence of tension but (also) the presence of justice." Dr. King ends where he begins, calling on us to step forward as a people and with other oppressed and progressive peoples of the world, continue to weather the hurricanes of history and to wage the ongoing struggle to create the good world we all want and deserve. "The battle is in our hands," he tells us, "the road ahead is not altogether a smooth one. There are no broad highways that lead us easily and inevitably to quick solutions, but we must keep going."

2006 January 19

Malcolm X:
Eternal Message, Immortal Man

It is written in the sacred *Husia*, that "to do that which is of value is for eternity. A man called forth by his work does not die for his name is raised and remembered because of it." Surely the imperishable character of Malcolm X and his meaning to us and the world lies unavoidably in his tireless and self-sacrificing work and struggle to transform himself, liberate his people and bring good into the world.

I had met Malcolm in the summer of '62 while I was a student at UCLA. We had brought him to campus. He and I talked at length after one of his lectures at Mosque #27 and at the Shabazz Restaurant and afterward he had given me a ride home. From that time until his martyrdom, we talked when he came to town. And in that time, I developed a profound respect for him as a leader, elder brother, incisive intellectual, and world historical person. He was a man among men and equally a man among women. And he was a man among the machines that masquerade as men, imitating and extracting our humanity in continuing and alternating bouts of racist insanity and planetary suicide. It is to these moneyed-machines that Malcolm spoke saying, "I'm the man you think you are. And if you want to know what I'd do for my freedom, think what you'd do for yours. I'll do the same, only more of it."

Malcolm's life and his enduring lessons are about liberation on a personal, collective and world level. Thus, his teachings and practice are an ethical and spiritual project. As a project of liberation, it is a struggle which is both a process and promise of human freedom and human flourishing. Malcolm's religion was Islam, an earth-based practice with the promise of liberation first here on earth. In his days in the Nation of Islam, taught by Messenger Elijah Muhammad, Malcolm reminded us to understand that in a real sense "heaven and hell are conditions reflecting one's moral and material conditions here on earth." Given all that is to be done on earth to end suffering, free the oppressed, and bring justice in the world, "no one's mind should be in the sky." Indeed, he said, "in Islam everyone works. Heaven demands hard work. There is no room for laziness and no room for ignorance."

Malcolm talks here about *jihad*, the internal and external struggle for self- and world transformation in the interest of freedom, justice and good in the world. Malcolm's project has three basic dimensions to it, summed up in his call to "wake up, clean up and stand up." The first dimension is a coming-into-consciousness which is a struggle against both ignorance and illusion cultivated by the dominant society. And it is equally a struggle for the acquisition of knowledge of: (1) self as a person and as a member of a world historical community and as a bearer of dignity and divinity; (2) God as a divine being, appearing in our own image and acting in our own interests; and (3) the oppressor as an enemy of human life, freedom and flourishing. Waking up precedes and makes possible each of the other steps. For Malcolm teaches, "when a man understand who he is, who God is, who the devil is...then he can pick himself up out of the gutter; he can clean himself up and stand up like a man should before his God."

To clean up is for Malcolm to live a moral life, speak truth, do justice, avoid all vices and addictions—chemical, behavioral or psychological, and constantly strive to do what is right and good for ourselves, our people and the world. Here it is important to note that Malcolm believed deeply in the possibility of self-transformation regardless of how low one has fallen. He notes that before his own transformation thru Islam, he "was addicted to and enslaved by the evils and vices of this white civilization—dope, alcohol, adultery and even murder." He was, he said, locked at the bottom level of life "buried up to his neck in the mud of this filthy world with very little hope, desire or intention of amounting to anything." Indeed, he says, he was so low and lost he was actually "walking on his own coffin."

But as he recounts in his autobiography, Islam gave him a faith, a community and a cause that enabled him to lift himself up, overturn himself, and dedicate his life to lifting up others and living a life worthy of his human and divine nature. Here, then, is where his call to stand up is so essential, even indispensable and urgent.

Malcolm's moral call and challenge to us to stand up speaks to each of our need and obligation to create the world we want and deserve to live in. Malcolm's teaching on standing up, like his other ethical and spiritual teachings, are rooted in and reflective of his own personal recovery and reconstruction. For him, standing up is offering one's life and death as a "testimony of some social value," in a word, being willing to live and die as a mirror and martyr for liberation, freedom, justice and good in the world. It is a morality of sacrifice, he teaches here, a morality and self-giving in which we offer our hearts and minds, time, efforts, material goods and ultimately our life and even our death, if necessary, for a greater good.

Finally, it is important to remember that Malcolm asked us to understand and assert ourselves as we are, a world historical people, "part of a global rebellion of the oppressed against the oppressor, the exploited against the exploiter." And thus for ourselves and humanity, we must imagine a new world and be the self-conscious fathers, mothers and midwives of history who, with other struggling and progressive peoples, bring it into being and make it flourish.

2006 May 18

Working in the Wilderness of North America: The Legacy of Messenger Muhammad

This is the 109th anniversary month of the birth of the Honorable Elijah Muhammad, Messenger of God (Allah), teacher of the people, institution-builder, a leaver of a legacy unique in its form and enduring in its content. No one in the 60's, who was aware and active, can seriously say or truthfully claim they were not influenced in some meaningful way by the teachings, initiatives and achievements of Messenger Muhammad and the Nation of Islam (NOI). The ideas of the centrality of Blackness, the severe critique of White supremacy and savagery, the focus on economic control, development and ownership, political self-determination, the right and responsibility of self-defense, reparations, liberation theology, education for liberation, draft resistance, the idea of a Ten-Point Program of "what we want" and 12-point program of "what we believe" and the struggle against police brutality and for justice and freedom for political prisoners, are all part of his earliest teachings and the practice of the Nation of Islam.

The Messenger had come up from the slaughter-fields of Georgia with his wife, his first believer and his constant companion, Sister Clara Muhammad, and his children, escaping the routine racist bloodletting, barbarism and brutality which posed and passed as White civilization. But when he came North, he soon noticed that wherever he and his people went, they still were in what he called the "wilderness of North America." And this, he noted, was not a natural wilderness but a social one, a place where human predators lined up daily to leap on the vulnerable, where Whiteness, wealth and power were the real trinity, and the concept of God was trotted out regularly to justify genocide, holocaust, and other crimes against humans and humanity.

At an early age, he had felt a sense of mission. His mother had dreamed of his divine mission and his grandfather had named him Elijah and predicted he would become a prophet. Later, Muhammad would understand and assert himself as a Divine Messenger, raised up from among his people to bear special witness to their divinity, their rightful religion and the right path to pursue for freedom, justice and equality. He taught us that "the first and foremost teaching for us"

92

from God, himself, is "accept your own and be yourself." Accepting ourselves and being ourselves requires that we know ourselves as divine, know our oppressor as evil and reverse the world order established during the rise of White supremacy. "We are of God," he stated, "and our oppressors are of the devil." Thus, we must work for good in the world, avoid evil, and "do for self and kind." Then, we can enjoy the good of the earth "which belongs to (us) divinely as much as it does to other nations of the earth."

For the Messenger, Islam was the way to success and respect in the world. For him, Islam gives Black people "a sense of dignity," "makes them fearless," "destroys superstition and removes falsehood," and "has the divine power to unite us and save us from destruction." Muhammad taught a religion rooted in the reality of daily life. God was a God in our own image and interest and the devil was the oppressor. Hell was the oppression, brutality and savagery we suffered at the hands of our oppressor. And heaven was a life of freedom, justice, and equality, a space and time "we can call our own, . . . (and) . . . hold up our heads with pride and dignity, without the continuous harassment and indignities of our oppressors." In a word, a place where we understand and assert ourselves as bearers of dignity and divinity in the strongest sense of the words.

Also, Messenger Muhammad taught the need for a liberational education, saying "I want an education for my people that will let them exercise the right of freedom . . . elevates them . . , creates unity and makes us desire to be with our own and build for our own." Moreover, he said "the education my people need is that knowledge, the attribute of God, which creates power to accomplish and make progress in the good things . . , the righteous things."

Finally, Messenger Muhammad taught a strong commitment to the principle and practice of self-determination and self-reliance in every area of life. "If we want freedom, justice and equality we must look for it among ourselves and our kind, not among the people who have destroyed and robbed us of even the knowledge of ourselves, themselves, our God and our religion," he said. Thus, we must defend ourselves against injustice and oppression. Indeed, the *Quran* says, "For those who struggle against oppression there is no blame." Speaking to the freedom struggles in the South, Messenger Muhammad taught that Black people are "justified by God and the divine law of self-defense to fight and defend themselves against dog and human attack."

In terms of development, Muhammad always linked moral grounding, education, and economics. In his economic program, he stressed the centrality of Islam and education, and offered five practical steps in building an economic base for the Black community to develop and flourish. These included "unity and group cooperation, pooling of resources, stopping criticism of all that is Black-owned and Black-operated, avoiding jealousy, and working hard in a collective manner and making no excuses for failure."

The Hon. Elijah Muhammad came as a Divine Messenger, reading signs and causing wonders, and building on the legacy of the Honorable Marcus Garvey and the Noble Drew Ali. He taught the good way of the ancestors to walk in the world as bearers of dignity and divinity. He straightened the bent back, cleared the cluttered mind and freed the enslaved spirit. He challenged us to be men among men and women among women—righteous, productive and deserving of the highest respect. He taught and mentored Min. Malcolm X, gave foundation and framework to Min. Louis Farrakhan and brought Min. Khalid Muhammad into being. And he informed, fostered and profoundly influenced our Movement for Black Power. We can perhaps best sum up his message and mission in these, his words, "Love yourself and your kind, refrain from doing evil to each other; love each other as brothers and sisters, do for self and kind, accept your own and be yourself, practice unity, and do good and righteous things" in and for the world.

2006 October 19

Rosa Parks, Her People and the Movement: Honoring the Person, the People and Their Struggle

The passing of Mrs. Rosa Parks calls immediately to mind the long, hard and heroic struggle waged by African people to expand the realm of freedom and justice in this country as well as the people, great and small, who made it possible. Mrs. Rosa Parks was one of the great ones, whose life we hold up as a lesson and legacy for both ourselves and the world. She was an ordinary person, called by history and heaven to do an extraordinary thing in the ongoing African ethical obligation to bring good in the world. And she accepted this dual invitation with strength, dignity and determination.

It is written in the sacred text of our Yoruba ancestors, the *Odu Ifa*, that we are all, every human being, divinely chosen to bring good into the world and that this is the fundamental mission and meaning of human life. Likewise, there are critical junctures in history when we, as persons and a people, already chosen by heaven are also chosen by history. That is to say, we are given an invitation and opportunity to do great things and in cooperation with others achieve a great good in the world.

But even as we are chosen, we must also choose, choose to accept the invitation and seize the opportunity to do good in the world. Mrs. Rosa Parks accepted the invitation of history on December 1, 1955 in Montgomery, Alabama. She tells us of that decision and act of defiance saying, "I knew there was a possibility of being mistreated (i.e., beaten or worst), but an opportunity was being given to me to do what I had asked of others." Thus, she accepted this invitation and dared struggle with and for her people.

It is important here to stress that the invitation of history to Mrs. Parks was handed at the same time to her people and they accepted the invitation also. Thus, the ground of her greatness and the spark of the Movement, lay not simply in her refusing to surrender her seat, for she and many others had done that before. What was important was not only that she remained seated on the bus, but that she also stood up in society and in a Movement with her people and with them resisted a brutal racism that wreaked havoc not only on her life as a person, but also on our lives as a people.

Moreover, it is important to note that she had a long history of struggle for human and civil rights and social justice. She often gave honor to her mother and grandparents who taught her to defend her rights and dignity, her husband, Mr. Raymond Parks, who helped cultivate her activism through working together in the NAACP, and all the women and men in the Movement who embraced and supported her.

And yet the established order has packaged and presented her as the lone and lonely heroine, sitting in "quiet dignity" with no history of struggle behind her, no future of struggle in front of her, no people in struggle around and with her and no Movement which gave ground, support and meaning to her actions and initiatives. By doing this, they seek to mask the strength of the masses and hide their capacity to produce and nurture the great persons they need.

In contrast to this, Mrs. Parks tells us, she had "a life history of being rebellious against being mistreated because of my color" and that she and others in Montgomery had been struggling and "planning for freedom all our lives." We must remember, then, that her honor is a shared honor that she herself shared with her people and the many persons who helped her become a giant in a generation of great leaders, i.e., Fannie Lou Hamer, Malcolm X, Ella Baker, Martin Luther King, et al.

The meaning of Mrs. Parks to us lies, like all our history and historical figures in: the lessons she has left us; the spirit of possibility she provides us; the model of human excellence and achievement she offers us; and the morality of remembrance she gives us an opportunity to practice. The first lesson for her life is that of the indispensability and unavoidability of struggle. Second, we learn from Mrs. Parks that even as we are chosen by history and heaven, we must also choose. At a critical juncture, Mrs. Parks said she "had been pushed as far as I could be pushed. . .I had decided I would have to know once and for all what rights I had as a human being and a citizen." And that knowledge and reaffirmation could only come in resistance to the White supremacy that would deny those rights.

A second area of meaning of Mrs. Parks' life for us is the spirit of possibility she provides for us and reminds us to look within for the strength needed to accomplish both small and great things. Mrs. Parks clearly served as a spark which inspired a Movement and thus, she serves as a reminder that one spark in the right season and situation can set a whole forest on fire.

A third lesson from Mrs. Parks' life is as she said, "each person must live their life as a model for others." And they must work, build and struggle, as our ancestors taught us, conscious of the fact that "every day is a donation to eternity and even one hour is a contribution to the future."

Finally, Mrs. Parks teaches us to appreciate, learn and carry on the legacy of those who walked and worked before us. It was her belief and hope that "memories of our lives, of our work and our deeds will continue in others." And at the center of those memories must be the ongoing moral obligation to constantly struggle to bring good in the world and not let any good be lost.

2005 November 3

IV

Holocaust, Katrina and Reparations

It is both an irony and unique invitation of history that we are both the injured person and physician, both an oppressed people and our own liberator, both midwives of history and the sons and daughters who must give birth to our new selves and bring into being a new history at the same time. Indeed, it is the sacred teaching of the ancestors in the Odu Ifa that "If you are given birth, you must bring yourself into being again."

We are, then, the injured physicians who will heal and repair ourselves in the process and practice of repairing the world, transforming it into an ever-expanding realm of freedom, justice and human flourishing. For we are indeed our own liberators. Given this understanding, as we've said so often, there is no remedy except resistance, no medical or social strategy that does not privilege and promote struggle and no future or possibility of flourishing except that forged on the battlefield for a new world and a new history and hope for humankind.

Reparations

Reaffirming the Rightfulness of Reparations: Repairing Ourselves and the World

In the historic struggle for reparations for African peoples, nothing is more important than that we ourselves frame and forge the process by which we understand and approach it. Indeed, we must be clear about the larger meaning of this struggle. Clearly, it is not what the media and other sources of similar interests and ignorance tell us. It is not about the quest for a handout or to inspire, reinforce or perpetuate a sense of victimization among Black people or to divert attention from so-called more serious issues. Nor is it simply about money and the crass concern for dollars more than human dignity, freedom and justice.

On the contrary, *the struggle for reparations is a struggle for justice for a people, accountability for the oppressors, and an ethical model for the world of how to treat a grievously injured people.* It is a struggle to repair the gross historical and ongoing damage done to us as African people in the Holocaust of enslavement, to rebuild and reinforce our ongoing movement for liberation and ever higher levels of human life and to create a continuing expanding realm of human freedom, justice and flourishing in the world. And this is to be achieved, not simply by what we are given by our oppressors, but more importantly by what we gain and give of ourselves in and for the struggle itself. It is a struggle based on the psychology of Frantz Fanon and the social ethical teachings of Malcolm X: (1) that we can only heal and repair ourselves in struggle; and (2) that struggle must be not only against the conditions which caused the damage, but also to expand the realm of human freedom, justice and flourishing in the world and initiate a new history of humankind. This process and ethical practice is called *serudj ta* in the ancient Egyptian Maatian tradition and means to heal, repair and transform the world with the understanding that in the process we heal, repair and transform ourselves.

For our struggle for reparations to be more than a quest for back payments rightly owed, then, and for it to be more than a deceptive

101

dependency on the actions of the oppressor, we must understand and approach it, as a people, in its most meaningful and expansive form. That is to say, as a critical site and source of our ongoing struggle to create engaged and empowered communities of African people, just and good societies wherever we are, and a good and sustainable world for our ancestors, ourselves, and the generations which follow.

Regardless of the eventual shape of the evolved discourse and policy on reparations, there are six essential aspects which must be addressed and included in any meaningful and moral approach to reparations. They are public dialog, public admission, public apology, public recognition, compensation, and preventive measures against the recurrence of holocaust and other similar forms of massive destruction of human life, human culture and human possibility.

First, there must be a *public dialog* in which Europeans (Whites) overcome their acute denial of the nature and extent of injuries inflicted on African people and concede that the most morally appropriate term for this utter destruction of human life, human culture and human possibility is holocaust. Secondly, there must be *public admission* of Holocaust committed against African people by the state and people. By holocaust is meant a morally monstrous act of genocide that is not only against the targeted people, but also a crime against humanity. This moves the issue from one of commerce or trade gone bad with collateral damage to a moral issue of holocaust.

Thirdly, once there is public discussion and admission of the nature and extent of the injury, then there must be *public apology*. Moreover, the state must offer it on behalf of its White citizens. For the state is the crime partner with business and corporate interests in the initiation, conduct and sustaining of this destructive process. It maintained and supported the system of destruction with law, army, ideology and brutal suppression. Thus, it must offer the apology for the Holocaust committed.

Fourthly, public admission and public apology must be reinforced with *public recognition* through institutional establishment, monumental construction and educational instruction through the school and university system and the media directed toward teaching and preserving the memory of the horror and meaning of the Holocaust of enslavement, not only for Africans, but also for humanity as a whole.

Fifthly, reparations also require *compensation* in various forms. Compensation does not automatically mean simply money payoffs either individually or collectively. Indeed, it is a multidimensional demand and option and may involve not only money, but land, free health care, housing, free education from grade school through college, etc. But whether we choose one or all, we must have a communal discussion of it and then make the choice. Moreover, compensation as an issue is not simply compensation for lost labor, but for the comprehensive injury—the brutal destruction of human lives, human cultures and human possibilities.

Finally, reparations require *preventive measures*, i.e., institutions, processes and practices to preclude the reoccurrence of such massive destruction of human life, human culture and human possibility. This, again, means that we must see and approach the reparations struggle as part and parcel of our overall struggle for freedom, justice, equality and power in and over our destiny and daily lives.

Our struggle for reparations is and must be, then, an *inclusive project* which seeks to repair the gross and ongoing injury of one of the greatest holocausts in human history, the Holocaust of African enslavement. And this essentially means to produce in the midst of struggle a process by which we, the injured people, not only self-consciously understand and assert ourselves in ongoing efforts to restore a sense of wholeness, well-being and freedom in our lives, but also rightfully see ourselves as continuing our ancient ancestral struggle of expanding the realm of human freedom and flourishing and bringing good into the world.

2006 June 20

The Collective Vocation of Reparations: Repairing Ourselves and the World

N'COBRA, the National Coalition of Blacks for Reparations in America, met in Los Angeles, last month (October 27-29) at California State University-Dominguez Hills and the African American Cultural Center (Us) to map out and mark off the fields of focus and action necessary to continue and strengthen its forward movement and achieve its intermediate and long-range goals. Led by its co-chairs, Kibibi Tyehimba and Milton McGriff, and accompanied by the elder statesman and founding member, Dr. Imari Obadele, and one of its major theorists and national board member, Wautella Ibn Yusef, N'COBRA held both organizational and public discussions on critical issues the reparations movement is addressing and the need to constantly expand the way it understands and asserts itself. As both a member of N'COBRA and chair of Us, I gave a focal lecture on October 28 on operational unity and coalitions and alliances. Moreover, Us hosted and I chaired and presented on a panel with Dr. Obadele, Ms. Tyehimba and Mr. Yusef, titled "The Ethics, Politics and Practice of Reparations." Below are some of the ideas I shared and developed out of these discussions.

Clearly, this is a constantly dangerous, sometimes distressing and always demanding moment of history in which we live. It is dangerous because of the global human and environmental wreckage and ruin the powerful and wealthy bring in their coming and leave in their wake. It is sometimes distressing because of the magnitude of the damage done, the some-times seemingly unsolvable nature of the problems they produce, and the periodic and progressive erosion of the will to resist, even among some of the most seasoned soldiers and committed activists. And it is a demanding moment of history because of the life-and-death nature of the issues involved and because we all know, as Hannibal told us after crossing the Alps and before his decisive victory over the Romans, "we must win, for if we lose we're lost."

Clearly, the world is being damaged every day, as are the masses of people in it. Unfreedom, oppression, injustice and exploitation are the order of the day and everywhere there is this ever-present and urgent need to repair our damaged world, heal the gross and grievous injuries we have suffered and free and empower the oppressed and disempowered peoples of the world. There is no doubt, then, there is an urgent and compelling need to repair our world. The evidence is overwhelming: the ongoing genocide in Darfur; the continuous catastrophe of Katrina; the centuries of suffering in Haiti; the savage occupation of Palestine, Iraq and Afghanistan; the enduring and unnecessary hunger and homelessness in the world; the increasing spread of AIDS and other devastating diseases; sexual and labor enslavement; the continuing predation on women and children; the progressive degradation and destruction of the environment; and the daily "peaceful violence" of global systemic oppression.

All of this requires a process and practice of reparations which in its larger and ethical sense involves our not only healing and repairing ourselves, but also healing and repairing the world. Indeed, it is in the process and practice of healing and repairing the world that we heal and repair ourselves. This is Min. Malcolm's and Frantz Fanon's teaching on regaining our full sense of manhood, womanhood and humanity in the struggle against the system and social forces which would deny and diminish them. But reparations as a world-encompassing ethical ideal and practice also goes back to our ancestral sacred teachings found in the *Husia* that we are morally obligated to constantly repair, restore and renew the world, making it more beautiful and beneficial than we inherited it. This is called in ancient Egyptian the moral obligation of *serudj ta*.

As a righteous practice of repairing, restoring and renewing the world, *serudj ta* provides us with an expansive concept for understanding and approaching our work and struggle in the world. Indeed, it translates as reparations in a most expansive sense and roots us in a world-encompassing ethical project worthy of our collective vocation as a people. And we do need a new collective vocation as we had in the Sixties, a common commitment every-one knew and embraced, regardless of affiliations, i.e., the collective vocation of struggle for freedom, justice, equality and power.

It is the expansive meaning of reparations as *serudj ta*, healing and repairing ourselves in the process and practice of healing and repairing the world that insures and proves our movement is more than a mobilization for money; that it is not tied to the mistaken idea that concessions from our oppressor will heal and repair us; and that we are all clear about how we define reparations as an ethical principle, pursue it as a personal and social practice and achieve it as a goal of *Maat*, rightness and good in and of the world.

If reparations is to be our collective vocation, we must involve our people on every level, expand our presence in the major institutions of our community and society and dare to impact and shape social discourse and policy. We must pose another way to imagine and engage the world than that of the established order. We must craft, teach and practice a uniting ethical vision that fosters human well-being, wholeness and flourishing, eliminates the destructive division between the natural and social, builds and supports organizations and alliances concerned with and committed to good in the world, and become and be a worthy model of the cooperation and caring, work, struggle, service and institution-building we advocate.

It is both an irony and unique invitation of history that we are both the injured person and physician, both an oppressed people and our own liberator, both midwives of history and the sons and daughters who must give birth to our new selves and bring into being a new history at the same time. Indeed, it is the sacred teaching of the ancestors in the *Odu Ifa* that "If you are given birth, you must bring yourself into being again."

We are, then, the injured physicians who will heal and repair ourselves in the process and practice of repairing the world, transforming it into an ever-expanding realm of freedom, justice and human flourishing. For we are indeed our own liberators. Given this understanding, as we've said so often, there is no remedy except resistance, no medical or social strategy that does not privilege and promote struggle and no future or possibility of flourishing except that forged on the battlefield for a new world and a new history and hope for humankind.

2006 November 9

Katrina

Riding Out the Hurricane:
Reaffirming the Resilience of the People

We, as a people, have survived and prevailed over one of the greatest holocausts in human history, the Holocaust of African enslavement; only the Native American Holocaust is comparable. And we will survive and prevail over the horror, hardship and devastation of this combined natural and man-made disaster. But as we move forward to bury our dead, bandage our wounds, recover our lost ones and rebuild our lives, let us first pause to pay homage to the many thousands dead, to mourn especially the many who died avoidable deaths, casualties of criminal neglect by the established order. Let us reaffirm the uniqueness and equal worthiness of each of their lives, as the *Husia* teaches, and remind all who would deny it that they were and remain equal bearers of dignity and divinity, regardless of the value a racist society or callous government assigns them.

In the prayerful words of our ancestors let us say: blessed are those who have gone but remain with us. Surely, we share the profound personal loss of their relatives and loved ones and the great collective loss of our people. May the joy they brought and the good they left last forever. May all their loved ones be blessed with consolation, courage and peace. And may the beloved departed ones rise up in radiance and be welcomed warmly in the afterlife among the ancestors, among the doers of good, the righteous and the rightfully rewarded. Hotep. Ase. Heri.

Let us also praise the people for their resilience in the face of such immense and overwhelming devastation, for their courage under water, fire and the gross failure of their government to serve and save them, and for their kindness and compassion toward each other. Praise is due to those who shared their meager food and drink and sacrificed seats to evacuate others, to parents who stayed behind to send their children to safety, to younger people who watched and pushed the wheel chairs of the ill and aged, and to those who deferred in line to the elderly, the ill and the infant.

Let us also praise the national African American community as a whole for its immediate outpouring of unity, empathy and aid on every level, and who acted swiftly to issue the call for aid and began at once to mobilize and organize to deliver it: funding groups, professional organizations, activist organizations, religious institutions of all faiths, artists, actors and athletes and children as well as adults. They knew that, in the final analysis, we are our own liberators and must heal and repair ourselves in the process of repairing the world.

Let us also praise other national and local groups and persons of good will and the international community for their quick and valuable support. Arab and Muslim peoples who are regularly profiled, harassed, arrested, and held without trial gave hundreds of millions in aid. Little Cuba offered doctors which are among the most proficient in the world and Venezuela offered medical teams, tons of food and water, and generators which the Bush administration rejected in their continuing irrationality at the expense of us and others.

Clearly, the horrific and heart-wrenching devastation by Hurricane Katrina, was compounded by the callous, incompetent and criminally slow response to it by the national government. Indeed, the whole world watched in disbelief and moral disgust as the so-called single superpower in the world stood still coldly, then stumbled and staggered like a drunk towards New Orleans, stopping on the way to offer press-conference promises, instead of providing the real relief and rescue efforts needed.

Let us not be afraid or hesitant, then, to speak of the race and class character of Bush and company's response. Obviously, their political determinations of worth and need, don't include Black and poor people in their calculus of care and concern in the way they do the wealthy, White and vote-rich regions of Florida. Unlike in Florida, the people of New Orleans were crudely called refugees in their own country, and denied immediate aid, conjuring up images of the brutal treatment of devalued peoples like those in Haiti, Palestine and other places which Bush and company call the "dark corners of the world."

Bush also knew about the problems of environmental degradation and weak storm protection and levee systems, but he denied and reduced funds for five years. He transformed FEMA into an arm of his so-called war on terrorism, diverted monies and attention from natural disasters, and went around the world war-mongering, wasting lives, personnel, and vital resources necessary to prevent disaster and promote development.

Let us also criticize the corporate media for profiling Black people as criminals rather than courageous victims while presenting Whites as models of cooperation. Also, the media confused "looting" with the desperate and compelling search for food, drink and other survival supplies the government denied them and corporations would not give them although these were damaged by water and would eventually spoil. And they conflated the lumpen or criminal element with the masses themselves, conveniently ignoring that in every crisis, street and corporate criminals emerge to prey on the people under different guises.

Finally, let us remember again, that we must work and struggle to build the world we want and deserve to live in, a world of freedom, justice, power of the masses and a genuine peace. With this in mind we must continue to prepare for the 40th anniversary Nguzo Saba 2005 Conference of Us, September 8-11, and the Million More March and Movement, October 16. And we must recommit ourselves to get organized, rebuild our Movement and pursue the historic tasks before us which are: to know the past and honor it; to engage the present and improve it; and to imagine the future and forge it.

2005 September 8

Weathering the Hurricanes of History: Repairing Ourselves and the World

Even as we continue to find and bury our dead, wash and treat our wounds, rebuild our lives, and renew and recover our courage to go on, we know there will be other hurricanes, those that arrive from the sea and those that arise in society. And we must work and struggle together to weather them all and build a society and world where the hurricanes of history—the savage and destructive realities of oppression, injustice, domination and war—won't leave us so vulnerable and damaged, and thus so easily devastated by the forces and fury of nature.

Indeed, Hurricane Katrina stands as a metaphor for the destructive hurricanes of history, past and present, which have wreaked havoc on our lives. The metaphor is one of deadly fierceness and devastating fury, of relentless battering and cold and uncaring destruction. It is difficult at times to imagine or accept that humans would act this way, but history is replete with such realities, regardless of our reluctance to recall or concede them. Witness the Holocaust of African enslavement, the Native American and Native Australian Holocausts, and the imperialism and colonialism which were the parallel and pitiless systems that produced these Holocausts. Witness also the current and sustained savaging of the people of Haiti, Palestine, Iraq and Afghanistan, the high tech terrorism and vicious wars against the vulnerable peoples of the world. And think too of the virulent and resistant strains of racism and its sinister symbiont, class oppression. Think of how they have ravaged and ruined our lives and left us vulnerable to major and minor disasters and diseases, ill-equipped and impoverished and devalued and disregarded by the rich and the racists who rule us.

And then, to wash our open wounds in the salt and savagery of caustic comment, comes along Nurse Barbie Bush, matriarch of the Bushmen that masquerade on good days as government. With the aged arrogance and ignorance of wealth and a withered mind, she claims she fears that we find our displacement and virtual imprisonment at a sports stadium preferable to our own homes and communities and the sense of dignity and rightness we derive from these. She reminds us of her foreparents who swaggered in the midst

110

of our enslaved ancestors at the auction block, stripping us naked, poking and peering at our genitals, fumbling with our mouths and muscles, mocking and denying our suffering, and justifying our enslavement and their barbarism with convenient quotes from the Bible.

The hard lessons of history are there then, readable and unerasable, written on a mountain of evidence that will not go away. And thus we know that our defense against the devastating hurricanes of nature and destructive hurricanes of history depend not on the willing assistance or a change of ways of our oppressor. Rather our defense and development, our liberation and even our lives depend on our own efforts. Indeed, as we say in Us, the oppressor is responsible for our oppression, but we are responsible for our liberation. And part of our responsibility is to hold the oppressor responsible, to leave him with no illusions of the rightness of the damage he is doing to us and the world, and no sign of our acceptance of or submission to his oppression. Instead, we must make him know he will never have security until we are free, never know peace until we have justice, and never be at ease until he is no longer an oppressor and we all can enjoy the Good of and in the world.

Therefore, in the midst of global oppression, imposed poverty, world plunder, and willful human and environmental degradation, we will meet in great mass in Washington, D.C. on October 16, 2005; not only to commemorate the historic Million Man March/Day of Absence of 1995, but also to launch the Millions More Movement. It will be a Movement sensitive to our past and current suffering, to the damage done to other peoples and the world by those who have ruled and ruined our lives so long. And it will have as its central motivating thrust the unrelenting struggles to heal and repair ourselves and the world and build an ever-expanding realm of freedom, justice, power of peoples over their lives and lands and peace in the world.

More than ever, we need the March and the Movement. For we need to build a just society where we are not oppressed and impoverished because of our race, where we won't have to live in poverty below levees we know won't hold, wait in vain on housetops and highways for rescue and relief that never come, be herded and dumped in a sports stadium, without provisions or protection and be blamed for atrocities that never happened to exonerate those who never came. But to achieve this, we must rebuild the Movement and in the face of the destructive hurricanes of human history, create a counterforce for good in the world. We must harness the energy and activism of our people, join forces with other oppressed and progressive people, and create in struggle a hurricane of history only the oppressor needs to fear, Marcus Garvey's whirlwind of rightfulness and justice that envelops and frees the world.

Cabral counseled us to claim no easy victory; Mandela warned us there is no easy walk to freedom; and Maria Stewart taught us the urgency and unavoidability of our entering the field of action and building the world we all want and deserve to live in. Now is the time; there is no other. Struggle is the way; there is no alternative. We are the ones, there is no avoiding it.

2005 September 29

Aborting Racism, Ending Oppression and Giving Birth to Justice

The evil winds of race and class continue to blow our way, ravaging and reordering our lives and encouraging us to be silent and collaborate in our own oppression. Last week two cowboys from the Crawford ranch and a location somewhere west of reason, rudely reminded us we must constantly struggle to abort the intentional unending rule of racism, end oppression and give birth to a justice enjoyed by all the people of earth. At the root of our oppression in this country are the disadvantages inflicted and the penalties imposed for belonging to the wrong race in a racist society. Certainly, class combines with race to aggravate and further diminish our status and limit our opportunities and life-chances. In New Orleans, both race and class determined who was evacuated, escaped, drowned or was left behind.

Last week, William Bennett, former Secretary of Education, slipped on the banana peel of irrational and immoral reasoning and fell on all four. Trying to prove a point he could not make, he said that "I do know that is true that if you wanted to reduce crime you could, if that were your sole purpose, you could abort every Black baby in the country and your crime rate would go down." Here he claims a racist "knowledge," reminiscent of the so-called "knowledge" of Black possession of small brains, large genitals, natural rhythm and a criminal nature especially revealed in our resistance to oppression. Even though he denounced the idea and claims it was only a technique in argument, it is a morally monstrous thought and certainly takes on another degree of terribleness in the context of a country whose history includes Holocausts against the African and Native American and subsequent years of bloodletting, lynching and racist rampages.

Moreover, he says in his denunciation "that it would be an impossible, ridiculous and morally reprehensible thing to do, but your crime rate would go down." Notice how the moral issue is left last and the impossibility and ridiculousness of it are declared first. Genocide is not ridiculous or impossible; it is a morally monstrous fact of history and current life. It is thus hardly an idea a morally concerned and sensitive person uses even as a hypothesis. Also, it is a clear example

113

of the double White standard, the selective morality that allows savaging of peoples of color verbally and physically, and then seeking safety, exemption and respect for Whites. Who would hypothesize about aborting Italians babies to reduce crime among them or aborting Jewish babies to reduce U.S. taxpayer debt, foreign aid and wars in defense of Israel? And who would defend the hypothesis as innocent and wonder why the Italians or Jews are so sensitive? Bennett racialized crime and then criminalized race, and thus a whole people. And then he introduced a concept of genocide without noticing or being able to concede the criminal callousness of it all.

And then along came Jones, Alphonso Jackson, Secretary of HUD, on a mission with a message to his people from the Big House. No need to say White House, for even if it weren't the color, it would be the kind—racially dominant and disregardful of others, claiming the right to rule regardless. It's a classic portrait painted by Malcolm, the Fire Prophet, in his "Message to the Grassroots," Lo, the house man cometh and not only does he bring the message, he is the message—a woefully willing instrument of White policy and display of power.

The bringer of bad tidings tells us "Whether we like it or not . . . New Orleans is not going to be as Black as it was for a long time, if ever again." Although Jackson talked as if he were there to study and then advise Bush, in reality it was he who had been already advised. Indeed, the corporate vultures had already gathered, having caught the scent of death and open wounds in the air. Bulging with billions from their murderous business in Iraq, Bechtel, Fluor, Halliburton, and Shaw had already come to town. And they have already begun to purge the poor from the list of those alive and well and living in New Orleans. They have also begun to claim and clean up what they call "eye sores" and "underutilized areas," better rebuilt for the rich and White. The coastal areas this time will be secure and safe for the *herrenvolk*, the master race and the rich, with some upper and lower middle class people let in to claim class, if not racial, diversity.

So hail, hell, the gang's all there, but there is no room at the inn for Black people. Indeed, there is no inn at all and no real inclusion. Black people, we are told, have no right to return, which is a standard and staple of international law whether in Naples, a New Orleans Parish or Palestine. And we are told the poor, in effect, have no right of presence. For the bulldozers are already busy destroying the sources of their past memories, current needs and future aspirations. The real looters have come to town and there is little left for the devastated locals, in spite of the brave faces around the table of the rebuilding commission someone has formed.

Now more than ever, we need the march and the Movement. New Orleans and the Gulf states are a microcosm for a larger disaster that has gone on officially unacknowledged for years. It is the progressive impoverishment and disempowering of the people, the privatization of public resources and the blatant increased enrichment of the rich at the continuing expense of the poor, and the unconscionable disregard for the present and future generations. The oppression is clear and will not end of itself. The answer is struggle; the means is the Movement; and the responsibility is ours.

2005 October 6

Witnessing the Worst, Working for the Best: The Tragedy and Crime of Katrina

It is written in the sacred *Husia* that we must bear witness to truth and set the scales of justice in their proper place among those who have no voice, i.e., the unfree and oppressed, the wronged and injured, the poor and unpowerful and those vulnerable to the peacebreakers and warmakers of the world. And so, as we gather together on the anniversary of this great tragedy and crime we call Katrina, let us bear rightful witness to the horror and hope of our people's passing thru the wilderness of the worst and working for the best to recover and rebuild their lives and the devastated places they still call home. And in these ceremonies of remembrance and recommitment, let us begin by paying due hommage to the dead who lost their lives in various tragic as well as unnecessary ways in New Orleans and throughout the Gulf Coast. Let our memory and love of them motivate us in all we do to honor their name, hold those responsible, accountable for their deaths and do our best to prevent the reoccurrence of such a terrible and needless tragedy. And let us stand in solidarity and struggle with the survivors in their efforts to seek the justice denied to them, repair the injury done to them and secure the restored and renewed life due to them.

And let us not forget the government's criminal neglect before the flood, its culpable conduct during the flood, and its indictable disregard for the rights, interests and needs of the people after the flood. For at the heart of this horrific event is not only the devastation of a natural disaster, but the severe aggravation of it thru the almost depraved disregard for the lives and rights of the people by those in position and power. Certainly, part of the way they were treated is because they were poor, unpowerful, and lived just below the levees in an insecure and "inconvenient" location in the city. But the lack and low level of response was and is also and especially, rooted deeply in considerations of race and racism. Considered expendable people, these Black people are not perceived by the White powers-that-be to be as worthy as the Whites and the wealthy. Thus, defective levees that would have been repaired for the White and wealthy are left as an acceptable risk and loss for the people of color and the poor.

So after all the posturing in the press about the country's being shocked by poverty, sharing grief and groceries with the poor, and a promised White House and White folk attack on poverty, it's back to racial business as usual. The promised assault on poverty has been preempted by the lust for waging war overseas and corrupt concessions to the corporate world at home. New Orleans is now re-envisioned as a center for White tourists, not a historical site for Black culture or Black people. It's the music they make, not the bothersome presence they promise that is wanted. The developers, chosen and blessed by Bush and company, have drawn up the plans, received the no-bid contracts and are slowly but surely removing the rubble and ruined people that stand in the way. New Orleans, as a reconceived city, will be transformed from one of the largest Black cities into a smaller White citadel. It will be in the service of "high-end clientele," fun seekers and free spenders, tourists out to see but not save the town. Blacks will be in the background as local color and their memories and culture sold as commodities detached from the people themselves. Indeed, Bush had early sent his Black representative as a bringer of bad tidings, warning Black people of their impending disappearance as a majority or major force in the future of the city.

But history does not have to happen this way. History is a very human thing. We bring it into being with our own hands and minds, with what we do and do not do, with the struggles we wage to push our lives forward and to create and sustain the good world we want and deserve to live in. As we always say in Us, we are our own liberators and a people that cannot save itself is lost forever. So regardless of the work of the army and city engineers, the people are their own levees; they are the walls that will hold back the water; they are the ones who will secure themselves against future dangers and repair and rebuild their lives, homes and communities. It is they who must insist that New Orleans be more than a White and tourist town. They must make it a place where people live full lives, work, worship, send their children to school and college, weather hell and hope for heaven, play the blues and take serious the Black, and always pursue the good.

There is a long list of demands we must make on ourselves and the people in power. Again, we must first accept the responsibility that it is on us to pick up and reassemble the scattered pieces of our lives, repair the physical and psychic damage done to us and our

117

communities, hold the people in position and power accountable for failure to respect and protect the life of the dead or the rights and interests of the living, and reclaim and rebuild the city and communities we care so much about. And we must remember we can only repair ourselves in the struggle to repair the world we live in. We must insist on the right to return safely and live lives of dignity and decency, the right to participate meaningfully and effectively in the process of reconstruction and to rebuild our lives and our communities, the right to remain a cultural community and to preserve our history and culture and the right to access the resources to achieve all this.

But again, there is no easy walk or way to recovery and rebuilding and we can only reach our destination and goal by traveling on the long and hard road of struggle. And as always, it is important to remember and reaffirm the urgency of the issue and the collective responsibility of us as a people wherever we live. In a word—the time is now; there is no other. Struggle is the way; there is no alterative. And we are the ones; there's no avoiding it.

2006 August 24

Post-Katrina Politics and Elections:
Recapturing Our Radical Spirit

Whatever else is fantasized, put forth, fought over, discussed and eventually done, post-Katrina politics should never again be politics as usual. For us as a people, the first and continuing catastrophe of Katrina must have a profound and enduring meaning. It must make us constantly conscious of the cost of freedom, the demands of human dignity and the sacrifice and struggle needed to protect, provide for and promote the best interests of our people. It was not simply about class, but also essentially about race, about the cold callousness of the ruling race/class, and its willingness to watch Blacks suffering and dying, and show a repulsively perverse disregard for the lives and rights of our people and other peoples of color. And it was, as Malcolm said, a sign for those who can see; those who look beyond the surface and look for the deeper and more instructive meanings in the historical unfolding of events.

Indeed, Katrina and all associated with it reaffirmed in stark and undeniable terms that there is something radically wrong with this society we live in; and that we must recover and reaffirm our sense of mission and meaning as a moral and social vanguard in this country and dare recapture that radical spirit of social change that interrupted and altered how White people once ruled and ruined our lives in the most racist of ways. And no election will ever achieve what our people accomplished in the fire and fury of our struggle for freedom and justice and a life worthy of living in this land.

We cannot let others make us uncomfortable talking about our identity, identifying with our people or demanding and struggling to achieve for them the rights and good they are due and deserve. No one tells Jews or even the many ethnic gentiles to give up so-called identity politics, nor do they tell Latinos, Latvians or Lithuanians. That conversation is reserved for those among us vulnerable to it. And so, if we were ever unsure of the need for our unity and common struggle as a people, the catastrophe of Katrina should have erased that. The need for us is to recognize and respond creatively and resourcefully to the facts that we are our own liberations, that elections aren't liberation, and that neither freedom nor justice is a gift, but each is a hard-won gain, constantly forged, protected and expanded on the battlefield for ever higher levels of human life.

It has been both a blessing and burden of our history to be a moral and social vanguard in this country. For even when we provide the momentum and margin of victory, we are often marginalized during and after the struggle to achieve it. But still, as our sacred texts tell us, we are morally obligated to bear witness to truth, to set the scales of justice in their proper place and to constantly bring and increase good in the world.

It is, then, our responsibility to speak the truth, tragedy, triumph and promise of our own history, to make sense out of the senselessness that surrounds us, and carve out of the hard rock of reality a place in which we and our people can stand, grow and flourish. And so we stand up in the midst of silence and fear and forge a path for those of good conscience to join us. This is the meaning and source of our standing up against the war in Iraq, not because it was unwinable as some would argue now, but because it was and is unjust, immoral, illegal and unworthy of support by anyone. And it is the source and meaning of our support and solidarity with the Haitian, Palestinian, Iraqi, and Afghan peoples and all peoples in their right to self-determination and their right to resist invasion, occupation and murderous oppression.

And so, let us rejoice at the defeat of Bush and his minions, allies and fellow-travelers in this one critical battle. But let's also recognize that the wider war has not been won. Let's pay hommage to our people who provided the margin of victory in three key Senate races and five House races. This has almost certainly assured five chairs in the House for African Americans: John Conyers, Judiciary; Charles Rangel, Ways and Means; Juanita Millender-McDonald, Operations; and Bennie Thompson, Homeland Security. But no one seriously thinks this is going to get done all we need to have done in a just and good society. The signs are everywhere that we need to intensify and expand the struggle. Indeed, the right-wing is already rallying around ideas waist deep in self-denials about the reasons for their defeat. The doors to compromise by the Democratic leadership have long been open, and the corporations like James Moody have been there and done gone.

Thus, we must put forth and pursue a self-consciously ethical agenda for ourselves, society and the world. At a minimum, we must continue to struggle for justice for the victims and survivors of Katrina, quality education, universal health care, economic and environmental justice, a comprehensive and just immigration reform, the end of the official savagery called capital punishment, and reversal of the Patriot Act and related legislation that paves the way for a police state. And we must struggle against the ravages of globalization and for reparations on a global level, as well as the end of occupation and for self-determination and peace throughout the world. And to do this, we must rebuild the Movement.

So, after all the shouting and sho nuff joy, after all the hugging, holding hands and singing songs of struggle and celebration from the 60's and 70's, there is still the greatest part of our work to do. And we are compelled to remember the life-lessons of our ancestors and teachers. As Fannie Lou Hamer taught us, we begin by questioning America; know from Malcolm X, the need to constantly study the lessons of history; remember from Frederick Douglass, there is no alternative to struggle for progress; and keep in mind from Amilcar Cabral, the lesson that we should "mask no difficulties, tell no lies and claim no easy victories." It is, then, on us and the alliances, coalitions and partnerships we build for the long struggle ahead, not simply for the election of 2008, but for a future framed in freedom, rooted in justice, blessed with peace, and dedicated to insuring people have power over their destiny and daily lives, and constantly flourish in possibility, promise and peace.

2006 November 16

V

Pan-African and Global Issues

There is no hope for Africa without the active engagement of its people, first on the Continent and then support from the Diaspora. This requires that programs be put in place and sustained which not only satisfy human need, but transform the people in the process, making them self-conscious agents of their own life and liberation. Yes, the people need food, but they also need freedom to speak out, assemble, organize and participate in every decision that affects their destiny and daily lives. They need housing and health care, but they also need a sense of their own capacity which they form with their own hands and minds in the process of work and struggle to build the world they want and deserve to live in. They must have control of their lives and resources...

In spite of the Bush administration's unilateral decision to wage war against Iraq, we must continue to resist and oppose it. For the war against Iraq is a war against the Iraqi people without justification and thus unjust, immoral and illegal. This position evolves from the ancient and ongoing tradition of our ancestors which teaches us to respect life, love justice, cherish freedom, treasure peace and constantly struggle to bring good in the world and not let any good be lost. This tradition rejects the policy of peace for the powerful and war for the vulnerable, dominance and security for the rich and right race and oppression and insecurity for all others in the world. For us, peace is the practice of justice which ends oppression and hostilities and provides security and well-being for all.

Africa and the World

African Liberation Day:
Hope Within the Hurricanes of History

May, the month of Malcolm, is also the month of African Liberation Day (ALD), established May 25, 1963 at the founding of the Organization of African Unity which later transformed into the African Union. It was declared as a day of reflection and rallying, remembrance and recommitment, discussion, fundraising, planning and reaffirming, in countless ways, the awesome responsibility to free Africa as a continent and world community, harness our human and material resources, empower the masses of our people and return to the stage of human history as a self-conscious and powerful force for good in the world.

Afterwards, the fires of freedom raged with revolutionary intensity on the continent and in the Diaspora, especially in the USA. And there was hope that reached toward heaven in its height and caused us all to imagine a Fanonian future, i.e., a new history for Africa and humankind. But the hurricanes and horrors of history have seemed to overwhelm us after such a hopeful, determined and bold beginning in the 60's. On the continent, ravished by imperialism, enslavement, colonialism, settlerism and the savagery that came with them, we see so much suffering of the people, famine, the pandemic of HIV/AIDS, vicious resource theft, disrupted and delayed development, continued civil wars and ethnic strife, and even genocide as dictators, collaborators and other deformities act in the image and interests of our oppressor.

And in the Diaspora in Haiti, we still see a most heroic people daring to struggle, refusing to be passive in the face of the brutal invasion and intervention by the U.S. and France seeking revenge and reparations for a devastating defeat that marked the Independence of the Haitian people. Then there is the barbaric treatment of the African people of New Orleans, the crass official and social indifference to their deaths, loss and injuries. But within the most

125

fierce of winters, there are always sparks and fires of freedom, stoked by the struggles of the masses to achieve justice, push their lives forward, free themselves and forge a future for their children. And if we are to maintain hope in the midst of the devastating hurricanes of history that bring such oppression, death, degradation and destruction, we must root it in the resiliency and resistance of our people.

Indeed, at this ALD, we must reaffirm and reinforce the internal power and promise of the masses of our people, their capacity to endure and overcome the obstacles of history before them. And we must continue the four-prong process of political education, mobilization, organization and confrontation that intensifies and sustains the liberation struggle, without which there is no real hope or future worthy of the name African and human. We must rebuild liberation movements among African people, defiantly put forth our aims, demands and ultimate goals and dedicate our lives to realizing them.

There is no hope for Africa without the active engagement of its people, first on the Continent and then support from the Diaspora. This requires that programs be put in place and sustained which not only satisfy human need, but transform the people in the process, making them self-conscious agents of their own life and liberation. Yes, the people need food, but they also need freedom to speak out, assemble, organize and participate in every decision that affects their destiny and daily lives. They need housing and health care, but they also need a sense of their own capacity which they form with their own hands and minds in the process of work and struggle to build the world they want and deserve to live in. It is not enough for the people of Africa to receive gifts purchased from years of theft of their own human and material resources. They must have control of their lives and resources and be educated and supported in their long hard suffering-filled journey to self-determination, self-reliance and sustained development.

Surely, we must include in this life affirming, freedom-focused, justice-grounded, power-enhancing and development-driven program: (1) life necessities for the people, i.e., food, clothing, housing, health care, etc.; (2) security and peace; (3) freedom on every level; (4) gender equality; (5) protection and promotion of human rights; (6) regional integration and cooperation for common good; (7) projects for sustainable development; (8) cultural reaffirmation, preservation and renaissance; and (9) alliance in struggle and cooperation with other peoples of the world in the interest of freedom, justice, power of the masses of people, and peace in the world. In addition, we must demand from our former enslavers and colonizers and current oppressors: (1) debt cancellation; (2) reparations; (3) end of resource theft by corporations through proxy armies, dictators and corrupt officials; (4) end of global fiscal policy impositions that impoverish the people, reduce human services and privatize public wealth; (5) recovery and return of riches stolen and compensation for the unrecoverable; and (6) end of violation of the sovereignty and self-determination of the peoples of Africa, Haiti and throughout the world African community.

The project of liberation from the deformed and deadly grip of oppression, then, depends above all on the consciousness, capability and commitment of the masses of our people. It is thru them that we will weather the hurricanes of history, overcome our oppression and build unbreakable and life-protective levees against the high waves and strong winds of suppression and seduction our oppressor will constantly send against us.

In a word, we must harness the energy and activism of our people, join forces with other oppressed and progressive peoples and create in struggle a counterforce and counter-wind of history. This is the meaning and motive force of Marcus Garvey's promised whirlwind of rightfulness and justice that envelops and frees us and contributes to the freeing and flourishing of humanity as a whole.

2006 May 5

Genocide in Darfur:
A Defining Moment for the World

It is a time-frozen fact that we are not fond of admitting when we want to be at our moral best. But in the morally counterclockwise way the current world turns, there are chosen people, favorite countries, favored nations and then the masses of plagued and pleading people for whom we feel little obligation and would like to think of less. Thus, there is genocide in Darfur, Katrina-like waiting in Washington, and small periodic conscience-cleansing performances and gestures in the rest of the world. Since 2003, 400,000 people in Darfur, Sudan have been killed; 2,000,000 uprooted, displaced and turned into refugees, countless raped, mutilated and maimed, victims of a wide range of savage violence. And the world will not intervene. It stands stymied, stuck in the mud and miasma of immoral and amoral calculation of their own interests, weighed against the interests of the poor and less powerful, the ill and aged, the stranger, and those who it seems are addicted to or destined for continuous suffering.

China is concerned with its oil interest in Sudan, Russia is concerned with its arms deals there, and no one is quite sure what is on the military maps and White supremacist-fantasy-filled minds of the Bushmen. So the UN stands ready but on hold. The African Union Mission in Sudan has offered some protection, but is poorly equipped, outnumbered and without a strong mandate to act decisively. It also has brokered the peace talks, but it clearly needs help on the ground and needs to engage the continent in greater assertion to solve its great and small problems.

The rallies in Washington and throughout the U.S. this weekend to call Bush and Congress to more decisive action and intervention are to be acknowledged. But more from all of us is required, especially from us as Africans. We must build and join coalitions, educate, demonstrate, mobilize, organize and confront more. In this regard, we must build on the divestment movement that has begun with universities and pension plans, as was done in the South African liberation struggle. We must confront Congress and the Bushmen who seem satisfied with having Colin Powell announce the fact of genocide without the needed efforts to end it.

Also, we must put forth and struggle around several basic points to bring a halt to the genocide, repair the lives of the people, rebuild the region and address effectively the reasons the people went to war against the government in the first place.

These include solid initiatives to: (1) protect and provide security for the people thru strengthening the African Union forces with more troops and a mandate to undertake all measures to stop the killings and assaults and to protect the people over time; (2) reinforce the African Union Mission with a UN force of at least 20,000 to protect the people and maintain the ceasefire and peace agreement; (3) restore funds and increase the amount of humanitarian aid and protect the aid operations and aid workers; (4) disarm and dismantle the janjaweed marauders who are the government's official killing machine which is directly committing the genocide against the Darfuran people; (5) facilitate the voluntary return of refugees and internally-displaced people; (6) support a just peace settlement involving: reparations for the people, unification and rebuilding of the region in a unified and political state, and effective and immediate sharing of wealth and power for Darfurans.

Rwanda is too recent for us to pretend the immoral forgetfulness we've grown used to toward the genocide/holocaust against the Native Americans and other Native peoples, and the Holocaust of enslavement which we're taught to think of as slave "trade," i.e., business gone bad with collateral damage. This case of genocide in Darfur is a defining moment for the world, determining whether intervention and protection from genocide, ethnic cleansing and other morally monstrous crimes against humanity are for just some chosen and favored nations, peoples and states, or a principle and practice for everyone in the world.

2006 May 5

A New President and Promise for Liberia: Searching for Signs and Wonders

The election of Ellen Johnson Sirleaf to the office of President holds great significance for the long-suffering and struggling people of Liberia, the Continent and world African community, and freedom-and-peace-loving people everywhere. This is not simply because she is the first woman elected president of an African country, although this is significant, especially in contrast to the U.S. and other countries which have not yet done so. Indeed, she follows in an ancient tradition of women leaders of Africa, from the women pharaohs of ancient Egypt such as Hatshepsut to ruler queens and queen mothers throughout Africa, such as Nzingha of Angola and Yaa Asantewa of Ghana, and women leaders in the modern liberation movements like Winnie Mandela and Elizabeth Sibeko of South Africa.

So, it is not simply a question of women in high places, as Condeleeza Rice reminds us in her loving loyalty to Bush or Hillary Clinton in her relentless rush to the presidency, alternately ignoring and disclaiming the rights and oppressive realities of the peoples of occupied Haiti, Palestine, Afghanistan and Iraq. What is more significant, then, is the promise she holds not only for women, but also for the people of Liberia who see in her possibilities of a new leadership and new opportunities to build a new democratic and people-serving society.

The people of Liberia who elected her see in her a peace-maker, unifier and builder, a professional who knows the ways of men, women and the world, having spent thirty years in the rough and raw politics of Liberia, the savage circles of international financial organizations and corporations, and the diplomatic halls and peace and development projects of the UN and the African Union. And they see in her in the ancient African tradition, a mother and sustainer of the people who will give them justice, heal their wounds of war, help them rebuild their shattered lives and suffering society, provide them with needed human services, and guide them honestly and quickly toward the life of dignity and decency they so deserve.

But as Amilcar Cabral reminds us in our liberation struggles, we should "mask no difficulties, tell no lies and claim no easy victories." Indeed, the President, herself, has told her people "there is no easy fix" and it is "a long hard road to recovery." For there is a heavy burden of history to bear on this rock-strewn road to recovery.

Founded in faith and hope in the midst of the Holocaust of enslavement in 1847, Liberia was to be a haven of freedom for formerly enslaved Africans from the U.S. who were repatriated to the Continent. Later, Edward Wilmot Blyden, one of Africa's great statesmen and pan-Africanists, called on Africans in the Diaspora to come there to build a refuge and realm of freedom and development for all Africans. The Hon. Marcus Garvey also explored the possibility of Liberia as a central site for redeeming and rebuilding Africa.

But history does not always happen as we would wish. And thus instead of this special African refuge, Liberia became a colonial outpost of U.S. economic and political interests in Africa with all its dire and disastrous consequences. Emerging to establish and defend U.S. interests and their own, a ruling class of Africans born in the Diaspora set up a system of domination that lasted until a bloody military overthrow of the government in 1980. This military government was in turn overthrown in an equally brutal manner in 1990 and this initiated 14 years of civil war, bringing widespread death, devastation and displacement, and abuse of children and women in the most terrible ways of war.

The President brings with her also a history of bitter struggle with opponents and the problem of reconciliation. Also, her long history of work with and for the international financial institutions and corporations is seen as an asset in expertise, but could be a problem in politics, if she takes their advice and imposes policies which please them and disable and disempower the people.

To end the hardships and horrors of history and rebuild Liberia, she must from the beginning put the people first. This means putting in place policies to address the immediate and long-term needs of the people, secure the peace and insure security, rebuild the infrastructure of the country, i.e., its systems of health, education, water, electricity, communications and roadways, bring back exiles with skills and capital, and engage the masses in meaningful and life-sustaining work which rebuilds their lives and society at the same time.

In addition, there must be land reform, return of the nation's stolen wealth, and an end to personal and corporate corruption, and to corporate theft of the country's natural resources. And there must be special attention to the needs of women and youth, real respect for human and civil rights, and continuing UN and AU presence and support, as well as support from other Africans on the Continent and in the Diaspora.

Malcolm X, a deep reader and respecter of history, taught us to be diligent students of history. For he said, as history unfolds, there are signs for those who can see. So, we look here for signs and wonders in the changing face of history, hoping that in our Sister/Mother President Johnson Sirleaf, there are signs of coming relief, repair and rebuilding for the people. But we also know that in the final analysis, there will be no miracles except those the masses of people make as they slowly and patiently overcome the overwhelming odds against them, repair and reverse the ravages of war, poverty, destitution and disease, push their lives continually forward, forge a future and life worth living, and leave a legacy that offers hope and promise for the peoples of Africa and the world. This is the ultimate meaning of President Johnson Sirleaf's statement to her people in her inaugural address that, "the future belongs to us, because we have taken charge of it."

2006 January 26

Black Mothers, White Madonnas & Green Money: Adopting Africa, Parenting the Poor

Even if we listen to Oprah and readily or reluctantly accept her advice and give Madonna the benefit of the doubt about the motives and terms of her adoption of an African child, that still does not solve the problem. For it is not simply about Madonna and Malawi or the child, David, and his baba, Yohame Banda, but about Africa and African people, and practices and processes which threaten, disrupt and destroy their lives and deny them the lives of dignity, decency and forward development that they deserve. And it's about the urgent need to repair the injuries and horrors of history and correct the current injustices rooted in globalization practices highly immune to the personal outreach gestures Madonna, Angelina Jolie, Bono, Bob Geldorf and other entertainment personalities make to address some critical issues.

Although the issue is larger than Madonna and what she has done and is doing, it's important to deal with the larger issue by engaging the problems raised by her in the larger framework of concern. First, any White persons, regardless of how well-meaning they are, should be historically conscious of and morally sensitive to Africa's and African peoples' relationships to Europe and European people. It is a relationship rooted in a legacy of imperialism, colonialism and the Holocaust of enslavement and the open wounds of current and continued exploitation of Africa's human and natural resources by the transnational corporations they and others control.

Thus, it's a bad choice for Madonna's project to be called "Raising Malawi" as if the whole country needs parenting and the people's poverty gives donors the right to impose rules, regulations, and labels on their lives. Such a suggested program of adopting Africa and Africans and parenting the poor passes over the facts and foundations of the people's conditions and their need as a whole for real relief from oppression and exploitation, and for reparations of themselves and their world in the most urgent and ethical sense.

Parental vulnerability is another problem with this case, for the father's decision was not a free and informed one. Indeed, he said at first when he gave his consent for the adoption, he did not know it would deprive him of his son forever. And though he shifted from assent to dissent and then seemingly back to assent, it's clear he was vulnerable to manipulation by both the coercive pull of money and the compelling push to have a better life for his son. But suppose those who would help had not asked him for his son in exchange for their help, and instead helped him make a good life for himself, his child and others right there? Would he have chosen to send the boy to what he imagines will be a better life or been glad to join in a cooperative effort to build community and keep his son with him?

And then there is the reality that the introduction of money in such an exchange and linked to the adoption, taints good intention and has the immoral appearance and odor of flesh peddling. This is one reason in most countries, we don't and can't buy children or people in general. The need here was to avoid appearing to turn the child into a "celebrity accessory," a thing to get to enhance the status of its owner, not to serve the interests of the child himself. This also conjures up images of human mascots at court or other human specimens collected by colonialists and enslavers in their vampiric voyages to Africa and Native America.

No one doubts the devastating effect AIDS and war have had on Africa with orphans as some of their most tragic consequences. An estimated 43 million orphans, mostly from these twin dragons of death and destruction, populate Africa with 5 million in Ethiopia alone. It is reported that "babies have become Africa's fastest growing export" and this too reminds us of the Holocaust and the killing, kidnapping and incalculable casualties, i.e., the morally monstrous destruction of African life, culture and possibility.

Moreover, we can commend a person for a good will and good-intentioned act and still believe it would be better to act another way. Our concern is the whole of Africa and African people, not at the expense of or oblivious to the rights and interests of our children, but expressly because of our commitment to them. And we are confident that the most ethical and effective way to deal with the issue of orphans and other issues rising from the horrors of history and current catastrophes is to improve the lives of the mothers, fathers, families and people as a whole, not lift out one and feel justified, good or numb in leaving others behind.

The media and society focus on personalities; but we must focus on the masses of people who struggle daily to repair their lives and the world around them, push their lives forward and together forge a future for their children and themselves. It cannot be done by long-distance adoption by famous persons. Even the claim of their raising awareness begs the question of awareness of what and a series of related questions like what is to be done, how best to do it, and who will dare begin? Surely, the problems are not solved either by Hollywood joining in programs and partnership with transnational corporations to create the image of a "caring capitalism" and "consumerism with a conscience." Indeed, this masks the damage these corporations have done and continue to do and a percentage of some products bought does not begin to pay the reparations due Africans and other peoples of color.

And so Oprah, Madonna and all those who mean well, it's not just about adopting an orphan or two but about uplifting the life of the parents and the people. Indeed, it comes down to the will to wage a larger struggle beyond personal adoptions and donations, and percentage purchases to the struggle of African people's for control of their own resources, the return of their professionals, effective involvement of the people at every level, and sustainable systems of social welfare, work and building. In a word, it is about the struggle of African people to take control of their destiny and daily lives, diminish and end poverty, and carve out of the hard rock of reality a future that has the presence and face of their children and coming generations, smiling and moving forward in their own communities and countries and through their own efforts.

2006 November 2

White Hawk Down and Disabled:
Issues of Peace, Security and Self-Determination in Somalia

The disrupted state of Somalia serves as a sad and sober reminder of the ravages and historical residue of the white and black hawks of imperialism and oppression and the massive ruin they bring to the lives and lands of the people. It is a terrible irony and almost obscene twist of history that Africa, the original home of humanity and human civilization, should be so brutally savaged by external and internal oppressors. To be a son and daughter of Africa, to know its history of grandeur and greatness, and to see it now as it is, is to get an unsettling sense of undermined magnificence, ruined possibility, and resultant deep-rooted suffering. The state of things is aggravated by the steady stream of stereotypes in the media, the half-truths and outright lies, and the daily portrayal of people plagued by poverty, famine and disease, dead and dying in the midst of ancient, medieval and modern ruins without any indication that this is not the whole truth of Africa and its people. There is no counterbalancing report on the unsurpassed resiliency of the people, their hard and heroic daily struggles to improve their lives or the horrors of the imperialist history that brought them to this place and condition.

Indeed, if the nightly news and the daily deceptions that pass as papers stop hiding history and start telling the truth, we would have a whole 'nother picture of the complex processes that undermine Africa's right and ability to rule itself, harness and use its own resources, and uplift and empower its people. One would see that if so many of the peoples of Africa stand now naked and in need, it is because they are historical and continuous casualties of a brutal colonial unclothing and imperialist rape that extracted their human and material resources and left them artificially poor on the richest continent in the world. And we would also see that the home-grown thugs, who litter the African landscape, wage civil wars and lay waste the lives, lands and hopes of the people, are most often proxies of an unseen and savage corporate and political presence in whose image and interest they act.

From the beginning of its domination, Europe structured Africa's underdevelopment, enslaving its people, exploiting its labor, extracting its wealth and striving to reduce it to a permanent customer and non-producer and eliminate its capacity to ever become a serious competitor, economically or politically. Thus Africa, weakened by centuries of colonialism, imperialism and the Holocaust of enslavement, finds itself torn from within and mercilessly attacked from without. And there is in the media no hint that in spite of the overwhelming odds against them, the peoples of Africa still struggle to end their oppression, secure the peace, push their lives forward, and forge a good future for themselves and their descendants.

For the Somali people the long and difficult struggle for peace, security and self-determination took a decisive turn this June with the Islamic Courts Union's capture of the capital, Mogadishu, and the defeat of the bandit militias and their leaders who ruled and ravaged it under the name of Alliance for the Restoration of Peace and Counter Terrorism. They were rogue remnants of the political militias that had helped overthrow the dictator, Siad Barre in 1991 and then for 15 years conducted a reign of extorting, robbing, raping, looting, engaging in regular shootouts, and feeding the U.S. false reports on imaginary terrorists in order to keep the dollars and arms flowing.

The Islamic Courts Union emerged in response to calls and support from the people and business community, longing for peace, security and the rule of law. They began by curbing crime and establishing legal processes for justice, marriage and divorce, property transfer, and conflict resolution. They promoted Islamic law and values, local leadership and the people's right to choose their leaders. In his first statement to the world, the leader of the ICU, who was then Sheikh Sharif Ahmed, said "we want to restore peace and stability. We are ready to meet and talk to anybody in the interest of our people." He also sent a letter to the U.S., UN and European Union calling for "friendly relations based on mutual respect and mutual interest," and reaffirming the Somali people's right and commitment to self-determination. The ICU has renamed itself the Somali Supreme Islamic Courts Council with Sheikh Ahmed as head of the Executive Committee in charge of day-to-day affairs and Sheikh Hassan Dahir Aweys as its new chairman.

Thus, both the defeat of its allies and the election of Sheikh Aweys, who the U.S. claims, without offering evidence, has ties with terrorists, has caused panic, increased fear peddling and pathetic whining from the White House. Trying to free itself from the memory and legacy of the disastrous intervention in Somalia in 1992 to 1994, monumentalized by the movie and book "Black Hawk Down," it finds itself facing another collapsed strategy, easily called "white hawk down and disabled". Routinely resistant to learning the lessons of history, the U.S. will undoubtedly continue to intervene trying to shape Somalia in their own image and interest even in the face of repeated failure.

But the future of Africa and the Somali people does not lie in London or Washington, but in the will and ongoing struggle of the people. Thus, the rebuilding of Somalia is first and foremost the right and awesome task of the Somali people, aided by the African Union, the regional group of African states, the Intergovernmental Authority on Development, the UN and the international community. It is important here that the current leaders of the SSICC, the Transitional Federal Government, Somaliland, Puntland and other Somali interests honor their obligation to serve the people, negotiate among themselves and together build a just and good society. And this requires that they not imitate the historical oppressors of Africa who came in the name of God and acted in the interest of the devil, doing damage to the rights and hopes of the people and distorting the real message and meaning of the religion they represented.

2006 June 27

Africa on Our Mind:
Mwalimu in Our Memory

The impending visit of His Excellency, President Jakaya Kikwete of the United Republic of Tanzania represents an important historical moment for the city, and especially for us as an African people. For the city, it's about important new business opportunities and perhaps some educational and cultural exchanges with an African country. But for us, African Americans, it must and does have a deeper meaning. For it is a family affair, *jambo la jamaa*, and an opportunity for an even broader exchange in our long and ongoing quest for pan-African unity and cooperation for common good. Indeed, it puts Africa at the center of our mind and reminds us of the legacy of a legend and man called *Mwalimu*.

It was the early and enduring pan-African hope of the great ones like Maria Stewart and Martin Delaney, Marcus Garvey and Mary McLeod Bethune, that we keep alive and vibrant our consciousness of being African, anchor ourselves in the best of our culture, and work together to free and rebuild Africa and its people in ways that enabled them to live good and meaningful lives and contribute to the future and flourishing of humankind. Such a pan-African project is, of necessity, multidimensional, i.e., political, economic and cultural. It requires strengthening of relations, investment, trade, assistance, political support in the proper places, exchanges of all kinds, and above all a sense of deep-rooted relatedness and self-conscious partnership in a historical and ongoing shared project for common good. And so, the African community awaits President Kikwete's arrival with increasing expectation and meticulous attentiveness and we wish him well in his tenure.

But President Kikwete's visit also calls to mind another president and predecessor who for so many years personified Tanzania, represented the best of African leadership, and was one of the greatest statesmen of our time, Marehemu (the late) Mwalimu Julius K. Nyerere. Mwalimu, which means teacher in Swahili, was his honorific name. It indicated not only his first and favored profession, but also his dedication to teaching the people the possibilities within themselves, reminding them of the rich values and visions rooted in their own history and culture and pointing and urging them toward a good future forged with their own hands, minds and indomitable spirit.

It is in these roles as teacher and leader that he embodied, expressed and advanced the hopes and aspirations of the people of Tanzania and Africa for freedom and lives of dignity and decency in a context of democracy, development, peace, security and self-reliance. And he represented the best of African leadership by refusing to be president for life, by always putting the people first in any project and by spending the last years of his life as an honored peace-maker and a tireless teacher of the good and the possible.

I came into consciousness in the Sixties reading and studying the works of Mwalimu Nyerere and other continental leaders like Sekou Toure, Kwame Nkrumah, Jomo Kenyatta, and Frantz Fanon, as well as diasporan leaders like Marcus Garvey and Malcolm X. From each I learned valuable insights which I later incorporated in my philosophy of *Kawaida*. From Mwalimu I learned especially the principles of *Ujamaa* (Cooperative Economics) and *Ujima* (Collective Work and Responsibility) and put them within the *Nguzo Saba* (The Seven Principles). And so, at this occasion of President Kikwete's visit, I remember and raise up a few of these important insights.

At the heart of Mwalimu's social teachings is the priority of the masses of people. He argues that the only justification for anything we do and dare lies in its benefit for the people. He tells the educated that our education does not give us any rights over the people, but rather increases our responsibility to them. He goes on to say "unless we who have power—whether it be political or technical—remain one with the masses, then we cannot serve them" and cannot righteously serve ourselves in any moral or meaningful way. For our destiny, like our duty, is a shared one and we stand up or stay down together.

Moreover, Mwalimu stressed the importance of *Ujima*, collective work and responsibility. He emphasized the need to empower the people, to enable them to become self-conscious and self-reliant agents of their own life and development. And he teaches us that the benefit a people receives from any society or project "will depend upon their contribution to it—their work, their cooperation for common good and their acceptance of each other as equals and brothers (and sisters)."

Speaking to issues of *Ujamaa*, economic development and the acquisition and accumulation of wealth in relationship to the people, he reminds us that wealth should serve the interests of humans and not vice versa. And he teaches us that we must act with the understanding and commitment "that there are more important things in life than amassing riches, and that if the pursuit of wealth clashes with things like human dignity and social equality, then the latter will be given priority."

Finally, on the subject of pan-Africanism and African unity and cooperation which are indispensable to it, he again puts priority on the freedom, dignity and development of the people. He says, "all the reasons for African unity can be summed up in one phrase—the welfare of the people of Africa. Their greater freedom is the objective, that is, the freedom from outside oppression, from poverty and from the possibility of inter-African wars."

As a global pan-Africanist as well as a continental one, I read this as relevant not only in terms of the unity of the African continent, but also for the unity of the world African community. And I take seriously Mwalimu's position that "the people of Africa (continental and diasporan) are the only justification for African unity and they are also the only means through which it will be attained." And again, it is on us—all of us, continental and diasporan Africans to reach out, reinforce the bonds between us and together in work and struggle, build the good societies and world we want, need and deserve to live in and leave as a legacy for future generations.

As Mwalimu taught us, "Let's all go forward (then); the road to African freedom and unity is long and rocky, but it is not impassable. When a bridge is washed away, we can rebuild it. When a mountain blocks our path, we can go around it or cut through it. Our tools are our hands, our brains and our spirit. And these will suffice, if we have courage, patience, stamina and vision."

2006 September 21

Africa and Global Justice:
Beyond the G-8 Scam in Scotland

No one who thinks seriously or critically about the problems and ways of the world could possibly imagine the recent G-8 Summit in Scotland was really about Africa or even about the weather. Indeed, in spite of the transparent fig leaf of concern for the vulnerability of the planet and some of its poorest inhabitants, the summit was really about the health and wealth of White supremacy in the world. Thus, although we say G-8, it's really the G-7 with Japan in tow and in tandem. For it is a group of countries which are the pillars of White power, the captains of world capitalism and a repentant Russia, with Japan assuming the role it played in apartheid South Africa as honorary Whites in a White man's club. As an accommodating ally, Japan is there and counted among the self-anointed "chosen" not simply because of its economy, but because it also serves and usually shares White interests.

There they were: Bush and Blair coupled in a corner discussing their slow dance of death and unraveling in Iraq; the Frenchman, Chirac, frowning at Bush about warmongering in Iraq but joined to him at the hip in the savage suppression of Haiti; the Germans and Japanese swapping old and new visions of empire and war and exploring reasons for rearming; Russia exchanging the red wine of communism for the "white lady" of capitalist and European inclusion; Canada and Italy huddled in hope for larger roles the U.S. might graciously assign them. And all were concerned about the fierceness and resiliency of resistance to their domination and exploitation in Haiti, Palestine, Venezuela, Iraq, Bolivia, Afghanistan, and around the world and of the global justice movements and the progressive people in their own countries and thus they hid themselves behind a wall of 10,000 police.

Then there were the Africans, Asians and Latin Americans, convenient color in an otherwise colorless project, decidedly marginal at a meeting in which they were, at least for PR purposes, billed as a central concern. It was all sham and showboat, an immorality play that could easily be titled "Scammin' in Scotland." But as Malcolm taught, the oppressor is the master image-maker, making criminals into victims and victims into criminals, invaders into defenders of democracy, debtors into creditors, creditors into debtors, and bandits into benefactors, and palming off a revised version of continued global theft as a genuine gesture of generosity.

The staged gesture of generosity was a cheap charity of previous promises masking a major deception. It was first to soften the warmongering, world-dominating and earth destroying images that has dogged White supremacists and empire addicts since their emergence in history. Secondly, it was designed to preempt and divert attention from the demands of the reparations and global justice movements for more fundamental change. Thirdly, it was a counter to Islamic and other radical initiatives in Africa and the world by seeming to alleviate conditions which draw a stark line between oppressed and oppressor. And finally, it was a deceptive package of promises and conditions which increased wealth concentration and extraction and perpetuates domination and plunder by the favored few—the rich and the powerful countries, global corporations and international financial institutions.

There are several flaws in the fake gesture. First, on the issue of debt and debt cancellation, it begins with an illegitimate claim. For it is not Africans and other people of color who owe the rich White nations of the world, it is they who owe us. Moreover, if the fictitious debt is to be cancelled, it must be unconditional and for all countries, not a selected few. On the issue of aid, it is too little, too conditional and never directed toward development. Aid offered and given is never beyond welfare, never enough to develop infrastructure and technology, reduce poverty, educate the people, truly improve their health, and empower them to take control of their destiny and daily lives. It is always emergency aid, drawn from cast off and surplus food and supplies wasting away in warehouses and used at appointed times as weapons to wring concessions from vulnerable populations and corrupt governments. In a word, it is directed toward structural underdevelopment. For there must be no Singapore, South Korea, Japan, Taiwan or China in Africa to compete and threaten the monopoly on wealth and power Whites enjoy in the world.

For the oppressed, then, there is no relief except in resistance and no real future except one which is forged in struggle. Thus, we urge Africans, other peoples of color and all progressive peoples to cast away illusions and intensify the struggle to achieve the following goals: (1) cancellation of debt by the real debtors for all needy countries without conditions; (2) payment of reparations for the Holocaust of enslavement, colonization, imperialist plunder of resources, labor exploitation, and environmental degradation and destruction; (3) end of resource theft and plunder by global corporations through proxy armies, dictators and corrupt officials; (4) shift in priorities of world laboratories to developing of medicines, vaccines and health strategies for African and other needy nations; (5) end of conditions and policies which impoverish and disable the people, reduce human services, privatize public wealth, services and utilities, increase trade imbalances, encourage exports at the expense of domestic needs, and open up the countries for greater exploitation; (6) recovery and return of riches stolen and deposited in foreign banks with the complicity of collaborating countries, corporations, private banks and international financial institutions, and compensation for that which is unrecoverable; (7) respect for the sovereignty, self-determination and the need for democracy of and in these countries and the end of cultivating, cuddling and protecting collaborators by foreign forces at the expense of the people; and (8) putting forth and fighting for a policy based on the ethics of sharing in the world— shared status, shared knowledge, shared space, shared wealth, shared power, shared interests and shared responsibility in building the good and sustainable world we all want and deserve to live in and for which we struggle in the interest of global justice.

2005 July 28

Hurricane Hugo Hits Landfall:
Telling the Truth & Shaming the Devil

It may not be the month of May, but I heard echoes of Malcolm X and even Messenger Muhammad in the recent UN speech of President Hugo Chavez of Venezuela. It's the way the word "devil" was used against those who for so long demonized the dark-skinned people of the world and how it now comes back to haunt them with the overwhelming evidence of history against them. Moreover, it's about how Malcolm taught that being revolutionary and responsible to the people makes you dangerous and "irresponsible" to your oppressor. And it reminds us of Malcolm's standing up in the midst of mummified silence, and speaking truth to power and especially to the people, in a way others were afraid or unable to do. It is clearly in the tradition of our own ancestors who taught that we are to "tell the truth and shame the devil" and that we are to "bear witness to truth and set the scales of justice in their proper place among those who have no voice."

Rising from the South and roaring like a hurricane of righteous anger, President Chavez hit landfall and rushed to the podium at the UN to report that Bush, the Devil, was in the house, and he could still smell the sulfur Bush left in his wake. It was a metaphor for the active and ongoing evil of imperialism in its various racial, religious, cultural and class forms. And it was also a reminder of how it leaves the stench and stain of bloodied, mutilated and murdered bodies, an awesome evidence of the wasted lives and gutted lands of the weak and vulnerable by the powerful, predatory and perverse.

Bush and company need to stop whining and wailing about Pres. Chavez's blunt language, his courageous contempt for evil in high and low places and his relentless and unadorned exposure of the unconscionably evil things they have done and do to the people of the world. Moreover, it is they who introduced a language of preferential religion and chosen race in the politics of global exchange, not Chavez. It is Bush who first talked about an "axis of evil" and waging a "crusade" against the "evil ones," in the "dark and uncivilized corners of the world."

And it is Bush and company that long ago abandoned any diplomatic niceties of public discourse designed to shield the behind-the-scenes savagery that the powerful impose on the weak. It is they and their right-wing radio hosts who rant and rave against the peoples of color and publicly push to legalize torture. Even their religious leaders call for the assassination of heads of state and any other real or imagined enemies of the U.S. and Israel. So it's the height and depth of hypocrisy to be moaning and groaning about Chavez's lack of respect for rules of diplomatic engagement which the right-wing rulers of this country and their allies have long abandoned and only appeal to when they are the subject of such severe and on-target criticism.

Chavez justifiably criticized the U.S.'s "imperial hypocrisy," its talking peace and making war, its talking of democracy and attempting to impose it by force. As he says, it is "the false democracy of elites,...a strange democracy...that's imposed by weapons." President Chavez also dares to do what few large or small countries dare to do, i.e., repeatedly criticize Israel's aggression and brutality against the Palestinian and Lebanese people.

Chavez also rightfully raised the issue of race, saying that whenever Bush looks, he sees extremists and extremism which is really the politics and color of resistance. Turning to the Native American President of Bolivia, Evo Morales, Chavez says, "and you my brother, he looks at your color and he says 'oh, they are extremists'." Indeed, he says "the imperialist sees extremists everywhere." But "it's not that we are extremists. It's that the world is waking up. It's waking up all over, and people are standing up." And he said to Bush, "I have a feeling, dear world dictator, that you are going to live the rest of your days as a nightmare, because the rest of us are standing up...rising up against U.S. imperialism . . . shouting for equality, for respect, for the sovereignty of nations. Yes, you can call us extremists, but we are rising up against the empire, against (your) model of domination."

It is in this spirit of rising up and resistance that Chavez rightfully rejects Bush's paternalistic lectures to the peoples of color of the world "as if he owned the world" and all of us in it. What quintessential racist arrogance to give us garbled and self-stroking instructions, issue annual report cards on our conduct, and dare indict anyone except himself!

But regardless of what the White corporate media says or does to caricature Chavez- and confuse the world about his meaning and mission, the world is listening and applauding as the international audience at the UN demonstrated. For he speaks to the international anger and worldwide resistance to Bush's attempt at U.S. dominance of the world, his savage assault on Iraq and Afghanistan, his illusion of imposed democracy thru military dictatorship, his gulag of secret CIA torture chambers and prisons, his crude attempts to reinterpret the Geneva Convention, his support of Israel's war crimes against Palestine and Lebanon, and his globalization policies with their destructive effects on the lives, lands, economies and futures of peoples of the world.

Chavez is a democratically-elected president, an anti-imperialist, a socialist, and an extremely popular leader of his people with an approval rating of over 80 percent compared to Bush's 30 something percent. He has used his oil wealth to help people in this country and around the world, forged alliances the U.S. opposed, and he is not afraid of the "big bad wolf of the north."

Moreover, Chavez is an African and Native American Latino, a descendent of two peoples who have suffered the greatest Holocausts in human history and he is conscious of this history and committed to the struggle to end oppression in the world. His mission is to resist the U.S. drive for world dominance, reform the UN in the interest of the masses of people of the world, build alliances of struggle and development, and dare help usher in a new history of humankind. And this tends to frighten oppressors and make predators preach forgiveness and moderation.

2006 September 28

Peace, War and Resistance

Peace, Justice and Resistance to War

In spite of the Bush administration's unilateral decision to wage war against Iraq, we must continue to resist and oppose it. For the war against Iraq is a war against the Iraqi people without justification and thus unjust, immoral and illegal. This position evolves from the ancient and ongoing tradition of our ancestors which teaches us to respect life, love justice, cherish freedom, treasure peace and constantly struggle to bring good in the world and not let any good be lost.

This tradition rejects the policy of peace for the powerful and war for the vulnerable, dominance and security for the rich and right race and oppression and insecurity for all others in the world. For us, peace is the practice of justice which ends oppression and hostilities and provides security and well-being for all.

Although Bush claims to be waging a just war, his real reasons are transparent and tragically self-serving and reveal a post 9/11 imperial offensive with colonialist conversations about "civilizing missions," "crusades" and "dark and evil nations." Our ethical tradition requires several conditions for a just war which his self-declared war against the Iraqi people does not meet.

These criteria are: a just cause; collective considered judgment; just means; consequences of common good and; last resort. There is no just cause in an unprovoked preemptive war of aggression which is a crime against peace and the people against whom it is directed. Moreover, the current war is not a war of self-defense, but of self-aggrandizement, a war of vigilante aggression, resource acquisition and imperial expansion.

The collective considered judgment of the world is that the war is immoral, illegal and unjust. The UN has rejected it as illegal and illegitimate despite attempts by the U.S. to bribe, bully and threaten other states into compliance.

The principle of just means requires a conscientious effort to reduce the deaths, damage and devastation of war, especially harm to innocent civilians. This demands discriminate and proportionate use of force, a condition not met by the Bush administration's plans for the largest and most devastating bombing raids on Iraq since those of WWII. Boasting of the use of catastrophic weapons which will "shock and awe," they insure massive civilian deaths and injuries and the extreme devastation of the civilian infrastructure and the environment.

There are no consequences of common good for such an unprovoked, unjustifiable and unjust war. It is grossly wrong and does not benefit the world or the American people to kill thousands and thousands of innocent Iraqi civilians; to conquer and occupy their country; to seize their oil, water and other resources; to contaminate and degrade the environment of Iraq and neighboring regions; to violate international law and weaken international institutions; to destabilize the region and the world; to cause unnecessary casualties among U.S. and Iraqi soldiers; to provoke retaliatory attacks against the U.S. and its people; and to divert needed resources for social well-being in this country.

The principle of last resort grows out of a predisposition for peace and a presumption against war. By definition a pre-emptive war is not a last resort, but the first even prior resort. For to preempt is to act prior to—prior to discussion, negotiation and the pursuit of alternatives to war. Bush's fundamentalist faith-informed approach to issues of peace and security for the U.S. and the world reeks of messianic and chosen race notions of U.S. power and place in the world and the role of war in maintaining them.

But there is no security without peace, no peace without justice, no justice without freedom and no freedom without the power of people everywhere over their destiny and daily lives whether in the U.S., Afghanistan, Iraq or Palestine.

2003 March 27

King and the Question of War, Peace and Justice

It is the teaching of our ancestors that "to do that which is of value is for eternity. A person called forth by his work does not die, for his name is raised and remembered because of it" (*The Husia*). So are the eternal work and name of Dr. Martin Luther King, Jr. As we raise and remember his name and work this month, let us reflect on his meaning to us and the world and ask ourselves how can we honor his legacy by embracing the lessons of his life and work.

Certainly no issue which confronts us now looms larger than Bush's presidential preaching and promising of war, his arrogant assumption of the right to wage preemptive wars of aggression against any country deemed a threat, to violently overthrow governments, to assassinate leaders and citizens of other nations designated as enemies of his interests, to suspend and dismiss constitutional rights and protections under the camouflage of national security, and to cultivate through fear a patriotism of raised flags, lowered vision, controlled conversation and indictable dissent. Clearly, Dr. King's life lessons and teachings on war, peace and justice offer us insight and encouragement in addressing this issue in concrete, moral and meaningful ways. For as he says during the Vietnam War, "we are deeply in need of a new way beyond the darkness that seems so close around us."

King is against war and states war "cannot be reconciled with wisdom, justice and love." But he is especially critical of unjust wars against weaker and vulnerable peoples as evidenced in his opposition to the Vietnam War. Yet, he also realized that peace and justice, like freedom and security, are inseparably linked. Without justice for the peoples of the world, there can be no peace for the world and without their freedom, there can be no security in the world. Indeed, King says "True peace is not simply the absence of tension; it's the presence of justice." And he says, "oppressed people cannot remain oppressed forever. The yearning for freedom eventually manifests itself."

For King the evil of war is rooted in the devastation and ruin it wreaks on human life–the magnitude and moral monstrousness of the physical, psychological, cultural and spiritual destruction and deformation it leaves in its wake. Thus, he argues that an indispensable step in opposing war and securing peace and good will among the peoples of the world is the "affirmation of the sacredness of all human life." This position reaffirms the ancient African ethical teaching that all humans are bearers of dignity and divinity, equally worthy of the gift and promise of human life.

This means that all hierarchies of race, class, gender, religion and nation that exalt a person or a people over others and make them more worthy of life or dignity, freedom, justice, peace and other goods are immoral and indefensible. Thus, the Native American, the African, the Latino and the Asian are no less worthy of life and the goods of life than the European. And the people of Iraq, Afghanistan and Palestine are as worthy of life, freedom, dignity, security and justice as those of the USA and Israel. Given this, a selective morality that mourns loss of white life and denies or dismisses the savage and sustained destruction of the lives of peoples and persons of color is vilely hypocritical at best and at worst criminally complicit. For as King taught "to ignore evil is to become an accomplice in it."

King offers his most complete critique of the Vietnam War and by extension all unjust war and ultimately war itself in his historic address "A Time to Break Silence." It is given on April 4, 1967 at the Riverside Church in New York exactly a year before the month and day of his martyrdom. King begins by reaffirming the fundamental principle that in the face of wrong, injustice and evil, "a time comes when silence is betrayal," a betrayal of our highest moral principles and even more so of the victims who suffer the grievous injury and devastation of war. Surely, the proposed unjust war against Iraq confronts us with the moral urgency to oppose it as did the Vietnam War. King tells us that he realizes how difficult it is to oppose "government policy, especially in times of war." Indeed, he says speaking up for peace and justice in such times is "a vocation of agony, but we must speak," moving beyond an easy "patriotism to the high grounds of a firm dissent based on the mandates of conscience and the reading of history." "We must encourage creative dissenters" whose "fearless voices" thunder above the "blasts of bombs and the clamor of war hysteria," he counsels us.

Moreover, "Those of us who love peace," he says, "must organize as effectively as the war hawks. As they spread the propaganda of war we must spread the propaganda of peace." We must then mobilize, organize, "demonstrate, teach and preach, until the very foundations of our nation is shaken" and we "lift this nation we love to a higher destiny, a new plateau of compassion, to a more noble expression of humaneness." Therefore, King says, "When evil men plot, good men must plan. When evil men burn and bomb, good men must build and bind. When evil men shout ugly words of hatred, good men must commit themselves to the glories of love. Where evil men would seek to perpetuate an unjust status quo, good men must seek to bring into being a real order of justice."

Finally, Dr. King tells us that if he were to sum up his opposition to the injustice and devastation of that unjust war, it would be because of his sense of an interrelatedness with the Divine and other humans and the "vocation of sonship and brotherhood" this gives him. Within this expansive ethical understanding of our interrelatedness, he and we are called to stand up and speak in the interests of humanity as a whole. Thus, not only are we to speak for the welfare of our country and its people, but especially are we "called to speak for the weak, for the voiceless; for victims of our nation and for those it calls enemy, for no document from human hands can make these humans any less our brothers (and sisters)."

2003 January 16

Pledging Allegiance to the USA:
One Nation, Under Illusion

There is something eerie and unsettling about the infantile addiction to illusions and the mature commitment to lying that affects the "head" table at the White House. Coldly without conscience or concern for consequences to others, they have woven a web of lies that would put a spell of confusion on a spider. There in some fortified, fear-peddling and detached-from-reality room, the Bush-men seem to meet daily to develop the lies and illusions they will believe in and sell to the country. They are illusions rooted in equal amounts of ignorance and arrogance, reflecting also a mystical belief in White hegemony and the omnipotence of their military might. Thus, even in the face of failure and exposure, they hold fast to their lies and illusions and swear everyone else has lost the way.

And so on the third anniversary of the second invasion of Iraq and the unjust war against the Iraqi people, they hold fast to lie and illusion and ask us to pledge appropriate allegiance to them. They had predicted the war would be quick and easy and they had prematurely declared it over. But now they are bogged down and befuddled, wondering why the flowers they expected as self-proclaimed liberators blew up in their faces and set fire to the illusions they had hoped to live by. They had deluded themselves into believing they would simply slip in, slit throats and leave quickly before the blood flow fell on them. Or better still, they believed they could rain down missiles and bombs from on high, "shock and awe" and escape the blood splatter, and drown out the cries and voices of the victims.

But the tables turned and they are now in shock and awe over the fierceness, tenacity and rootedness of the resistance to their occupation and their inability to ransack and rob the country in relative security and pretend liberation of a population that refuses to let them. They have discovered what they could and should have learned from the lessons of history, even from their ally Israel, which has for over fifty years failed to defeat the Palestinian people or destroy their will to resist even against the most overwhelming odds. It is an old and enduring lesson: where there is oppression there is resistance; weapons are essential, but the will of the people is paramount. What is important is that the people fight and refuse to be defeated, dispirited or diverted. This is the lesson of all liberation struggles whether in Africa, Haiti, Vietnam, Palestine, Cuba, Iraq, Afghanistan or other places.

It all started with the illusions and lies about the reasons for the war of aggression they had chosen. It was, they said, because of the threat of WMD's and links to Al Qaeda. Having failed with this fantasy, they turned to the masquerade and illusion of being liberators and bringers of democracy. And to keep up their illusions, they have brought to Iraq a new terror, torture, daily bombing, ruthless and random murder and mutilation, radiation poisoning, and the continuous impoverishment of the people. They have killed more people than the dictator before them, imposed a military dictatorship and called it democracy, destroyed the country and pretend now to rebuild it. They have manipulated the media and minds of the people of this country, constantly cultivating fear, anxiety, uncertainty and hatred, and eliciting support for an international gulag of prisons and a long list of atrocities against the Iraqi people and the world which will return to haunt all of us. For they have linked us to their corporate killing and attempted conquest and cowering of the world.

This is why it's so important to stand up, step forward and massively resist this infantile addiction to illusion and lies and the real, extensive and in some cases, irreversible damage the Bush-men are doing to and in the world. And this rejection and resistance requires, above all, a new way of thinking about this country and the world and a long hard struggle to change the way we act, live and relate within them.

Inherent in resisting, not just the war but also changing the direction of national and international policy which are linked, is to honestly face and discuss openly and thoroughly the real reasons the Bush-men took the country to war of aggression and international banditry which had neither the sanction of law or morality and why so many people accepted it.

The real reasons for this war of naked aggression were: (1) to seize and control the oil fields, water and strategic position of Iraq; (2) to expand and consolidate U.S. dominance of the Middle East and in the process strengthen Israel in its occupation of Palestine and in its status as the dominant power in the region; (3) to enhance the U.S.' and Israel's capacity to dictate limitations on the inevitable state of Palestine; (4) to terrorize and cower other states and people who oppose U.S. policies; (5) to weaken and hopefully reverse, in the guise of globalization, the rise in Muslim resistance to European dominance, which is the only world force capable of offering creditable resistance; and (6) to reaffirm and insure White hegemony in the region and the world—militarily, politically, economically and culturally.

Also, we must not be diverted to a discussion of a fantasy democracy and claim of rebuilding of Iraq and overlook the moral obscenity of invaders claiming to save a people they are savaging. The U.S. has no right to be in Iraq, let alone to dictate the lives and future of the people and pretend their destruction and devastation are an improvement. Also, we must discuss what some call the constant "invisible elephant in the room," Israel, and the Israeli lobby's role in urging and supporting this war, mistakenly thinking it's in Israel's interest. It is a difficult and divisive issue, but must be dealt with. This inevitably leads to the discussion and support of the liberation of Palestine from Israeli occupation and the establishment of an independent, secure and viable state of Palestine.

And finally, we must build and sustain a massive progressive movement in this country, directed toward creating a just and good society, a good and sustainable world, and a new history of humankind hostile to oppression, illusions and lies.

2006 March 23

In the Middle of East, West and War: Palestine, Lebanon and Malcolm X

The heavy and merciless winds of war are blowing our way. Rising in the east, they are moving relentlessly toward the west with a sure, certain and unsettling rhythm. And if history holds any lessons we can learn from, any evidence we can rely on or any signs we can see and reliably read, we should approach this escalating crisis in a more just and rightful way. It is not enough for oppressors to rant and rave about rightful resistance or keep on killing, increasing human suffering, and imagining that they can hold back history or blot out the sun by shutting their eyes. There are these hard, fast and treasured things called freedom, justice, self-determination and rightful resistance, these unfinished items on the agenda of history that must be dealt with to the satisfaction of the oppressed and deprived. And there are these struggling people throughout the world who will not be defeated, dispirited or deterred from their quest, regardless of the savagery of oppression which surrounds and daily assaults them. Like the people of Palestine who are prisoners in their own country, locked in and bombed out, they will not accept their oppression meekly in hopes that the horror of their lives under Israeli occupation will be eventually lessened thru the grace and earned gratitude of their oppressor.

And then there is Lebanon, being also brutally bombed and destroyed for the "sin" of solidarity shown by Hezbollah for their Palestinian brothers and sisters. Like the Palestinians under the leadership of Hamas, they understand resistance as both a moral right and responsibility and argue they will not accept security for the Israeli soldiers and civilians while Israel inflicts state terrorism and imprisonment on Palestinian and Lebanese soldiers and civilians. The Palestinians point out that not only is Israel brutally occupying their land, but has also captured their soldiers, kidnapped and carted off to Israel duly elected members of their Parliament and have unjustly imprisoned 10,000 Palestinian children, women and men. But where is the discussion of Palestine and the rightful struggle of the Palestinian people to end Israeli occupation, live free and meaningful lives and leave a future for their children of freedom, peace and prosperity? In spite of this, as the Lebanese Prime Minister reminded us, regardless

156

of the great efforts to hide and deny it, this war begins and will only end with the liberation struggle of Palestine.

However, we cannot grasp what's going on, if we allow the media and image makers Malcolm X warned us about, to be the source of our insight or sentiments concerning these issues and the unfinished struggles which have recently imposed themselves on the consciousness of the world. Malcolm taught that critical and independent thinking is not only our responsibility as moral agents and activists, but that it is also indispensable to our liberation—both psychologically and politically. In fact, in a lecture at Harvard, the high seat and prized citadel of Eurocentric learning, he said that in our struggle to understand ourselves and the world, free ourselves and forge our future in our own image and interest, we must develop a new logic of liberation.

Thus, we enter any conversational and analytic space with a healthy questioning and routine rejection of the established order's version of things, knowing its race and class interests are always packaged and presented as truth, its violence against the vulnerable as self-defense, and justification of its injustice and evil as human nature.

We take an Afrocentric stance, a stance that is culturally and ethically grounded. It is a stance for truth for knowing and living, freedom for the oppressed, justice for the wronged and injured, power for the masses of people over their destiny and daily lives, and peace in and for the world. We thus oppose the oppressors and warmongers who weave worldwide webs of half-truths and whole lies held together by encouraging ignorance and illusion in various forms.

An Afrocentric stance is, of necessity, an ethical stance, representing the best of what it means to be African and human in the fullest sense. It draws on both our ancient ethical and spiritual teaching and is informed by the best of our current moral reasoning and experience in the world. Thus, we begin with a stance of self-conscious solidarity with the oppressed, the poor, and the vulnerable. Indeed, the *Husia* teaches us that we are morally obligated "to bear witness to truth and set the scales of justice in their proper place among those who have no voice." And who are the voiceless here; and who is denied presence and presentation in the media and academy— surely, not the oppressors of the world. For us, then, the oppressor can never have the moral status of the oppressed. Moreover, the oppressed has both the right and responsibility to resist. And regardless of their demonization by the oppressor, freedom fighters are not terrorists, guerillas are not gunmen and there is no righteousness in freedom and security for just one race or religion.

Also, we must contextualize what we see, hear and read. We must ask not simply what's going on, but what is its origin; not simply what's in front of us, but what's hidden in revised or unrevealed history; and what's rendered irrelevant or reduced to marginal importance by the established order's media and academy? Is the war waged by Israel against Palestine and the Palestinian people about a captured soldier or to enforce its occupation, destabilize and destroy the democratically-elected government of Palestine headed by the Hamas resistance movement, impose an unjust solution to the rightful demands of self-determination and a viable Palestinian state and support the U.S. in its drive to dominate the Middle East?

Finally, in this time of turmoil and tension, let us stand in solidarity with the struggling and suffering peoples of the world. And let us bear witness in the way we walk and work in the world that there will be no end to struggle, nothing settled, and no oppressor or oppressive system safe, until freedom and justice are the norm for all people and human flourishing, unimpeded, envelopes and enriches the world.

2006 July 20

Rampaging in Palestine and Lebanon:
A Strange Sense of Self-Defense

Surely it speaks to the shame and shallow moral commitments of religious and political leaders who offer a betraying silence or give vote-and-funds-pandering support for Israel's recent savaging of Lebanon and its ongoing occupation and brutalization of Palestine. In a similar situation during the brutal U.S. war against Vietnam, Martin Luther King, Jr. stood up in courage, in spite of the cost, and called for an end to that unjust war. He said that there comes a time when silence in the face of injustice and oppression is a betrayal of our highest ideals and that we must thus, put forth "a firm dissent" to official and popular positions "based on the mandates of (our) conscience and reading of history." Indeed, he taught us, "we must find new ways to speak for peace...and justice throughout the developing world."

In his usual pre-school problem with complexity and his adolescent grasp of the world, Bush has declared, as an appropriate response to Israel's rampage in Palestine and Lebanon that every nation has a right to defend itself. As he should know and the world has stated, self-defense is one thing, savagery is another. Even if he and Israel believe literally in the early-man morality of an eye for an eye, common sense should tell them that you should not take twenty eyes for one or blind a whole city or bomb and destroy a whole nation to satisfy some strange and primal sense of vengeance as justice.

Of course, he does not mean Palestine, Haiti, Iraq, Lebanon, Afghanistan and other nations under occupation and attack have the right to self-defense. Only the chosen, the elect and favored of the races and religions and his allies in evil and injustice enjoy this right. That is why he has given Israel the green light and a "grace period" to kill and destroy as it sees fit, after which he says he can no longer provide it with diplomatic cover. So he has vetoed numerous resolutions by the U.N. criticizing Israel and trotted out Condi Rice to say a ceasefire will not solve the problem, even though the problem is Israel's massive destruction of the lives and living conditions of the peoples of Palestine and Lebanon.

And so, the world watches while Israel, acting like Bulgaria for the old Soviet Union, does the U.S.' wet work on small and larger scales. It seems they, the rulers of the U.S. and Israel, have decided that now is the time to assert their hegemony decisively over the region and destroy or diminish the perceived threat of a rising Islamic initiative and counterweight.

Israel has said it is responding in Palestine to the killing of two and the capture of one of its soldiers. But it kills and captures Palestinian civilians and soldiers regularly as an acceptable, even necessary, aspect of its occupation of Palestine. It holds ten thousand Palestinian prisoners, including children, women and men, and recently kidnapped half the cabinet of the Hamas-led Palestinian Provisional Government and 60 members of its Parliament. The reality for Palestinian and Israeli relations is the occupation of Palestine by Israel. And we cannot talk about recent capturing of soldiers outside of the prior and ongoing occupation of Palestine. So every conversation must start with and be set in the context of the brutal occupation and the continuing struggle against it.

Likewise, even the military action by Hizballah was linked to Israel's occupation of Shebaa Farms and its holding of Lebanese and Palestinian prisoners since its occupation of Southern Lebanon in 1982. The guerilla action was called "Operation Truthful Promise" and was to free these prisoners and show solidarity with the Palestinian struggle. In fact, Hizballah had stated then it reserved the right to capture Israeli soldiers until the Lebanese and Palestinian guerillas were freed. It is here, then, that one gets the sense of the real right to self-defense, the right of resistance against occupation and aggression on a total and terrorizing scale. So, it is not the oppressor who should invoke the right of self-defense, but the oppressed. The need is for a ceasefire, an exchange of prisoners, the end of occupation, and a comprehensive Middle East peace plan with a free Palestine at its center.

Indeed, the war Israel has been waging in Palestine prefigured the destructive kind of war it would wage in Lebanon. It is all there, the disproportionate response, the bombing of civilian populations, collective punishment, death-squad assassinations of religious and political leaders and intellectuals, the kidnapping and false imprisonment, destruction of farms, trees, and water systems, the seizure of lands, the merciless bombing of airports, apartments, homes, hospitals, schools, shops, power plants, fuel depots, roads, bridges, gas stations, communication systems, food transports, emergency vehicles and even the use of phosphorous and cluster bombs.

Part of Israel's vicious response, as one of Israel's daily papers notes, is due to a sense of recapturing "lost dignity," damaged by guerilla groups and resistance movements they cannot seem to crush, and who constantly demonstrate an enviable adaptability to their lack of weapons equivalence. But it is a willful self-deception to imagine that they can defeat Hamas or the Palestinian people after trying and failing since 1948. Nor will they defeat Hizballah. For in spite of the media manipulation of history and reality, the struggle is about self-determination, about the end of occupation, about self-defense of the oppressed against the oppressor, about freedom, security, justice and power of the people over their daily lives, and peace for everyone not just a few.

And so, the long hard and difficult struggle continues. In spite of the bombs, the invasions and the hegemonic illusions that inspire and accompany them, there is a heavy storm named freedom steadily rising above the horizon of history. And along the almost forgotten roads of revolutionary struggle, there are weather signs which serve as warnings to the oppressor and inspiration and promise to the oppressed. And they read in every language: whirlwinds, tornados and hurricanes ahead, rough and muddy roads, thick ground-level fog and guerillas in the mist, always among the people and thus, as immovable as mountains.

2006 July 17

Rice and Beans in Rome and Israel:
Hot Air and the Cold Calculus of War

History is rightfully hard on the willing servants of masters of any kind. Only the self-conscious servants of the people reaffirm their dignity in the dedicated performance of their duty, and honor the ancient African ethical obligation to heal, repair and transform the world, making it more beautiful and beneficial than we inherited it. U.S. Secretary of State, Dr. Condoleeza Rice, went off to Rome last week, wading in the blood-soaked waters of the Middle East wars, claiming to be searching for a solution to bring peace. But there she stood alone against the wishes of the world and refused to support an immediate halt to hostilities which would have saved lives while diplomats took their time in debating the political issues. Instead, in the cold calculus of war, she repeated the Bush men's "Kill Bill" litany against Hizballah, ran routine interference to suppress condemnation of Israel's rogue state behavior in the region, and gave it another green light and "grace period" to continue its bloodletting in the killing fields, into which it has turned Lebanon and Palestine in the futile hope to defeat Hizballah and Hamas.

Rice, it was reported, was saddened even "sickened" by the news of the carnage in Qana in which approximately 60 children, women and elders, seeking refuge in the basement of a house, were killed last week by the Israelis, while she was in Israel talking to its leaders. But Rice must know that the U.S. cannot provide permission, immunity and protection for Israel to wage an unrestrained and unrestricted war and not expect it to commit all kinds of atrocities and violations of international humanitarian law. Indeed, this is why the U.S. is seen as a lapdog and clone of its client, Israel. Rice was to visit Lebanon, but Prime Minister Fouad Siniora of Lebanon disinvited her immediately afterwards and said a ceasefire and cessation of the slaughter were the order of the day, not Rice's imaginary plans for an imposed pax Americana-Israeliana on the region. And Secretary-General, Kofi Annan, spoke for both the UN and virtual universal consensus when he said that Israel's attack on the innocent civilians of Qana was brutal and unjustifiable and should be condemned by the Security Council and the world. But again the U.S. insisted on Israel's "immunity" from criticism.

162

It is rumored that Rice wants a more open and effective foreign policy, but she is imprisoned by the small minds that mingle in the tight space of Cheney and Rumsfeld's ruminations about the threats and woes of the world. She finds herself linked with the neo-conservatives who worship weapons, idolize Israel, perceive the Pentagon as a sacred place, assume that one's race, religion and power determines one's relevance and right, and believe that war is the indispensable way to hegemony, happiness and the endless pursuit of resources and riches. But she too dotes on Israel at the expense of reason and moral sensitivity to others. And though she has argued for talking to Iran and North Korea, she, like those before her, does it out of begrudging respect for their nuclear and military capacity, not out of moral concerns for peace and human cooperation. Moreover, she can't even say the word, Palestine, let alone concede that there will never be peace in the region or security or legitimacy for Israel until Palestine is free and concedes this legitimacy.

So whether she likes it or not, she is stuck with an old boys' network whose foreign policy in the region is rooted in three basic concerns and commitments—oil, Israel and dominance. Thus, Rice has found herself boxed in, blowing hot air in a stuffy room in Rome and a blood-stained region called the Middle East. And she is caught up in the disorienting illusions that the U.S. and Israel can dictate the destiny and daily lives of the people, kill without being killed, invade countries without being attacked themselves, deny others security without losing it also, rule irrelevant any leader or negotiating partner they want, and expect the people will accept it without resistance and struggle.

The carnage in Qana and the larger crisis in the Middle East opens a window of opportunity for a comprehensive peace plan. But there are several requirements necessary, including: (1) an immediate halt to hostilities; (2) humanitarian aid to the people of Lebanon and Palestine; (3) Israel's and the U.S.' abandonment of the illusion of their ability to defeat the Palestinian and Lebanese resistance; (4) a negotiated ceasefire; (5) withdrawal of Israeli occupying forces from Palestine and Lebanon; (6) placing of a UN International Peacekeeping Force between Palestine and Israel and Lebanon and Israel; (7) honest and open negotiations with all parties involved, including both the states and the resistance movements; (8) placing Palestine and its rightful demands at the heart and center of the comprehensive settlement, including the establishment of a viable, strong Palestinian state; (9) reparations and international aid for rebuilding Palestine and Lebanon; and (10) withdrawal from Iraq and Afghanistan.

The warmongers in Washington and West Jerusalem will not land their war planes or put away their bombs willingly. The quest to dominate by oppressors with superior weapons is a potent addiction even in the face of their continued failures and the iron refusal to be defeated of resistance movements from Haiti to Hamas and Hizballah. So the peacemakers in these countries and around the world have a heavy work to do. Thus, no state, people or persons can have an immunity from criticism and confrontation; no people is superior, more chosen, more elect or more deserving of the goods of the world than any other; and we must struggle continuously to affirm, secure and insure this.

Condi Rice, then, is not to be seen as a representative of the best of our moral and progressive tradition, but rather as an ally and appointment of the established order. She has made her choice and must, as a matter of moral agency, accept responsibility for what she does and supports and we must steadfastly resist her and her allies. Thus, we as a people should not feel responsible or be held responsible for the mad and immoral acts of her day-dream savior and our nightmare oppressor, but rather bear the burden and glory of our own history in struggle.

2006 August 4

Beyond the Mystification of 9/11:
Reflective Remembrance and Rightful Mourning

It is clearly right and morally required that we remember and mourn the loss of life, even of one person, not to mention hundreds, thousands and even millions. And so as the country turns this week to remember and mourn the tragic loss of life of 9/11, let us honor the dead and offer an important lesson to the living thru reflective remembrance and rightful mourning. This requires that our remembrance move beyond presidential propaganda and mystification as well as media trivialization of the larger meaning of 9/11 and the wrong road the country has been led down in response to it.

No matter how difficult it is, we must look at the larger picture of human suffering and human evil in the world without denying our own tragedy or the wrong the country has done and does in the world. And we must also recognize the great good this country could do, if it abandoned its current preference for war and began the difficult work of peace and development in the world. The need, then, is to approach this memorial with an expanded sense of our own humanity and of our relatedness in life and loss with others and imagine and seek to bring into being a new history of humankind.

So, in the midst of our rightful mourning, let us mourn not only for the 3,000 plus in this country, but also for those who have died and die needless and tragic deaths in other lands: 500,000 in Darfur; 4 million in the Congo; thousands in Haiti, Iraq, Afghanistan, Palestine, and Lebanon. And let us ask ourselves what brought us to this place, 9/11? And was the waging of an unjust and illegitimate war against and the occupation of Afghanistan and Iraq the right path to pursue? And is it right for Bush and crew to sacrifice other people's children on the altar of their infantile illusions of global empire, invincible power and endless profits?

Surely, if 9/11 is to have any real and lasting meaning for U.S. society, it requires a sober assessment and rejection of the disastrous policies Bush and company have imposed on this country and the world. And we must recall how far he has taken the country away from the empathetic position it held in the hearts of the people of the world right after 9/11. It was an opportunity he had that will not come again for him, but perhaps there is an opportunity for the country, if it is conscientious and courageous enough to transform and transcend its current deceptive self-understanding and destructive self-assertion in the world.

Bush and his warmongering crew squandered all this good will by lying to the people, perverting national purpose, violating and eroding civil and human rights, and reducing patriotism to shared fear and hatred, flag-waving, and automatic agreement with any policy he proposed. Indeed, he went forth with a kind of "kill Bill and Bonnie" policy, waging war at great cost in human life and life-sustaining resources, claiming religious inspiration for an imperial rampage and finding treason and traitors in every sign or sound of opposition and dissent.

Bush has bumbled his way thru a play called "the president," and assumed an arrogance his level of intelligence doesn't support, and an air of brutal self-righteousness only those from a religion of thugs would think moral or appropriate. This man has ruined so many lives, laid waste so many lands and will never be able to live down or explain away his criminal neglect and abandonment of the people of New Orleans and the Gulf Coast before, during and after Katrina. And we must free ourselves and the country from the heavy burden and debt he and company have placed on us.

Still, there are lessons to learn from all this, and the first one is that the only remedy for this and other similar social ills we suffer is resistance, resistance to unjust and endless wars, violation and erosion of human and civil rights, the pimping of patriotism, and the fostering of fear and hatred to mask a myriad of wrong, evil and ultimately insane policies and practices in this country and the world. Secondly, let's not lie about how 9/11 created a "season of sorrow and solidarity" across race and class lines. We were not all equal in life and thus were not all equal in death. Before the buildings had finished burning, racism had reared its unholy and omnipresent head. Relations between first responders, coverage of casualties, difference in insurances payments, recognition of Blacks and other people of color for their sacrifice, differential reporting on the diversity of persons and peoples involved, and certainly the vicious attacks on Arabs, Muslims and so-called Middle East types, excluding Israelis, all speak to the race divide. So let's not declare solidarity; let's build it in the process and practice of working and struggling for common good.

Also, we must reject the selective morality that privileges select races and religions and bear witness in word and practice that we are all bearers of dignity and divinity, and thus, deserving of the highest respect and a rightful share of all the good and goods of the world. This means also that every people has the right to self-determination, freedom from invasion and occupation, and the right to the resources of their own people and lands.

We must also be clear about the use and misuse of the term terrorism. It can be practiced by a group or a state, by Al Qaeda or the U.S., Israel or Iceland, Germany, Pakistan or Poland. To invade and occupy a people's land, repeatedly bomb its population, send death squads among them to assassinate its leaders and citizens, to inflict regular and ruthless collective punishment, capture and torture its people, and wall it up from the rest of the world to hide crimes against the people and humanity is clearly terrorism. And if even one lacks the political courage to call the name of the offending states, we should muster the moral courage to at least condemn the acts themselves when and wherever one finds them.

Finally, as Frantz Fanon says, "let us reconsider the question of humankind." And in that reconsideration, let us imagine a continuing expanding realm of human freedom and human flourishing and dare build it. And as we say in Us, "if not this then what; and if we don't do it, who will?"

2006 September 14

167

VI

Confrontation, Coalition and Consciousness-Raising

Above all, we must stay rigorously active and rightfully attentive to every aspect of the process. For we know from historical and current experience, how easily principles are trumped and trounced by the perverse use of power and how rights are rendered null and void by money and might. But regardless, we must be defenders of the lives and legacies of our people, of their unquestionable right to justice, well-being and human wholeness. And there is no way to pave the road and reach these goals and good ends or realize their promise except thru deep-rooted and relentless struggle.

Confrontation

The Unfinal Fact of Freedom: The Ongoing Struggle for Justice

Whenever I think of the labor movement and the sacrifice and struggle of the masses of workers to win a better life for themselves and their families, I think of A. Phillip Randolph, one of the greatest leaders and most skilled organizers of the labor and civil rights movement. I think of the rich lessons he left in both word and deed, especially the emphasis he placed on the labor movement as a key means, not only of achieving economic justice, but also social justice in the larger sense. "Social and political freedom cannot be sustained in the midst of economic insecurity and exploitation," he said. "Freedom requires a material foundation. Social justice and economic reform have become inextricably intertwined in our time."

And so, when the word came last week that the four-year struggle which the Service Employees International Union and the community had waged to win the right of security officers to unionize in the buildings of the largest property owner in downtown Los Angeles had been won, I thought of him. I thought how he would interpret this beginning but meaningful victory in the larger ongoing effort to organize all the security officers in Los Angeles and in the whole country.

Certainly, he would begin by reminding us to give proper praise to the masses of our people who marched and rallied in rain and heat, who blocked streets, who were arrested in civil disobedience, who occupied buildings and disrupted daily business as usual, and who participated in the negotiations to defend and secure the security officers rights. He would tell us that Mayor Antonio Villaraigosa's later intervention was important, but without the struggle of the masses in their own interest, neither the Mayor nor the rich employers would have had any reason or push to negotiate, regardless of how worthy the cause. Indeed, Mr. Randolph said, "The virtue or rightness of a cause are not alone the conditions and cause of its acceptance." It is the "power and pressure . . . from the masses" that are decisive.

Praise, then, is due to the Stand For Security Coalition which was composed of security officers, SEIU and a broad range of community organizations, activists, clergy and politicians including the Los Angeles Alliance for a New Economy, Bethel AME Church, Say Yes to Children, Community Call to Action and Accountability, SCLC, the Organization Us, the NAACP, Mt. Gilead Baptist Church, the Nation of Islam, Community Coalition, Clergy and Laity United for Economic Justice, Ward A.M.E. Church, Agenda, New Frontier Democratic Club, Congresswomen Maxine Waters and Diane Watson, Assemblymembers Karen Bass, Mervyn Dymally, Mark Ridley-Thomas, Jerome Horton and others.

Also, we learn from Mr. Randolph that in the struggles for economic justice, we must not see it as just a struggle between employees and employer, but as a historic moment and matter of interest for the community itself. Thus, the struggle around unionizing security officers was posed and pursued in terms of three basic and yet broad issues: justice for the security officers, respect for the community, and security for the public.

The struggle is first about justice in a broad, deep and demanding sense. Certainly, it is and remains about decent wages, affordable health care insurance and other benefits, and advancement opportunities, professional training —none of which they had. But it was in a larger sense about the right to respect, as men, women and workers, worthy without question, of living lives of dignity and decency and of having the means from their work to do this, to care for their families, and be free from unwarranted fear for the future of their children. And this, of necessity, is tied to their right to choose and organize a union of their choice and to be represented in defense and promotion of their rights and interests.

Second, the struggle is about respect for the African American community in several ways. It is about: respect for the rights of all its members to freedom, justice, equality, shared power and decision-making in the workplace and for the community's interest in strong working families, the economic strength that well-paid workers bring to the community and what these things mean in terms of the health and wholeness of the community and each and all of its members. And it is about the community's commitment to economic justice as an indispensable principle and practice of a just and good society.

And finally, there is the issue of security for the public itself and the contradiction of having a security force which is insecure itself and lacks the employment conditions and training to do the security work for which they are hired. It is clearly in the interest of the public, the building owners and the security officers themselves to be well-paid, justly treated, professionally trained, and effectively linked with other similarly-engaged agencies as first responders in coordination and cooperation. They, of course, have none of this and thus the need and urgency of struggle.

But if the victory in this battle is going to be a solid step in the larger struggle for justice for the workers and the rebuilding and strengthening of the labor movement, certain things still must be done. First, the union must insure that African Americans who have won this important struggle and who represent 70% of the security officers are not replaced in manipulation by employers or current organizing emphasis of the union which is mostly on Latinos. Moreover, it must build projects of cooperation among African Americans and Latinos and not imitate employers by initiating policies which divide rather than unite them. It must also allocate an equitable amount of resources for organizing and training Black workers; put more Blacks in leadership positions; place the organizing and training of Blacks in the Black community as well as build cooperative projects with and in the Black community. For this will build a strong alliance with labor. As Mr. Randolph told the AFL-CIO Convention in1963, if the labor movement embraces the "(Black) struggle for freedom . . . it will rise to its full moral stature." And if they do this, "when labor's rights are threatened, you will see an outpouring of Black Americans into the streets in defense of their own rights."

Finally, Mr. Randolph, who made history organizing the Brotherhood of Sleeping Car Porters in the midst of raw-meat racism and ice-cold terror (1925-1937) reminds us not to mistake the victorious battle for a truly won war and to remember we are our own liberators and must continue the struggle until final victory. "Salvation for any race, nation or class must come from within." He said, "Freedom is never granted; it is won. Justice is never given; it is extracted. Freedom and justice must be struggled for by the oppressed of all lands and races and the struggle must be continuous—for freedom is never a final fact, but a continuing evolving process to higher and higher levels of human social, economic, political and religious relationships."

2006 April 19

In Defense of King/Drew:
A Triumph and Promise Born of Struggle

The establishment of the Martin Luther King, Jr./Charles Drew Medical Center (KDMC) in 1972, seven years in the wake of the Watts Revolt, represented for the African American community a triumph and promise born of struggle. The name of the Center itself was a statement of profound historical, cultural and social significance. It was a monument to the two men whose name it bears, to the life-affirming cultural values they and the community embrace, and to the struggle for social justice and self-determination which brought it into being. At this place there was to be an unquestioned obligation of the hospital and each health care provider to preserve life, treat illness, relieve suffering, and promote the well-being of the people. And they were to do this with competence, conscientiousness, compassion and commitment.

At this hospital, born of the battle for the community's control of its vital institutions, respect for the life, rights and dignity of persons and the people would be enshrined in policy, affirmed in instruction and embodied in practice. For we would not deprive, damage, and disregard each other like the dominant society had done and continues to do in far too many places and cases. And at this place, we thought and declared, health care would be accessible and affordable and the community would enjoy the full range of preventive, curative, rehabilitative and educational services a first-rate hospital should have and provide.

And now after all the struggles of the Sixties, after the heavy hope, the hard work, and enduring faith, it has come to this. Poor supervisorial oversight and management, disillusioned and dispirited staff, needless deaths and injuries, and a record just raw enough for the *Los Angeles Times* to paint or imply a stereotypical portrait of gross racial incompetence, blow things out of proportion and seek the institution's dismemberment and demise. After the alarm had been sounded and Congresswoman Maxine Waters took leadership in organizing the community into the Save King/Drew Coalition, and after their laudable and strenuous struggle for two years to elicit accountability and change, after all the testimony, recommendations and requests at the many meetings of the L.A. County Board of

Supervisors and assurance things would be different, we have come to this. The Board of Supervisors did not correct the problems even though they spent over $14 million on consulting firms who claimed competence in such matters.

Now the hospital has received a letter from the Center for Medicare and Medicaid Services (CMS), the federal agency responsible for oversight of hospital services, saying KDMC has failed its survey of compliance in nine out of 23 areas of concern and will thus be ineligible for the $200 million it now receives per year in federal funding. To appease them and maintain the money, the Board of Supervisors has decided to radically restructure the hospital and its relations with the community. It intends to reduce services at King/Drew, transfer most of its staff to other county facilities and give Harbor-UCLA Medical Center, 10 miles away, oversight and control of it. Moreover, the plan includes possible closure of the center for the transition.

There is, of course, righteous anger and restrained apprehension, for this means more than the possible loss or gain of money, sorely needed for quality health care. It also means the possible loss of a legacy, a disabling reduction of a vital community resource and steady erosion of the rights of the community to affordable and accessible health care. And it means that instead of holding others responsible for their failure of oversight and corrective measures, the powers-that-be will end up punishing the people.

There is a strong and steadfast sense in the community that all this journalistic and belated administrative assertion of concern, and this so-called radical restructuring to save the federal funds, have more to do with political posturing and positioning, and reinforcing racial stereotypes than a real ethical regard for Black life and health. Some point to the existence of similar problems of practice in other hospitals without a similar radical response from the county and federal governments. Moreover, they note that there were ongoing community complaints and requests for assistance, training, incentives and added resources and yet no real response from those responsible. And they also point out that closures and reductions at King/Drew, i.e., the trauma center, have benefited other hospitals in other areas for other people obviously deemed more worthy.

Some rightfully admit problems at the hospital, but feel also it was singled-out for various unsavory and racialized reasons. Others respond saying, even if they concede the problems, any solution that threatens or ends the community-based delivery of quality health care is not justified. They correctly think that people have a right to affordable and accessible health care and any solution which does not foster and facilitate this is a violation of human rights.

But respect for our rights will only come from our conscious and constant struggle. Thus, we must stand and struggle in solidarity with Congresswoman Maxine Waters and the Coalition to Save King/Drew, as well as other legislators like Assemblyman Mervyn M. Dymally, Congresswomen Juanita Millender-McDonald, Diane Watson, Lydia Sanchez, and others, who have taken up the cause of the people. We must keep King/Drew a public hospital where the impoverished, uninsured and underserved are treated with dignity and decency and the highest level of care. We must reaffirm the human right of everyone to health and health care, and public health services in their own communities. And we must insist on due process for the staff in their mass transfers to other county facilities, request an extension for the deadline from the CMS, and cooperate in any way we can in the restructuring and re-strengthening of KDMC under a new ownership and management.

Above all, we must stay rigorously active and rightfully attentive to every aspect of the process. For we know from historical and current experience, how easily principles are trumped and trounced by the perverse use of power and how rights are rendered null and void by money and might. But regardless, we must be defenders of the lives and legacies of our people, of their unquestionable right to justice, well-being and human wholeness. And there is no way to pave the road and reach these goals and good ends or realize their promise except thru deep-rooted and relentless struggle.

2006 October 5

In Defense of Life:
Unmasking Official Killing Posing as Justice

The death sentences hanging over the heads of Mumia Abu Jamal, Stanley "Tookie" Williams, as well as the many others similarly situated raises serious moral and social issues for us as a people and for the country as a whole. For in the midst of the calls for the freedom and new trial for Mumia and the petition for clemency for Tookie Williams is the moral imperative to abolish the death penalty and end the barbaric practice its application allows. Indeed, we must see and approach the abolition of the death penalty as part and parcel of our ongoing defense of African and human life and our struggle for justice in and for the world.

Much of the world that calls itself democratic and respectful of human life has recognized the difference between justice and public vengeance and has attempted to punish those who commit murder in a way that is humane, just and proportionate without trivializing the undeserved death of victims and the suffering of their families. The U.S. stands as an odd and unjustifiable exception in numbers of imprisoned and its primordial attachment to bloodletting as an official policy.

Our opposition to the death penalty is grounded first and foremost in our respect for the sacredness and dignity of every human life, even of those who we believe or have proven to have committed the most gross offenses. At the heart of African ethics is the ancient teachings found in the *Husia*, the sacred text of ancient Egypt, that humans are bearers of dignity and divinity and that there are certain things we cannot do to them without violating that special status. Killing human beings as a private and personal practice or a public and legal one is such a violation. Human life deserves the ultimate respect, requires the best protection possible, but the death penalty denies human dignity and degrades human life.

Even for the most serious of crimes, an increased international sentiment and stance against the death penalty has developed. Thus, the International Tribunals on Genocide for former Yugoslavia and Rwanda and the International Criminal Court has excluded the death penalty as a punishment option. In fact, the UN has called the abolition of the death penalty "a contribution to the enhancement of human dignity and the progressive development of human rights."

Secondly, given the sacredness of life, the proneness to error, and the irreversibility of killing someone, the risk of killing the innocent becomes a central and unavoidable moral concern. What could be more horrible and horrifying than the official murder of the innocent by the state while pretending to protect them? Recently, DNA evidence has demonstrated how wrong the state can be in its conviction and condemnation of the innocent.

Also, tied to the moral problem of executing or running the risk of executing an innocent person is the irreversibility of the act. For no matter what reconsideration is given existing evidence later and no matter what new evidence might be discovered afterwards, nothing can reverse an execution once it has been carried out. Given this and the human and institutional capacity for error, such a decision should be avoided and alternatives sought. Moreover, such a deadly decision and act denies in practice the capacity for reform and redemption so central to the moral and spiritual concept of what it means to be human.

In addition, there is the problem of retribution which reduces itself so often to little more than the state's carrying out personal and family calls for vengeance. It is argued that one who kills should be killed. But the early man morality concept of "an eye for an eye, a tooth for a tooth and a life for a life" is clearly not representative of our best moral reflection and values. It is a retribution approach of equivalence that taken to its logical extreme would require us to rape rapists, dismember dismemberers, maim maimers, kill the families of killers of families and revive and kill several times serial killers. Indeed, we have rightly rejected such equivalent or identical punishments except in the case of the commitment to killing itself.

Another factor arguing cogently for abolition of the death penalty is the flawed justice system that disadvantages by both race and class and even at its best, produces unequal justice. It is hardly deniable that race and poverty are major and continuing factors in determining who gets profiled, who gets arrested, who gets a fair trial and the severity of the sentencing for those convicted. The rich are rarely, if ever, found on death row and the people of color and poor are never absent from it and always in greater numbers. African

American men are clearly represented in disproportionate numbers among those in prison, those on death row, and those executed.

Surely, there is no justice in or justification for redefining children as adults and the mentally disable as mentally competent in order to kill them. In light of these raw and morally repugnant realities, and the great harm it has caused to both persons wrongly convicted and mistreated and wrongfully executed, a moratorium on official executions has been called for across the country and around the world.

Finally, we oppose the death penalty because there are alternatives which are morally justifiable and more effective in redressing disorder and injury caused by an offense, maintaining the common good and attempting correction. Preventing, restraining and punishing criminal conduct is both a fundamental obligation of society and an enduring and essential interest of the people. But we also have an obligation to and a profound interest in justice, a justice that is not arbitrary and unfair and excessively prone to error and injury to the innocent, the poor and the racially stigmatized. Official bloodletting is not a proper penalty. It only degrades the human person and society and involves the state in the practice of vindictive killing which should be opposed, not catered to or masked as justice.

2005 November 17

Regarding Stanley Tookie Williams:
Matters of Life and Death

The life and death of Stanley Tookie Williams offers a wealth of lessons worthy of being learned and taught in the community, society and the world. The first is the living lesson of Tookie, himself, self-described as once a "wretched and terrible man" and a purveyor of the most reprehensible and evil practice. But he was one also who overturned himself, turned himself around and became a teacher and broker of peace and harmony, a Nobel Peace Prize nominee, a writer of children's books, a mentor and teacher of ways to walk righteously in the world. It is a lesson and legacy especially suited for the millions of young Black men dealing with similar situations of origin, deprivation, alienation, violence turned inward, limited opportunities and lives of little hope. And likewise it speaks to those raised and ruined by the instructive model of violence, domination and destruction which has saturated this society since its inception, from its murderous children games to the top-gun, big-bomb and false-phallic posturing and policies of the small-minded men who rule this society and prey on the world.

There is a lesson too in the way Black people embraced his case and struggled to save his life, recognizing his redemptive transformation and the promise this held for turning other lives around. Special credit goes here to Barbara Becknell and others working with her for tirelessly gathering numerous supporters, and sharing the meaning and message of his case and life. Black people's embrace of this case and building of a multiracial coalition against the death penalty raised the issue to a new level of discourse and concern. And it reaffirmed both the need for our own internal initiative and outreach and alliance with other progressive forces in the country and world. For the struggle assumed an international reach with world leaders calling for clemency and an end to the death penalty.

What is equally important about this struggle is that Black people and their allies struggled against the greatest of odds and up to the twelfth hour. For we are a people tempered and tested in the fire of the Holocaust of enslavement and there we learned to feed on faith, self-heal thru hope and remain steadfast in and thru struggle, regardless of the odds or advice to the contrary.

There is a hard and unavoidable lesson too in the fact that Tookie was a Black man, thus many times more likely to be profiled, convicted, more harshly sentenced, and be executed than others, especially White men and even more so rich White men. And so no matter how we address or approach it, turn it around in our minds and talk about it in mixed or closed company, it's a race issue as well as a class and human one. And thus there is a need not only to continue to fight against the death penalty, but also and especially against the racist way it is applied.

Stanley Tookie Williams went to his officially-conducted death with the defiant dignity of a Black man at peace with himself. Rejecting advice to gain sympathy and advantage by denying his innocence which he had maintained since his arrest and conviction, he chose death in truth rather than life with a lie. As the ghoulish gathering of witnesses from the press peered from their places from behind a protective wall, Tookie turned toward them with a defiant gaze, reaffirming his lack of fear even in the face of certain and impending death. But a White reporter was unnerved by such defiance, finding it intimidating, although Tookie was taped down and strapped in, lying on his back. It is a testimony and metaphor for White men's fear of Black men, their need to see them humbled, hat-in-hand, frightened, cringing and crying about the official fate Whites have defined and determined for them. It is too much for the seriously White mind to take, for a Black man to impatiently take over his official murder and advise his executioners where to find the right vein so they can speed up their quest to kill him. Such defiant fearlessness unnerves the oppressor and defeats his intention to terrorize the prisoner and the people into submission.

Lesson four begins with the recognition that we live in a society violent from its inception, violent in its best concept of itself, as a super and imperial power with no law except its own, no morality except in its religious text and deceptive talk, and no obligation to respect the rights of the less powerful. And so the lesson within this context is that the oppressor will not put down his butcher knife or become a Buddha because we and the whole world appeal to him. He will stop only when the people rise up in resistance, rewrite the laws and reorder the way we live and die in this land.

And so the last lesson, in fact the first and last lesson, is the lesson of the indispensability and unavoidability of struggle. Indeed, it was never simply about clemency for Tookie, but about justice, about ending the death penalty and practicing a justice worthy and respectful of all the people.

Tookie's life, death and struggle are lessons to others who walk the way he once walked, to turn their lives around, to stop the killing, pursue and build the peace, respect the lives of the people and give the oppressor no more excuses to take our lives under the camouflage and color of law. But it is also a call to all of us who love freedom, cherish justice and appreciate and pursue peace to move from seeing Tookie's case as a source of mourning to understanding it as an inspiration to movement. In this way we honor him and his legacy by continuing the struggle to abolish the death penalty, and the overall struggle to bring freedom, justice and other good into the world.

2005 December 15

Andy on the Altar, Wal-Mart on Trial, and Society in Acute Denial

There is something horrifyingly hypocritical about a society that teaches racism with such a savage commitment in word and deed, and then sits in pretentious judgment over its intended victims and accidental students. It is a society that suffers from enduring acute denial about its contribution and complicity in the routine racialized and racist acts that daily undermine its inflated claims to being a just and good society. Anyone with a modicum of historical memory and the morality to admit it knows Andrew Young is an integrationist and universalist from his heart. His choice of corporate family and friends is clearly deplorable and in dire need of reconsideration, but his opposition to racism and his embrace of diverse persons and peoples is on record and is not erased by his recent use of what he calls "racial shorthand".

The current criticism of Andrew Young comes from three basic sources. It comes first from those who genuinely oppose negative references to all people and have misunderstood Young's "racial shorthand" assertion. There is no need to justify Young's shorthand racial reference to Jews, Koreans and Arabs or anyone. And he immediately apologized and distanced himself from such a broad sweep which sounded similar to the collective indictment made against us in routine racial references we are often advised to accept and learn to live with by both liberals and racists. But it is necessary to put the remarks in perspective and avoid the pretension that this is simply a case of harmful racialized speech and that historical problems of racist instruction and oppression by society, the disproportionate share of businesses owned by others in the Black community and the existence of exploitation, high prices, low quality goods and inferior services in communities of color are solved in superficial and contrived outrage about racialized speech by a repentant Black liberal. Indeed, it tends only to hide and divert attention from the greater problem of racist practices by the ruling race/class of this country.

Secondly, the criticism comes from those who see this as an opportunity to punish Young for his indefensible defense of Wal-Mart, and to further indict and isolate Wal-Mart, itself. This partially-contrived controversy evolves in the ongoing effort of union and other activists to expose and indict Wal-Mart, and Young is caught in the crossfire, a sacrificial victim whose choice of corporate company has caused him repeated condemnation and harm. There is no moral or meaningful way to defend Wal-Mart with its low wages, pro-forma and unaffordable health care, pathetic approach to diversity in its upper ranks, its anti-unionism, its riding roughshod over rural communities and its strong-arm expansion in urban ones, and finally, its unconscionable exploitation of cheap labor in China.

And finally, the criticism comes from those who are practicing a selective morality, who have never defended Koreans and Arabs before and who are now doing so only as part of a defense of Whites included in Young's statement. Indeed, these people remain embarrassingly silent in the face of the daily doses of racism against Arabs and Muslims as well as Koreans, not to mention Native Americans, Latinos, other Asians, and the ever-available African "suspect and sinner".

Moreover, they pretend shock at the racial shorthand of speech in this racialized and racist context in which people don't stop to qualify what they say to avoid seeming to indict a whole group. It goes on daily against people of color, especially Blacks, and we are told not to be too sensitive. But we are supposed to be immediately outraged when it happens in reference to some Whites. Clearly, ideas don't drop from the sky; they don't grow from the earth, and they don't float in from the sea. They come from the society in which we live. And racialized speech is part and parcel of a racist society which problematizes the presence and life of peoples of color.

Again, no one can doubt the need for verbal civility, respect in speech for ethnic, racial and cultural diversity. But in placing so much emphasis on racialized and racist speech out of context and in isolation, at least two things happen. First, Whites and their allies can and do argue that people of color can be as prejudiced as Whites and thus have no moral advantage or just claims as the oppressed. And secondly, it diverts attention from the real danger and destructiveness of what racists actually do as opposed to what anybody might say. After all, although words can injure, if we had to choose between being called a name and being killed, profiled, fired or excluded, the choice would be clear. Moreover, we shouldn't even have to choose. But we must make a clear distinction between a negative attitude and insensitive or injurious expression and the capacity and will to impose one's hatred and hostility as public policy and as "normal" social practice. The first is called racial prejudice; the second is racism.

Finally, there have been merchants of various colors that exploited our community even as there were those who brought needed services and products to it. In spite of his failure to observe a needed protocol, Young pointed to racial economic exploitation and economic disadvantage we need to address. His phraseology was problematic and his solution was outrageous in a large Wal-Mart way. We must not indict an entire people because of some among them who offend and oppress us, but we have the right and responsibility to name our oppressors and confront and resist them. Moreover, no one seriously thinks Wal-Mart can solve our problems or is a friend of the poor. It's the lies the corporate world pays people of stature, need or embarrassing gullibility to testify to and tell. But like all myths of race, class and state, the people will eventually see thru and destroy them.

If there is any good that comes from this, it is that Wal-Mart lost a defender it didn't deserve, and Andy Young resigned from a company unworthy of the record he had before joining them. And it reminds us that what is needed, then, is not a selective morality of episodic outrage about real, imaginary or alleged injury to only some groups, but the end of racism and genuine respect for the dignity and rights of all people in their various identities and on every level of life.

2006 August 31

Terror, Trials and Tribulations in Mississippi: Partial Justice and Ongoing Struggle

The trial and conviction of the Mississippi Klansman, E.R. Killen, of manslaughter for the murder of the three civil rights workers, James Chaney, Andrew Goodman and Michael Schwerner, hold for us as a people and the country critical lessons of history and struggle. The process served as a raw-nerve reminder of a terror-filled, blood-soaked and savage past in Mississippi and the USA, and showed how the racist past is still present as expressed in the jury's inability to convict Killen of murder, in spite of the brutality and premeditation of the act. But it also offered welcomed signs of a stubborn hope and continued struggle for the future and an important marker in the ongoing, unfinished struggle for the just and good society for which all of our people have longed, so many of us have died, and some of us still struggle. Thus, we must understand and approach the process in worthy ways.

First, we must pay homage to African people of Mississippi who in spite of White racist terror, rose up in struggle, undeterred by threats of death, firings, brutal beatings and burnings, and who gave and lost their lives in the unrelenting struggle for freedom and justice in Mississippi and the USA. Among these martyrs are counted most vividly James Chaney, Medgar Evers and Vernon Dahmer. But the real numbers are in the thousands and tens of thousands. Therefore, the trial provided us with an opportunity to practice the morality of remembrance and raise up the names and heroic deeds of those who sacrificed so much for us and others. For as that great freedom fighter and distinguished daughter of Mississippi, Fannie Lou Hamer, said, "There are two things we all ought to care about—never to forget where we come from and always praise the bridges that carried us over."

We also give credit to all those allies in the Civil Rights Movement who stood with us—Native Americans, Latinos, Asians and progressive Whites, and among the latter are Andrew Goodman and Michael Schwerner in this current case. But we must do this in a way that does not overshadow, minimize or suggest equal significance with the initiative and agency, suffering, sacrifice and loss of Black people. This is especially true with Whites, for example Goodman and

Schwerner, who have been the focus of the trial and whose murders have merited more consideration in the media and minds of many than does the horrible mutilation murder of James Chaney. Thus, news stories on the trial routinely focused on the bios and families of the two Whites and only mentioned James Chaney in passing. Surely, we cannot deny the unique condition, persecution and oppression of Black people simply because they belonged to the wrong race in the hate-filled minds of racists. Indeed, the racists determined that being Black and daring to demand respect and rights as a human being was a crime worthy of death. Therefore, *James Chaney was murdered and mutilated for being Black and acting human*; Goodman and Schwerner were murdered for association with him and support for his cause. Many Blacks who were brutally murdered and remain missing do not appear as a current and compelling case for legal pursuit, because there are no White victims associated with them. They died alone and devalued and, thus, could not derive the required relevance from Whites killed with them.

Finally, the lessons of Mississippi reaffirm the necessity of continuing struggle in the whole of the U.S. For the struggle for freedom for the oppressed, justice for the wronged and injured, power for the masses of people over their destiny and daily lives, and peace in the world remains unfinished and wanting. And we who struggle for these social and human goods must not be defeated, dispirited or diverted in our efforts. This too we must remember: *we are our own liberators and a people that cannot save itself is lost forever. Indeed, no matter how numerous or sincere allies are, those who would be free must strike the first, final and decisive blow.* Moreover, there is no alternative to struggle. For as Frederick Douglass tells us, "Without struggle, there is no progress." Thus, we must continue the ongoing historic struggle, as Fannie Lou Hamer taught us, "to bring justice and right where there is injustice and wrong." And this means moving from the impotence of simple complaint to progressive empowerment thru struggle, and from simply reliving the horrors of our history to healing and repairing ourselves and the world in an intensified struggle for social justice and good in the world. In this way, we truly honor those who walked, worked and struggled before us and insure that the good they have done on earth shall never perish or pass away.

2005 June 27

The Minister, the Movement and the LAPD: Police Violence and Community Resistance

There can be no justification for the recent arrest and savage assault on Minister Tony Muhammad, the Western Regional Representative of the Nation of Islam, by members of the Los Angeles Police Department. Regardless of the swift and persistent PR campaign waged by the LAPD to absolve themselves from the brutal and senseless beating of Min. Muhammad, they cannot shake their image and self-understanding as an occupying army in a conquered and hostile territory. Review the record of occupying armies in Haiti, Palestine, Iraq, Afghanistan or in former colonies of Africa and elsewhere, and you will find that their attitudes and actions are repulsively similar and familiar. Whatever other name or slogan we attach to police presence and practice in the Black community and other communities of color, it is always violent. And it is undergirded and informed by a racist ideology, (also embraced by some police of color) that cultivates contempt and fosters fear in the minds of the officers and often inspires a depraved and destructive disregard for the rights and life of persons of color.

There is in every occupied country or community always the racial profiling and violent roundup, the collective punishment, the lockdowns, the doors kicked down and the teeth kicked in, the shootings, beatings, bone-breaking, asphyxiation, maiming, killing and various other inventive ways to subdue and suppress the restless and resistant natives. And there is always the occupier's and oppressor's claim that their racist rampages are for reasons of security, self-defense and in response to the belligerence of the native, which is communicated thru rightful resistance to occupation and degradation; defiant looks, words and moves; and the outrageous audacity to question the offending officers and to demand respect or declare one's rights.

The brutality inflicted on Min. Tony Muhammad then, represents another example in a long history of daily horror imposed on an oppressed people who refuse to be docile collaborators in their own oppression. Thus, we must denounce it in the strongest terms as a violation of Min. Tony's civil and human rights, a disturbing escalation of police force and violence against communities of color, an unnecessary and dangerous provocation which could easily spin out of control and a call to conscience and action of all people of good will to defend the rights of all and preserve peace in the community and city.

First, the savage and senseless assault is a violation of Min. Tony's civil and human rights to be secure from arbitrary violence, especially that which is committed under the camouflage and color of law. Indeed, there is no greater violation of rights and no greater threat to life, freedom, justice and peace than arbitrary violence by governments and their officers. That is why it's not real nor rational to equate gang violence with police violence or to use gang violence as an excuse for police violence. They are separate issues and should not be linked. No one claims the need to criminalize and terrorize the Jewish, Russian, or Italian communities because of criminal gangs or mafia in them. These are called and treated as national problems, unlike in the Black community where they are defined and attacked as racial problems. Moreover, gang members operate outside the law and they are condemned and contained as criminals. But the police have a "right" to kill with impunity under the color of law and thus are more dangerous and deadly when on a racial rampage.

Second, it was also a clear continuing escalation of police violence which has become more indiscriminate and consistent. It is a statement of policy that everyone is vulnerable and a potential target: children—Devin Brown and Suzie Peña; women—Margaret Mitchell; men—Anthony Dwain Lee; and now a member of the clergy, a religious leader and teacher—Min. Tony Muhammad. For society and its guardians have racialized crime and criminalized race and in such a context, we are not only the usual suspects, we are also the customary and constant victims of the official violence reserved for occupied countries and communities.

It is also a continuing dangerous provocation of the community, a rash and racist act that could easily escalate out of control. For it tends to cultivate a sense that there is no hope of justice and no possibility of protection from those who claim to protect and serve. For it is they, themselves, from whom the community needs protection. Finally, this savage and senseless act is a call to conscience and action for people of conscience, the community and the whole city. It is a call to unite in struggle to end arbitrary police violence against the communities of color. Certainly, the religious community should be especially outraged by this unprovoked attack on a fellow member and minister and should stand together in opposition to it.

But again, the whole city should be concerned about arbitrary and abusive police violence because of its blatant wrongness, its devastating effect and its unpredictable consequences. Moreover, we know that evil unchecked spreads unchecked. And to paraphrase an old adage, if they come for us in the morning, without warrant and unchecked, they will certainly return to terrorize and take you at night.

It is in this context that the Nguzo Saba 2005 Conference of the Organization Us and the Millions More March and Movement take on special meaning. For they stress rebuilding the Movement, relief thru resistance, and freedom forged in constant struggle. In a word, they call on us to get up, get organized and intensify the struggle to end our oppression, repair ourselves and flourish in freedom in the world.

2005 September 1

Dreamin' With the Mayor; Wrestlin' With Reality

It was a good and promising beginning. Everyone was represented—the Native American, the African American, the Latino American, the Asian American, and the European American. Within the vast diversity of colors and cultures present at the inauguration, there was also a rich array of faith traditions—Buddhists, Christians, Hindus, Jews, Muslims, Sikhs and Tongva (Native American). There was also the walk among and with the masses, as a respect for origins and a reaffirmation not to forget where he came from and to be an active advocate for all those who brought him to this day and place of honor and awesome responsibility as Antonio Villaraigosa, the first Mexican Mayor of Los Angeles since 1872. In his inaugural address he restated his commitment to and concern for the poor and less powerful, the homeless, the undereducated and uneducated youth, and the insecure and vulnerable communities plagued by crime, gun and gang violence, and drug trafficking and use. Moreover, he promised to meet these challenges and asked the people to dream and work with him, and there was singing and dancing in the streets, and dreams and hopes were heavy in the air.

But in spite of the rightful rejoicing of peoples of color and progressives everywhere, we know that Mayor Villaraigosa can work no miracles or magic by himself. And his dream, like that of Martin Luther King, Jr., can easily end up as essentially a ceremonious reference with limited relevance in society. Whatever he accomplishes will be because he struggles and we struggle with him in a dual sense—as allies for the common good and as definers and defenders of our own interests as African Americans within that united struggle. And we must all struggle with him to keep his commitments and not be diverted by the rich and powerful whose dreams are often the people's nightmares. It is here that we must reassure the people, as Frantz Fanon says that, "everything depends on them, that if we stagnate it is their responsibility and if we go forward it is due to them." It is they who are the makers of miracles and magic and the essential means of doing this is thru their long, hard and relentless struggle.

Therefore, as Amilcar Cabral said, we should "mask no difficulties tell no lies and claim no easy victories." The corporations have already come calling and those who see Antonio as a possible governor or senator or even eventually president will counsel him to move slowly, keep to the center and say and do nothing which can be used against him later. And he will have to make a choice—to be "the mayor of all the people" as he promised or be the mayor of the moneyed men and women who finance and fix things, see the world strictly in terms of profit/loss analysis and routinely pursue private profit over public good.

To be the mayor of all the people means to have a public policy informed and driven by the best of our ethical thinking from all the ethical traditions represented at the inauguration as well as others. It must be a policy which puts in place a multiculturalism beyond focus on food, fashion and festival, beyond symbolic inclusion in ceremonies of unity, beyond expressions of self-congratulatory Americana and exhortations of episodic embrace of different and competing others. It will, of necessity, measure itself by how it treats the most needy and vulnerable and how it stresses cooperation over conflict, confrontation over passive compromise, social justice over an oppressive peace, and the politics of the common good of the many over the zero-sum politics of the few. And this requires values rooted and practiced in an ethics of sharing, which embraces the understanding that the greatest good is shared good, goods that rightfully and righteously belong to all the people.

An *ethics of sharing* as a public policy foundation and framework will focus on several indispensable areas and principles of sharing. These are: *shared status, shared knowledge, shared space, shared wealth, shared interests and shared responsibility*. The hub and hinge on which the ethics of sharing turns is shared status. For it posits every person, people and culture as a unique and equally valuable way of being human in the world, each as bearers of dignity and divinity and thus equally worthy of the good in and of the world. It is in this context that everyone is worthy of education and employment training of the highest level, quality neighborhood and environmental space to grow and live in, adequate resources to live a life of dignity and decency, and power over their destiny and daily lives. And it is in this context that we constantly pursue shared and common interests and dare share responsibility for building the city, society and world we all want and deserve to live in.

On this foundation and within this framework, the mayor and people of Los Angeles can begin the needed reconception and reconstruction of the city and meet the mentioned as well as unmentioned urgent challenges such as unemployment, immigration, ethnic conflict and cooperation, job skills training, and police abuse and misconduct. But again, there is no magic in the mayor's office, no miracles except those that the people make themselves in their daily struggles to improve and expand their lives and leave a legacy reflective of the best of their visions, values and social practice.

2005 July 14

Coalition

Gathering in Grief, Uniting in Struggle

It is neither wrong, irrational nor unrestrained to be morally shocked, emotionally shattered and righteously angered by the killing of children and other innocents. Thus, our justifiable outrage at the recent police killing of Suzie Marie Peña and earlier that of Devin Brown should be, in any moral mind, understandable and expected. Indeed, what kind of communities or people would we be, if we suffered in silence and hat-in-hand sat down and waited passively for a sign of contrition, confession, and conversion from perpetrators and oppressors? We are encouraged to mourn the taking and loss of innocent (and not so innocent) life among Whites here in this country and wherever else they are. But concerning such great and grievous losses all over Africa and in Haiti, Palestine, Iraq, Afghanistan and other places which Bush and company call the "dark corners of the world," as well as here in this country among communities of color, attempts are constantly made to desensitize, disinform and divert us.

We are given "reasons" why we should be calm, consider the circumstances, wait for an official interpretation of events and question the character of the victims and/or those associated with them. In spite of these efforts to deter and dispirit us, we must continue to struggle for justice and to end the oppression which consumes and kills us. Let us talk frankly and honestly, then, about the killing of Suzie Marie Peña and Devin Brown as well as the unjustified killing of all those before them by the police. This discussion must begin with putting the killings in context of both the larger society and the police subculture—a vicious racism which assigns people of color lower human worth and less social status and treats them accordingly.

In such a context the racialization of crime and the criminalization of races go hand in hand. And we and our children become victims of a pattern of reckless and often depraved disregard for the lives of people of color by the police in the process. One can argue that the killing of Suzie wasn't intentional, but it was certainly reckless and wrong in a moral and even legal sense. No one but police under the cover of law and racist reasoning could shoot so many times and so widely in such a small space and claim not to know it would kill both the targeted father and the child whom he was holding.

If the police argue it was wrong and reckless for the father to engage in the shootout with his baby in his arms, it is equally wrong and reckless for the police to participate in the shootout knowing the suspect was holding the baby. Did they see it simply as acceptable collateral damage? The reality is that the father chose wrongly and so did the police, but the baby had no choice. It is this reckless disregard for Black and Brown life that made the family and community rightfully raise questions of such an aggressive approach in a hostage situation, the brevity of negotiations, rejection of family intervention, differing methods in Watts and Westwood, and the apparent tendency of police to use force as a first resort rather than a last one.

The tendency of the police is to free themselves of responsibility for their own acts in several standard ways: attack the victim, attack their families or blame a third party or the community as a whole. Thus, Devin Brown and his mother are blamed and Suzie Marie Peña's father and family situation are blamed. Devin was joyriding, but he didn't deserve death for it. Even conceding the wrongness of Peña's acts, it does not prove the rightness of the police's decision to join him in it. If Peña was reckless in endangering Suzie Marie's life, the police were lethally reckless and culpable in taking her life.

Even in the worst of situations, we who struggle know we must search for and achieve some good. It is always good to see the masses of people standing up, demanding justice, and resisting oppression. And it is especially good to see the Brown and Black communities gathering in grief and uniting in struggle to accomplish this. It is an irony of history that this police killing and its challenge by the Brown and Black communities take place in Watts on the eve of the 40th anniversary of the Watts Revolt. It was, as the one in 1992 and virtually all the other urban revolts, the result of an incident of police brutality and injustice which served as the proverbial spark that ignited a prairie fire. It is only just and proper that we honor those who fought for justice and freedom then by continuing the struggle now.

Mayor Antonio Villaraigosa has called for a suspension of demonstrations until after the investigation into what happened. He is progressive, a person of color and as we did with Mayor Tom Bradley, we want to respect him and heed his advice as an ally. But unless challenged to do otherwise, he will act as mayor, stand in the center, call for calm, and try to avoid alienating either side. However, we are the communities suffering the injury and injustice and we are compelled to call for continuing struggle. His role is to calm troubled waters, ours is to make transformative waves; his is to stress peace, ours is to insist on justice; his is to call for patience in hope, ours is to call for perseverance in struggle; his is to call for investigation, ours is to call and struggle for changes in public policy and police practice that will yield equal regard and equal justice in the courts, our communities, and the larger society and point toward real justice in the world.

2005 July 21

Seeking Solutions to Interethnic Conflict:
Social and Institutional Issues

The current clashes in the L.A. county jails between African Americans and Latinos are both tragic and troubling, not only because of the deaths and harm they have caused, but also because of the damage they do to our sense of shared interests in life and struggle as peoples of color seeking a just society and a good world. Indeed, it is common consensus among socially-conscious activists, intellectuals and others, that people of color are natural allies, given our common condition of race and class oppression and our common interests in ending and transcending it. Although these clashes don't challenge this fundamental understanding, it does raise questions about the causes and conditions of the conflict and our role in solving the problem and pursuing the common good.

To correctly understand and effectively address this urgent issue, we must have a clear conception of the basis and nature of these conflicts. First, we must avoid the easy path of posing them as simply a racial problem. For although they contain a racial element, the issue is much more complex and rooted in a series of interrelated institutional and social conditions. It is ironic that we tend and are taught to explain every conflict between peoples of color by raising the issue of race. But in our negative relations with Whites, we are discouraged from doing so and told to look elsewhere for sources and solutions, especially within ourselves and our communities.

Secondly, we must not simply worry about what inmates will bring out of jail and prison, but also what they take in there from the society and communities from which they come. They do not enter naked and empty of mind and emotion, but rather fully clothed in the ideas and attitudes of society. Among these are racism, ethnic chauvinism, domination, aggression, alienation, hostility and objectification of others which denies their humanity and justifies any act against them deemed necessary. Thus, there is also an urgent need for societal and community self-reflection and self-transformation.

Also, then, we must always deal with the conditions of the institution itself which by its very structure and function produces a degenerative and tension-filled environment. Thus, treatment of inmates, living conditions, opportunities for meaningful activities, i.e., education, recreation, skill improvements; relations with guards and in-place policies to avoid, intervene in and solve conflicts in effective and non-abusive ways, all must be considered. The county jail clearly has problems in all the above areas. It is oppressively over-crowded and woefully understaffed, by Sheriff Baca's own admission.

The living conditions are thus breeding grounds for tension and hostility, and the cultivation and manipulation of ethnic or racial hatred by gangs, guards-gone-wild or others. Moreover, the tension intensifies in the absence of programs which would allow learning, recreation, skills acquisition, and other self-improvement opportunities.

Certainly, another important element which helps create and aggravate the situation is aggressive ethnic chauvinism which evolves when a positive appreciation of one's own ethnic identity and commonality turns into a perverse need to deny the equal worth and rights of others. This aggressiveness is emboldened by a numerical advantage. Thus, the Latinos who incite the attacks on African Americans exploit their numerical vulnerability. As reported, many Latinos don't share this aggressiveness or wish to participate in the attacks, but fear consequences if they don't cooperate.

It is important to note that many, if not most, fights start out as personal conflicts and confrontations over such issues as food, phone and sex access, bunk position, paper towels and toilet paper, or that perennial quest of men of color for recognition and respect so often denied by the larger society. But these incidents and issues are quickly taken up by racial provocateurs as insults and challenges to the group which must be avenged or answered in some macho-demanding way.

Key also to understanding and effectively dealing with this problem is recognizing the role some guards play in provoking groups, pitting them against each other, or letting them savage each other as a form of discipline, punishment, ethnic preference or self-saving in a violent and dangerous situation.

To effectively address this urgent issue and the interrelated problems, several things are necessary. First, given the obvious vulnerability and targeting of African Americans by some Latinos, the first step is to secure their safety and that of the innocent and uninvolved. This means at this point separating groups into distinct areas. However, if this is not possible, the sheriff should balance the numbers in given areas to create a balance of power which acts as a deterrent to those who prey on the vulnerable and less numerous.

In addition, the sheriff should: (2) separate and transfer those inmates who provoke and thrive on inter-group violence; (3) increase and expand focused programs which allow for classes in academic subjects as well as substance abuse, conflict resolution, anger management, and multicultural exchange; (4) stress preventive measures rather than post facto measures to quell conflict; (5) cultivate and strengthen existing groups and units who oppose interethnic and racial hostility and violence; (6) reintegrate the groups at a slow and measured pace with above measures in place; (7) monitor more closely the behavior of guards and discipline those found to be aiding and abetting interethnic strife; and (8) expand contact with and use of community groups and leaders as not only mediators in crisis, but regular reinforcement against divisive and destructive interethnic and racial views and behaviors.

Finally, we must rebuild the Movement. Indeed, in the midst of the 60's movements for liberation, there was not only less interethnic conflict between Africans and other peoples of color, but there was also less racial conflict between people of color and Whites. For there was a higher level of political consciousness and commitment to common struggle. Thus, the problems of jails and prisons must be seen as problems of the larger society and African American and Latino community leaders and members must organize and unite not only to solve the problems of prisons and jails, but also the problems of society. And this transformative process and practice we used to call the liberation struggle.

2006 February 26

The Ethics and Errors of Immigration: The Issue and Urgency of Justice

At the heart and center of the struggle around immigration is the issue of justice—justice not only for immigrants but for all concerned, especially the equally and similarly vulnerable. Indeed, it is the teachings of our ancestors in the sacred *Husia* that the righteous law and the most principled practice is that which does justice for all the people. So there is no justice in denying Latino or other immigrants' human and civil rights and marginalizing and mistreating them, regardless of their legal status. And there is no justice in denying, dismissing and failing to deal with the rightful concerns and needs of fellow African American and other workers and neighbors who are also working hard to provide for their families, send their children to school, pay their taxes, secure a living and decent wage and live a good and meaningful life.

Thus, somewhere beyond the racist ranting and raving of the right-wing, the vote-pandering-and-posturing of the average politician, the manipulative moves of big business in the background, and the unthoughtful embrace by most progressives of policies inadequately attentive to the real and rightful concerns and needs of the impacted communities, we must struggle to find a just and humane way to address this critical issue. And to do this we must, first, reject the language and logic of our oppressor and not talk and think in ways that are divisive and degrading, make villains out of fellow victims and injure our shared interests in social change, justice and the common good.

In the best of our ancient and ongoing ethical tradition, as found in the *Husia* and *Odu Ifa*, we are obligated "to bear witness to truth and set the scales of justice in their proper place among those who have no voice." We are to welcome the stranger, care for the vulnerable, shelter the refugee and seeker of asylum, and do justice for those we don't know like those we do know. And above all, we must treat all human beings as bearers of dignity and divinity, divinely chosen to bring good into the world. We thus stand in solidarity with the oppressed and struggling peoples of the world. And we uphold their right to live lives of dignity and decency in their home countries and to migrate to seek this in other places, whether they are from

Mexico, Haiti, Central and South America, the Caribbean, Africa, Asia or any other place in the world.

What we need, then, is a comprehensive immigration reform which includes: (1) respect for the rights and dignity of all immigrants, refugees, asylum seekers and exiles, regardless of documented or undocumented status and the rejection of criminalization of undocumented immigrants or of those who aid and advise them; (2) recognition and respect for the rightful concerns and needs of the receiving and impacted communities; (3) ways to prevent employer exploitation and manipulation of the labor and vulnerability of undocumented workers; (4) a just, humane and legal means of permanent and temporary entry for citizenship and work; (5) a border control policy which respects the immigrants' right to due process and dignified treatment and is directed against human trafficking and a justly regulated flow of legal immigrants; and (6) the strengthening of the economies and life conditions of the immigrants' home countries, devastated by historical and recent imperial policies and related poverty, oppression and armed conflict.

Within this context, Latinos, Africans and others must address key issues missing from the current progressive agenda and discourse on immigration. These include: application of the above policies to other immigrants in addition to Latinos, i.e., the Haitians, other Caribbean and Continental Africans, Asians and others; dealing effectively with employer preference for low-wage, vulnerable and pliant undocumented workers and its effect on employment, wages and working conditions for U.S. workers and especially employers' displacement and replacement of African American workers with them. And it is important to note here that it is not the case, as commonly argued, that African Americans don't want to do the work that Latinos do. It's only that they don't want to work for the low wages and degraded working conditions under which Latinos do it. Moreover, the potential misuse of the call for bilingual workers by employers and the Latino ethnic network which favors Latino workers both pose problems which require a just response. Thus, progressives and the labor movement must find ways to insure Africans have an equitable share of the jobs, training, economic opportunity and leadership in this rapidly evolving economic context.

As some sections of labor have conceded, the guest workers program is similarly problematic. For it creates a second-class vulnerable work force which encourages employers to transform regular jobs into temporary ones, lower wages and degrade working conditions. Also, a path-way to citizenship for those immigrants who wish to remain, must be developed, but it must be for all immigrants—Haitians, other Caribbean and Continental Africans, and Asians as well as Latinos. And justice requires that it not privilege Latinos or put them ahead of those already in the process.

Finally, whatever is done in Congress, the courts or closed corporate boardrooms, it's on us as Africans and Latinos first, who still must and will most often live and learn together, work together, and be locked down together and even compete in middle-class and corporate spaces across this country. And thus, we, more than any other groups, must find ways which serve our interests and achieve common good for everyone. The current mobilization by Latinos around this single issue does not overshadow our history nor threaten our future. It is rather a historical moment of possibility for both of us and the country.

Thus, we must not underestimate what we, African Americans, have done and continue to do in the struggle for justice, nor fear or inflate what Latinos are doing now. We have both mobilized millions in marches for justice in recent times, nurtured youth activism, and worked together on issues of common interests and common good. Now we must each rebuild our own movement and in the process, link our movements and with other struggling and progressive peoples, build a larger movement for fundamental and far-reaching social and world change based on an ethics of sharing—shared struggle and shared good in the world.

2006 April 13

Boundary Setting and Border Crossings:
Beyond Small-Minded and Mī-nute Men

This is the month of Min. Malcolm X, the Fire Prophet, teacher of the right and responsibility of resistance, caller to the prayerful practice of struggle and doing good in the world. It is Malcolm who taught us that there are signs everywhere for those who can see. And thus, one ought not miss a sign of the times reflected in White racists, small-minded and mī-nute men, coming to the Black community to recruit us to join them in gathering at the border to howl hatred and do harm to another vulnerable and victimized people. And this too is a sign, the spontaneous and then organized gathering of those who resisted them, reaffirmed the best of our social justice tradition and would not let them and their allies-in-hatred-and-harm misrepresent the larger African American community. The signs, then, are those of the constant challenge to confront and resist evil, injustice and wrong everywhere we find them, to uphold the best of what it means to be African and human, and to struggle earnestly and incessantly to bring good in the world.

Thus, even in the midst of great stress and strain, we must set boundaries for ourselves and not allow ourselves or others to cross them. As the *Odu Ifa* teaches, we must "speak truth, do justice, be kind and not do evil." And we must not let our oppressor be our teacher, nor evil men and women masquerade as our allies or seduce us into being theirs. Indeed, the *Husia* teaches we are commanded to struggle against those who struggle against us, protect the weak against the strong, and join with those of like mind and heart to repair, renew and transform the world in ever more beautiful and beneficial ways.

The immigration issue is real and pressing to us. And progressives do us no good by reducing the discussion to simple support for some immigrants (Latinos) without concern for others (Africans, Asians and others) and denying adequate attention to the consequences of massive immigration to the receiving and impacted communities and the often strained and unequal relations which emerge from this. Nor is there any value or justice in pointing to every negative thing said or done in the African American community concerning the issue of immigration at the expense of the good things said and done by those of us who understand the issue and seek justice for everyone. The responsibility of progressives is not to deny or devalue people's pain and discomfort, but to seek with them the proper care and relief. And it is not to deny they have real issues, but seek to help create a context and cultivate a national conversation in which mutual respect for each other's interests and the collective and constant search for common ground are principles and pillars of all our efforts.

Thus, the question is how do we address both the issues of all immigrants—Latinos, Continental Africans, Caribbean Africans, especially Haitians, Asians and others, and the specific issues of receiving and impacted communities, especially African Americans. It is an irony of history, a legacy of racism and a design and built-in dynamic of capitalism that the two largest ethnic groups find themselves at this historical junction more in unnecessary competition than in necessary cooperation, and lacking leadership initiatives from both sides which would lay an expanded basis for alliance and common struggle.

Still, we must forge ahead and build the good society and world we all want and deserve to live in. And from an African American standpoint, this means reciprocity in everything, i.e., mutual respect, mutual concern, and mutual support for each other. This translates in concrete terms as progressives working together to deal effectively with critical African issues including: (1) job loss and difficulty in finding employment because of employer preference for undocumented and vulnerable workers, as well as their tilt toward the Latino/a in critical spaces at other levels than low-skilled jobs for various given and hidden reasons; (2) neighborhood transitions and the quality of resultant relations; (3) equity and justice in public funds distribution; (4) changes in political representation; (5) union leadership and community focus in training, organizing and alliance; (6) a wide range of educational issues; and (7) respect for the sacrifice, suffering and struggle of the Black Freedom Movement and its contribution to the expanded realm of freedom in which others afterwards justly demand and demonstrate for rights achieved and reaffirmed in that struggle.

And so again, regardless of what decisions come out of Congress or the courts in the coming months and years, it's still on us whose lives and real issues are interrelated and which cannot be placed in external hostile hands, without serious damage to our interests and expansive understanding of ourselves. It is on us, Native Americans, African Americans, Latino/as, Asians and progressive Europeans to find common ground in the midst of our diversity, practice an ethics of sharing and think deeply and work together diligently to forge a future and world worthy of our highest principles.

2006 May 11

Consciousness-Raising

Raceball, Baseball and Unforgivable Blackness: Hank, The King and Barry, The Man

The great African American intellectual and leader, W.E.B. DuBois, wrote an editorial in 1914 in the NAACP's magazine *Crisis* in which he sought to identify the source of the deep and sustained White hatred and hostility directed towards Jack Johnson, the first Black heavyweight champion of the world. He noted that there were the usual pretensions that it was because Johnson's character was less than admirable. But as he said, it was no less so for many celebrated White athletes. "Why then, this thrill of national disgust" toward Johnson he asked? He concluded that its roots lay in race and racism. Thus, he stated, "It comes down, after all, to this, unforgivable Blackness."

I must admit I have no interest in sports per se. And thus I have turned attention to them only when an issue and discourse of race (the Lakers vs. the Celtics in the beginning) or of class (the Pistons vs. the Lakers) arise around them. Certainly, at the heart of the hatred and hostility directed toward Barry Bonds now and Hank Aaron earlier are the issues of race and racism, summed up in DuBois' cogent and compelling category, "unforgivable Blackness." Indeed, in a racist society, being Black in itself is unforgivable; being Black and excellent is intolerable, and being Black, excellent and defiant is outrageous. Hank Aaron is the first two; Barry Bonds is and Jack Johnson was all three.

In a racist society, Blackness is a crime of personhood, peoplehood and presence. Our very identity as persons and a people indicts us and our presence is suspect and provocative of fear and loathing and a miasmic mix of attraction and repulsion, depending on how they want to use us. One can "play dumb" about racism, as Bonds says, but the racism is there. It hangs heavy in the air like a thick and unsettling odor and penetrates our lives in countless savage and subtle ways. It's a brain fog in the minds of Whites who cringe, cry and howl hatred at seeing a Black man, Aaron then and now Bonds, force them to admit his excellence, recognize and respect it and free themselves from illusions of superiority.

They remember or read about a time when Blacks were excluded from these sports. For these were fields of White racial prowess and pride, marked off in the beginning by racial rituals resembling early man's (or animals') boundary-peeing, bouts of brutal power and primal screams. Now comes Black men, forcing them into racial and phallic fights, working within their rules and standards, defeating them, making them repeatedly long for a new White champion and destroying every great and small White hope Whites raise against them.

This beginning racialization of sports sets the stage for the racial hatred and hostility toward Johnson, Aaron, Bonds and others even though each case is unique and similar at the same time. The racism is palpable and pervasive in the media as it attacks Bonds and ignores Aaron, discussing and using Ruth as the standard as if Aaron didn't end Ruth's race-based reign three decades ago. And I say race-based reign because before Aaron and now Bonds, there was Josh Gibson, an African American whose career home run record is 900 and whose single season record is 84. The Hall of Fame concedes 800, but he belonged to the Negro (Black) League, deemed *minor* and unworthy of honors bestowed on White league players, intentionally called the *major* league.

Raism is clearly reflected in the way the media and others have been discussing Bonds' quest for kingship in terms of Ruth's record rather than that of Aaron who dethroned the White icon in 1973. Bonds, of course, noticed this and even declared, after his historic 715th home run, that though he felt good breaking Ruth's record and respected Ruth, "Hank Aaron to me is the home run king and I won't disrespect that." So, Hank the Hammer is home-run king (755); Barry Bonds is the man of the hour (715) and gaining fast; and Babe Ruth's record (714) was broken three decades ago by Aaron. Why then have supposedly sane and rational observers of the game been talking as if Ruth was still the standard and Aaron's surpassing his record doesn't matter?

It might offend the White sense of superiority and in some circles seem like a harsh and hurtful assessment. But in other circles, it is said that compared to Hank Aaron and Barry Bonds, Babe Ruth ain't nothing but a candy bar. Surely, it is only in a context where baseball is really raceball, that if you're White, even when you lose the title, you remain the champion and stay on as the standard.

Racism is also expressed in the daily death threats and harassment and the hypocritical outrage over Bonds' alleged steroid use and making him a sacrificial lamb in a country literally committed to drugs for life and living, taking them to go to sleep and wake up, to remove facial lines and restore phallic efficiency, and to pursue a happiness hardly imagined in the Declaration of Independence.

So they will continue to demonize Bonds and other Blacks who defy and dismiss them and whose excellence unseats them. And they will continue to pretend Ruth's record is still the standard, even though Hank is King and Bonds is the man of the hour, until they are challenged and forced to free themselves from such illusions. Because it meant so much to them, Barry said he wanted to break every record Babe Ruth had. But because Aaron meant so much to him, he said he won't mind not catching and surpassing him. To them, it seemed too race-conscious. To us, it just seemed like a Black thing, something sensitive we developed in the midst of our rich, beautiful and reputedly "unforgivable Blackness."

2006 June 1

Tragedy and Trouble in the House:
Reasoning Away Injustice

It might sound like the Sixties, that period of the awesome presence and liberating practice of a generation of giants such as Malcolm X, Fannie Lou Hamer, Martin Luther King, Jr., Ella Baker and others, but we must confront the reality and enduring nature of race, racialization and racism in this country. The recent brutal and dramatic police killings in New York and Georgia, the comedian gone-wild on stage in L.A., and the L.A. Mayor's veto of a just settlement for a Black fireman fed dog food in an historically-documented and conceded environment of racial and sexual hostility, harassment and discrimination, are linked by this unholy trinity of race, racialization and racism. Thus it is in our interest to revisit, confront and dare finish the fight against racism in every area of social life.

For the issue, evidence, and effect of race are there, whether in thin or thick disguises or under the cover and camouflage of comedy, religion and law or the ever-convenient concern for taxpayers' interests. Race is not only a socially-constructed identity, and an indication of status, life chances and treatment. It is also the foundation stone and standard of racism, a system of imposition (violence, domination, discrimination), ideology (justification of the imposition), and institutional arrangement (structures which facilitate, promote and make permanent the imposition and ideology). It is within such a system that the history, humanity and human rights of the people of color are devalued, violated and denied. Indeed to racialize is to assign race to an idea or practice in order to condemn or praise the people identified. Thus, to make "virtue" White and "crime" Black is to racialize virtue to praise Whites, and crime to indict Blacks. Moreover, to define crime as Black is not only to racialize crime but to criminalize a race.

The racist outburst of the comedian, Michael Richards, is not so much a mistake as an unguarded moment of self-exposure even White liberals and leftists, Jews and Gentiles, might have had. It is what some Whites whisper in public and talk openly in private. Richards' imagery of lynching and curious embrace of anal invasion as a particular form of racial violation and devaluation lacks only the customary preoccupation with Black men's penis, exaggerated sexual prowess and feared predation. Furthermore, he aimed to injure not only by the use of a degrading term, but also by linking Whiteness with wealth and worthiness and its opposite with Blackness in the use of the term itself. Thus, he asserted that when it is all over, he still would be White (i.e., worthy) and wealthy and Blacks would still be "N's". This speaks to a racist assumption of Blackness as a permanent stigma and lower status, regardless of wealth acquisition and yellow-wig attempts to alter one's identity and be acceptable to Whites. Furthermore, this is clearly injurious and must be repaired for the direct victims and Black people as a whole.

Whatever else comes from this, we must see the good of the self-questioning and discussion about use of the word "N" by us also, and the collective call and planned efforts of activists and entertainers to promote the disuse of the word. The reaction of Black people to Richards' unveiling undermines the conceptions among some that it is some kind of term of endearment, empowerment and solidarity and that it can be redeemed and salvaged from its savage history and offense to our humanity. Instructively, there are no efforts to claim the negative names for Jews and Gentiles—kikes, crackers, Hymies and honkeys, etc., as terms of endearment, empowerment and solidarity. And these names don't carry half the hellish history of the "N" word. Only persons disoriented by their oppressor and finally allowing themselves to be defined and taught by their oppressor would advance and argue such self-degrading thoughts.

The police killings in Georgia and New York clearly reflect an historical and ongoing pattern of reckless, even depraved disregard for the life and rights of Africans and other peoples of color. The repeated resort to use of deadly force reveals an assumption of societal sanction and tolerance of this approach to devalued communities. Indeed, they understand the rules of engagement as giving them not only the right but also the responsibility to search and suppress, profile and apprehend, capture and kill without fear of punishment or penalty.

In these and other cases, there is a problem of liberal hypocrisy which wants to hide and deny the extent of racism in the daily life of U.S. society and the minds of its people while claiming to be concerned about racism and racial discrimination. But clearly there are favored racial and religious identities. Here people of color and Muslims don't make this list and thus they are given lessons on accepting their losses and learning how not to be hurried in their centuries-long pursuit of justice and to prove themselves worthy of rights Whites take for granted.

Liberals, masquerading as progressives, are quick to confess that the cops use excessive force, have too often killed, beaten and battered into unconsciousness and ill-health too many, and that a comedian or fire chief can lose his way and should be chastised, and even punished. They are especially embarrassed by the early-man behavior of the guardians of their city, wealth and way of life. They know that everywhere there are innocent victims, but they offer easily accessible alibis for police aggression against them.

Moreover, they ask us to admit there are among us, these thugs and thieves, killers, burglars and bandits of all kinds which must be corralled, captured and killed before they kill them and us. This is a justification for police profiling and predatory pursuit of the racially indistinct offenders who walk and work among us and who must be savagely rooted out for all our safety. We are now introduced to an abstract offer of common ground, the shared fear, suspicious and justified suppression of our people.

It is this liberal advocacy of the established order and reasoning away injustice that undermine our will to resist, make us place our liberal allies' interests above our own and leave us doubting the justness of our claim and the rightness of our struggle. And only thru our radical rejection of this kind of irrational reasoning can we practice self-determination and pave the path through uncompromising struggle for the good world we all want, deserve and demand for ourselves and future generations.

2006 December 7

Steppin' Off Stage as N's:
Returning to History as Africans

The road to recovery from the Holocaust of enslavement is a long and difficult one, full of twists, turns, relapses and losses. But we are a resilient, steadfast and defeat-resistant people. We know that this ongoing struggle we wage to free ourselves is larger than the one to break physical chains or eliminate unjust and immoral laws. Moreover, we know it is about removing the residue of the Holocaust, segregation and other forms and features of oppression from hearts and minds. And it is about an ongoing and unfinished fight to secure our rights and establish conditions to live lives of dignity, decency and promise in our time and for future generations.

We know too that, as Amilcar Cabral says, that in our ongoing liberation struggle, regardless of the obstacles the oppressor puts in our path, the greatest struggle is the struggle against ourselves, against that in us which is in contradiction with our highest values and the choice we've made for liberation and ever higher levels of human life. It is in this context that the ongoing discussion of the use and disuse of the N-word must be placed. For it is part of the struggle to free ourselves, reconceive and reconstruct ourselves and our world in our own image and interests and join other progressive people in the awesome task of repairing and transforming the world.

The recent decision by some Black leaders to lead an assault on the use of the N-word then speaks to two levels of struggle—a personal and social struggle. The personal struggle is to break the monopoly the oppressor has had on our minds, think our own thoughts, understand ourselves in dignity-affirming and life-enhancing ways, and assert ourselves similarly. But a successful struggle on a personal level also requires a struggle on the social level to eliminate the conditions which produces not only the N-word but those who embrace it as their own and defend their oppression and oppressor. Indeed, the call for a free self-respecting language and person is at the same time a call and requirement for a social context conducive to freedom and self-respect, as well as respect for others. So it is not enough to announce the need to end the evil of social and self-degradation, it is imperative to wage a wide-ranging and deep-reaching struggle to end it.

In the Sixties, we used to say that "inside every Negro, there is a Black person struggling to get out," struggling to be his real self, and to realize her internal capacity for living the good and righteous life we all long for in our most divine and dignified moments. So when I think of Black people willfully using the "N" word or trying to justify it or experiencing other oppression-induced psychological disorientation and disorder, I remember the teachings of Frantz Fanon. An active participant in the Algerian liberation struggle, Fanon gained deep insights into psychological disorders and the way oppression works to erode and erase one's dignity and sense of self and to instill a will to identify with and defend both their oppressor and oppression in the liberation struggle in Algeria.

From his writings, Kawaida philosophy extracts four basic stages of personality erosion, disorientation and disorder in the midst of the most severe, savage and inhuman oppression. And this holds true for all oppressed peoples. Those who unravel and reject resistance, Fanon teaches us, go thru four basic stages: self-doubt; self-denial; self-condemnation; and self-mutilation. First, they *doubt themselves*, i.e., wonder if their oppressor is right in his assertion of their inferiority, incompetence, and unworthiness, personally and racially. Secondly, they *deny themselves*, i.e., refuse to accept the obviousness of their Blackness, or if they are mixed, privilege and promote the non-Black components of their identity, especially White, in order to escape the severe penalties for belonging to the wrong race in a White-dominated society.

Thirdly, they *condemn themselves*, i.e., accept and embrace the oppressor's definition and devaluation of them and their people, borrowing from and building on his racist vocabulary, view and arguments of indictment and devaluation of us and other peoples of color. In a word, they see themselves as "N"s. And finally, they *mutilate themselves*, i.e., psychologically and physically disfigure themselves with desperate and degrading alterations of mind, mouth, nose, eyes, speech, color and consciousness of self in order to look and sound like those who caused the pathology of self-revulsion and rejection in them.

Surely, it takes more than a day or night at the comedy club to become even an unconscious "N". But to become a conscious and willing one speaks to a history of heavy hurt and deep and persistent pain of victims for whom the righteously religious should pray and the

214

ethically sensitive reach out to with empathy and loving kindness and a therapy of self-confrontation and radical change of self thru personal and social struggle. For this perverse attachment to one's own statement and status of degradation reflects a radical break with reality in which the victim identifies with the image, interests and ideals of the victimizer and accepts them as his or her own. It is called in psychology the Stockholm syndrome and is expressed most clearly in persons captured, kidnapped, brainwashed and abused. And only in the process and practice of freeing oneself thru personal and collective struggle can this monstrous hold be broken and the person affected regain her/his health and wholeness again. Indeed, those who struggle are strengthened in this struggle and, as Fanon notes, learn new things about themselves, their worth, and capacity for positive and productive self-assertion in the world.

"Liberation is coming from a Black thing," we used to shout and share in the Sixties. It will come not on TV or in comedy clubs, football fields, basketball courts or even in the classroom of large or small universities. It will, as Malcolm taught us, Bethune informed us and Fanon, Cabral and Tubman showed us, come into being in the midst of struggle, in the midst of the battles we wage for the hearts and minds of our people and for the new and good world. In this free and dignity-affirming space, there will be no need for yellow-wigs, blue-eye contacts, and self-mutilating surgery on the nose, mouth or mind. There will be no sitting in a sewer of N-words and negative names, pretending it's a sauna and something special. And every self-declared and closet "N" will step off the stage of self-mutilation and return to history urgently aware of and committed to the awesome responsibility of being African in the world.

2006 December 14

Rough Riding With Reagan

The official memories and fanciful commentaries of last week served as Ronald Reagan's last script, but one he would not have to read or recite like the good and pliant political actor he always was. He had only to lie still an let the talking heads of the media work their way thru a week and maze of mystification, convenient omissions and outright lies to elevate him to the status of saint and savior. It was a weeklong drama of almost biblical proportions, pervasive and persistent, interrupting ordinary lives and regular radio and TV programming, insisting on involvement and due deference from all of us. Republicans, democrats and independents alike lined up to bear witness to this newly created wonder, this carefully crafted idol and image of unspeakable greatness. It was as if we were being asked to imagine that Malcolm X, Martin Luther King and Harriet Tubman as one person had died—Harriet, the audacious soldier and uniter; Malcolm, the master teacher and fire prophet; and Martin, the gentle warrior who challenged us to build the beloved community of equals.

Disregarding all pretensions of objectivity, the media dedicated itself to canonizing, even deifying their fallen hero. And if we were able to forget the facts and for a moment embrace the fantasies they offered us, we could, perhaps, see the halo instead of the horror and hardship Reagan had represented for us. Lighten and lengthen his hair, he could have been, in earlier times, a candidate for the white image of divinity we once placed on our church walls. But like the unmasking of that white image, if we look below the surface, we see not only Michelangelo's cousin who served as the model, but also ideas and evidence of white supremacy which requires us to see even our oppressors as saints and saviors, if not God.

It is here that the lessons of Malcolm X on the centrality of image-making in maintaining and justifying the established order are so relevant. For Malcolm says that one of the great powers of the rulers of this country is their "science of image-making" in which they can turn a victim into a criminal and a criminal into a victim, and of course, turn an oppressor into a saint or a savior. His example was the U.S.' murderous role in the Congolese independence struggle, but we can see it also in Reagan's invasion of Grenada and Bush's invasion and occupation of Afghanistan and Iraq, each of whom claimed they were making war on the people to save them. It is from this insight that we say in Kawaida philosophy that *one of the greatest powers on earth is the power to define reality and make others accept it, even when it's to their disadvantage.* Certainly, the established order seeks to define reality for us and make us accept it even when it's to our disadvantage. And this definition indeed, the redefinition of Reagan is such an example.

Deny Reagan what we will, however, he was, above all, a hero of white people, a white man's man. Indeed, he was seen as one who was called to return the U.S. to its place as a shining city set upon a hill, a promised land without the problems of problematic people—Native Americans, Africans, Latinos and Asians, the vulnerable, the poor and the less powerful. He had said it himself—with him, morning returned to America, i.e., the U.S. only. For him and his supporters, it was a return of the morning of the rulers and masters after a night of the underlings and oppressed—after the city-burning sixties and the bra-burning seventies, the divisive race and gender struggle for an undeserved equality. Peace at home and power abroad; victory over the defeat-in-Vietnam syndrome and reversal of the gains of the 60's and 70's were his watchwords.

It was for the religious right almost a sign of prophecy fulfilled. Behold a pale horseman, riding roughshod over the heathens and pagans, standing tall but with a slight John Wayne lean. Lo, a leaning white tower, talking about dark and evil people at home and evil empires abroad, laying the basis for future replicants and Republicans to build on, like Bush the Little with his rancid ruminations about evil people in the dark corners of the world, his preemptive aggression, his counter-constitutional Patriot Act and his commitment to the imperial occupation of Haiti, Iraq, Palestine, Afghanistan and elsewhere.

They said he was kind, gentle and a lover of humanity, but the record reads differently. Reagan offered no compassion for the poor, no hope for the homeless and no empathy for the unemployed. They saw it as a destiny that he would repair their world, the world of the political, economic and religious right. He would, in fact, try hard to reverse the gains of the struggling peoples of this country and the world. He would talk freedom and practice oppression, talk against racial injustice and make resurgent racism respectable, promise relief for the working people and cut out their jobs and dismantle their unions. He suggested that some of the poor and homeless were in this condition by choice and that people who really wanted work had only to look in the classified section of the daily papers. His administration reduced the number of families receiving needed aid for dependent children and suggested ketchup could be used as a substitute for vegetables in the meals of needy school children.

They have said he favored freedom, but like Bush, he practiced a selective morality, supporting dictators and oppressors against the rightful liberation struggles of their people around the world, especially in Central America—in El Salvador, Nicaragua and in Guatemala where over one million Native Americans have been killed. Moreover, his Contra project against Nicaragua, which involved pushing drugs for guns, is remembered by many as contributing to the increased spread of drugs in the African community. Also, he refused to join the international boycott against the apartheid regime in South Africa, accepted the regime's terrorist designation of the liberation groups, and favored a fellow racial exchange with the Boers. Limping from Lebanon with the loss of 241 Marines in an ill-advised imperial venture, Reagan diverted public attention from the disaster by invading Grenada, a 10 x 21 mile island of Black people who had no standing army and no way to defend themselves. It was an easy imperial victory and for all his talk about challenging the U.S.' enemies, he never attacked anyone but the vulnerable—at home and abroad. Indeed, even his claim of confronting and destroying communism is like his movies, insubstantial and dismissible. Soviet communism was already crumbling from internal contradictions. And it was Mikhail Gorbachov, not Reagan, who pronounced its death and officiated at its funeral.

Although aged and infirm himself, he had no empathy for those like him and instead reduced Medicaid recipients, put limits on Medicare and cut off Social Security disability benefits for 500,000 people, forcing the courts to step in and restore 200,000 of them. As governor of California, he turned out mental patients into the streets and as governor and president, he was silent on AIDS and HIV. With his trickle down economics, he cut taxes for the rich and jobs for the poor, eliminated the Comprehensive Employment Training Act (CETA) and thus 300,000 jobs for willing workers, increased the military budget, put more people below the poverty line, and left the country deeply in debt.

Dedicated to reversing the civil rights gains of the 60's and 70's, he kicked off his presidential campaign in Philadelphia, Mississippi, the site of a savage Klan murder of three civil rights activists. He opposed the national Martin Luther King holiday, cut the budgets of the Equal Employment Opportunities Commission (EEOC) and the Civil Rights Commission, appointed people on them who worked to subvert their original mission of racial and social justice and ordered the civil rights division of the Justice Department to oppose court-ordered measures to achieve this. He made a political gesture of giving amnesty to some Latinos to win political points and accommodate employers, but as Delores Huerta of the United Farm Workers Union pointed out, the amnesty excluded 20,000 Africans from the Caribbean. Like his ideological predecessors and descendants, he would use race to exclude, deny and deprive us, but try to outlaw our calling attention to it and using race in consideration of ways to correct the current and historical harm done in its name and interests.

And so Virginia, Reagan was no Santa Claus even on Christmas, no saint even on Sunday, and no savior for anyone anywhere. He was a latter-day White hope who rode roughshod over the interests and aspirations of the vulnerable and initiated a rightward turn of the country toward resurgent racism against people of color, a greater opulence for the rich, an increased poverty for the poor, and a reinforced White triumphalism and imperialism in the world.

This is the real legacy of Reagan, in spite of the media inflation and adornment of his image. And our task, in the face of this legacy and others like it, is to speak truth to the people and to work tirelessly with them to organize progressive forces into an unbreakable rock of resistance on which a new country and world can be built, a country and world without cowboys killing "Indians" and Iraqis, Africans, Afghans and others and in which all people can live lives of dignity and decency and in equal measure, enjoy the goods of freedom, justice, power over their destinies and daily lives and peace in the world.

2004 June 17

Rightful Concerns About the Funding of Faith

In the midst of the country's world-threatening lurch to the right, there is a rightful concern in the African American community about a small but increasing number of Black preachers who find themselves *in bed* and *out of Bible* with those who have engineered this. It is not only unsettling because it seems like a classic case of sleeping with the enemy/oppressor and thus posing political problems for a people in struggle. It is also disturbing because it raises the issue of the possible transformation of the Black church from a source of liberation to a site of collaboration. This in turn raises moral, spiritual, and political problems, not only for our ongoing social justice and liberation struggle, but for the country and by extension the world itself.

For whatever problems we've had and have as clear victims and ambiguous beneficiaries of this contradictory and self-congratulatory experiment called America, we've always kept an important conception of ourselves as a people as a moral and social vanguard in this country and the world. Indeed, we have launched, fought and won with our allies struggles that not only benefited us, but also expanded the realm of human freedom and became a model and inspiration for other oppressed and struggling peoples around the world.

It is thus an irony of history that the ideological and political descendants of our original oppressors should now seek to become our moral teachers. And we are compelled to ask: is God so busy that he has asked Bush to assemble us at the White House for a briefing on the latest illusion of white supremacy and morality in the world? And who is this God who Bush says has given him a green light to conquer countries, finance and support the occupation of peoples' lands, dictate his racialized concept of democracy, and masquerade as a missionary of the Most High in the world?

Furthermore, how do we speak truth to power if we embrace their view of us and the world and condone or remain silent in the face of the havoc they wreak on our lives and the world? And how do we speak truth to the people, if our faith is funded by the oppressor and we are paid by him to collaborate in the oppression of our people and others?

The first and foremost source of the Black preachers' susceptibility to the Bush embrace is the transformation in the last decades of the central message of the Black church from one of *social justice* to one of *personal prosperity*. God, the message goes, wants each of us to have money and material things and enjoy life. What one must do then is declare Jesus as one's personal savior, give all glory to God and little or no attention to the poor, oppressed and the vulnerable.

This leads to several interrelated moral errors. It elevates the personal over the collective instead of balancing the two. It detaches personal profession of faith from the ethical obligation to demonstrate it in the practice of good in the world. And it deemphasizes or omits entirely the common ground of our various ethical African traditions that teach us to feed the hungry, house the homeless, clothe the naked, care for the ill and aged, free the captive, liberate the oppressed, and constantly heal and repair the world. This essential and inclusive ethical obligation is not satisfied by an isolated anti-gang initiative and by misfocus and over focus on debatable personal sexual and reproductive practices.

The second source of this move toward the right by some Black preachers is the incentive of money. The gospel of prosperity, relieved of all pseudo-religious references, is a gospel of rank materialism. And materialism is a greedy and insatiable god. It requires a perpetual pursuit of money and things and more money for things. Bush's mentor, Karl Rove, counting the flocks and potential votes of the targeted pastors, put forth a *funds-based* initiative camouflaged as a *faith-based* one in order to take advantage of this financial vulnerability and the ideological conservatism that existed in these churches.

Once upon a time the Black church lauded itself as the one certain independent institution in the community. For its monies came mostly or totally from the Black community. Now times and talk have changed. It is clearly impossible, we're told, to fund the massive and many prestige and even basic projects of the church with just the monies of the membership and thus this requires outreach to other sources. But even conceding the need for outside sources, some of which are our own tax money returned, one still has to be careful concerning the conditions established for getting and keeping it.

Thirdly, Black preachers who collaborate with the white conservatives are encouraged by the acquiescence of their church membership. It is the membership that determines the kind of message they hear and the messenger who brings it. It is the Black church membership that embraces the market-driven ideas of a consumer society, sanctions their preachers' embeddedness with the right and accepts the move from an emphasis on social justice to personal prosperity as the central message of their sermons. And it is they who must push for the return to the best principles and practice of the church.

Finally, the preachers' vulnerability to the Bush embrace, as well as the membership's acquiescence, comes also in the context of the lack of a national movement in our ancient and ongoing social justice tradition. Surely, it is in the context of the Black Freedom Movement that we demanded a Black liberation theology with a God in our own image and interest, i.e., in the interest of freedom for the oppressed, justice for the wronged and injured, power for the masses of people over their destiny and daily lives, and peace for the world. And it is the rebuilding of the Movement that will enable the community to counter the rightwing seduction of these ministers and bring forth the best of what it means to be African and human in the fullest sense. It is what our history and spiritual and ethical tradition as a people demand. We can and should do no less.

2005 February 7

Rethinking Thanksgiving:
Beyond Big Turkeys and Small Talk

The histories and holidays of the oppressed, colonized and enslaved are, of necessity, different from the history and holidays of the oppressor, the colonizer and the enslaver. Likewise, their interpretations of those histories and holidays also differ, for they are lived and learned from different standpoints. Thus, the Palestinians call the conquest and colonization of Palestine, the *Nakba*—the Great Catastrophe, and the Israelis call it the war of independence. The Native Americans call the conquest and colonization of their land and the decimation of their people genocide and holocaust. The Europeans call it "discovery," "the move westward," "reaching the promised land," and other self-sanitizing words and phrases.

During the Holocaust of enslavement, Frederick Douglass, asked to speak on the meaning of the 4th of July, seen as Independence Day for Whites, told his White audience, "This Fourth of July is *yours* not *mine*. *You* may rejoice. *I* must mourn." For it is for the enslaved African "a day which reveals to him more than any other day of the year the gross injustice and cruelty to which he is a constant victim." Indeed, he goes on to say that for the enslaved African, "Your celebration is a sham," and a repulsive mixture of vanity, heartlessness, mockery and hypocrisy. And "your prayers and hymns, your sermons and thanksgivings with all your religious parade and solemnity are, to Him, mere bombast, fraud, deception, impiety and hypocrisy—a thin veil to cover up crimes which would disgrace a nation of savages." And finally, descendants of the Wampanaog in Massachusetts who first welcomed their White visitors and invaders, call what Whites call "Thanksgiving Day" the Day of Mourning, mourning for the millions killed and the memories erased and falsified about this great Holocaust.

We live in a country and world of brutal realities and comforting illusions, carefully crafted to mask and diminish the truth and tragedy of these realities. Certainly, one of the most comforting illusions we have in this country is the origins and meaning of the holiday of Thanksgiving with its big turkeys, small talk and scream-filled televised football games. Through both official and personal pretension, we approach Thanksgiving without its history of horrors and the uncomfortable calling to mind that more than turkeys were killed for the celebration of that first day and that its roots lie in the victory celebrations of European genocidal wars against the Native Americans.

So, as we sit down in celebration of the sanitized version of Thanksgiving, let us, as African people, honor our ethical obligation found in the *Husia* to "not turn a blind eye to injustice or a deaf ear to truth." Instead, let us remember the lives, cultures and whole peoples lost, and honor and share in the Native American Day of Mourning as they did our mourning and quest for freedom when we first met, joined and struggled with them against our common oppression and oppressor.

Giving thanks is not a problem, but celebrating genocide and/or oppression and the triumph of evil clearly is. Surely, it is an evil irony that the pilgrims who held the first White thanksgiving celebration in this country, did so to celebrate victory over those who welcomed and saved them; those who gave them food and shelter, those who taught them how to grow crops and offered them peaceful co-existence in their own land.

Moreover, it is worth noting that these people who came here running away from religious intolerance and persecution in their own country established a similar, if not more severe religious tyranny. They self-righteously saw themselves as puritans, pure and chosen by God, and in God's name, they condemned and burned their women as witches with repulsive regularity, brutally suppressed all dissent and created a White god and White religion in their own image and interest. It is with this false interpretation and inspiration from their racialized god that they went about they're devilish work of genocide, justifying it with biblical injunctions like, "slay the heathen hip and thigh, and make them hewers of wood and drawers of water." This racist ranting, posing as religion, was used also for Africans and other peoples of color.

Advancing conquest, occupation and imperial savagery as salvation or self-defense, they posed their plunder as the will and promise of God. Like their modern-day descendants, they turned god into a chooser of an elect and superior people, a ruthless real estate agent promising other peoples' land and resources, and an ally in the genocidal wars they waged to seize them. And they now, as then, pretend shock and outrage when the oppressed people rightfully and righteously rise up in resistance.

We might reason that celebrating the European thanksgiving day is all right because we're giving thanks to God not to the oppressor; reaffirming bonds between us; and it's convenient. Surely, it is always good to gather together to reaffirm the bonds between us. But do we have to do it on this day? And do we have to eat turkey, make small talk and act as if the official sanitized version of Thanksgiving is real and the Native Americans are not our brothers and sisters in life and struggle and their Holocaust, like our own, merits no place in our memory, hearts and homes?

Thanksgiving is a good and life-affirming practice and we should always practice it. But let us give thanks in our own way and on our own day and throughout the year. Let us give thanks for the good in and of the world, the good of life and love, of sisterhood, brotherhood, friendship, family and community, and the awesome beauty and good of the world. And let us turn our prayers of thanksgiving into the practice of good, especially for the poor and vulnerable among us. In this way, we honor the best of our moral heritage and open the way through struggle to a new history and a new world.

2005 November 24

Giving Thanks and Thankful Giving:
In Pursuit of an African Understanding

Last week the larger society celebrated another occasion for compulsive consumption and seductive sales and called it *thanksgiving*. Indeed, the corporations and smaller businesses had been busy early turning adults into toy-adoring juveniles who anxiously camp out overnight nearby, stampede into stores, and shove and shout obscenities at each other as they push and paw their way toward possessions that, by corporate design, will soon seem like a relic from another time. And this designed deterioration of use and value will only compel those addicted to repeat this ritual of raw-meat rage and passion to purchase and possess again next year.

Moreover, it is in the midst of this annual madness of holiday consumption and celebration sales that the established order indulges in a parallel ritual of myth-making and acute denial about the origins and meaning of this day called Thanksgiving. Hidden behind its pretty harvest scenes and neatly dressed pilgrims, there is the violent ugliness and bloody untidiness of the holiday's origins which mark a time of celebration of the triumph over and decimation of Native Americans.

As African people, we cannot deny the ethical and spiritual value and obligation of giving thanks and being thankful. Nor can we deny the sheer good of gathering together in harmony, to share a meal and enjoy the rich reward of each others' company or to celebrate the good of life in its many forms. But we must not confuse this particular day with our duty to give thanks and be thankful every day and in various other ways. Nor can we in good faith participate in the official forgetfulness of the established order, the cold and acute denial of the decimation of Native Americans and pretend it's just about gathering together in joy.

As the *Husia* teaches and reminds us, we are morally obligated "to bear witness to truth and set the scales of justice in their proper place among those who have no voice." Thus, our position is always on the side of the suffering, the poor and oppressed, the powerless and the seekers of peace and good for everyone. Indeed, it's not about having a special day of thanksgiving, but of having one built on righteous practice and rightful remembrance, not on acts of evil or

226

acute denial of them. For surely it is good to be thankful and give thanks.

In African culture, giving thanks is both a verbal expression and a social practice. The saying of thanks is imbued with a sense of the Divine, the sacred, and is ultimately a spiritual and ethical act. Thus, to say thanks in the languages of ancient Egyptian (*Dua-en netjer en-ek*), Zulu (*Siyabonga*), and Yoruba (*A dupe*) is to say implicitly or explicitly, "We thank God for you." Both "*dua*" and "*bonga*" also mean "praise" and suggest a reverence or deep respect that is given thru God or the Divine to the person(s) addressed. Moreover, to thank a person is to praise or thank God for that person, as well as for what she or he has done. Therefore, we thank the Divine for a person's goodness and the good they bring and do.

Also, this linkage with the Divine carries with it the concept that we always have something for which to be grateful even in the bleakest and most unBlack situation and times. In African tradition, life is a blessing and good in itself and open to all kinds of possibilities. Thus in Yoruba, the word for ingratitude or lack of thankfulness is *aimo oore* which literally means "without knowledge of good, blessings or kindness." To be without knowledge of the good in life is to be unaware of its existence and availability; unable to identify it when it's present; and incapable of grasping its deeper and wider meaning.

Among our people, we count small and large things as blessings and Divine-given good in the world. And we must hold fast to this fundamental foundation of our thanksgiving and the hope and inspiration it gives us in defeating any dispiritedness or despair that invites us to embrace it in our daily lives. This is the meaning of the verse in the *Husia* that teaches us it is wrong to walk upside down in the darkness of despair, dispiritedness and dislocation. Therefore, it says we must come forward today, indeed, each day and bring forth the love and light of truth and justice which are within us and struggle each day to restore, maintain and expand *Maat* (rightness and good) in the world.

Moreover, in the most inclusive sense of the world-encompassing ethics taught by our ancestors, we must also be thankful and show thankfulness for the good of and in the world itself. This means seeing the world as sacred space, and all in it as infused with the Divine and worthy of the greatest respect. The expansive ocean and awesome mountains, the beautiful butterfly and worrisome flea, the rock, river, star and stone, field, lake and woods, all have their function and form a unity and continuity of being with us. And so we give praise and are thankful for this world and life in it every day.

Finally, in the African worldview, giving and showing thanks is a contribution to the future in a real and positive way. In the sacred teachings of our Zulu ancestors, it is said "*ukubonga ukuzibekela*," i.e., "to give thanks is to provide for our future." The word "*bekela*" literally means *store up* goods or good things for the future. Thus, to be thankful is to do good in the world. Nakhetefmut says in the *Husia* that he did *Maat*, i.e., right, justice and good, in the world for he "knew that the result of doing good deeds is a storehouse which our children will find afterwards."

Again, it is important to remember thanksgiving is not simply a holiday or special day set aside, but an ongoing praise, appreciation and reciprocal giving in return for the good given to us. In Zulu ethical wisdom, there is the saying "*KwaZulu, sibonga ngezandla zombili*" which means "In Zululand, we give thanks with both hands." To give thanks with both hands is to give generously, willingly and with great gratitude, praise and appreciation for the good we've been given, get daily and will receive in the future. It is to give thanks joyfully by thankful giving and doing good in an ongoing practice that praises the Divine and the giver, reaffirms the sacred significance of the act, and forges for us and future generations, a constantly expanding realm of mutual giving and sharing of good.

2006 November 30

VII

Rebuilding the Family, Community and Movement

The wide sweep of history ultimately finds its foundation in the lives of the people who make it. At the heart of the history we make are men and women working in partnership to pursue, do and bring forth good in the world. And there is no greater good than the love and life they share and bring into being in the midst of the many and varied things they do with and for each other and the world. Thus, as we celebrate this second month of Black History with its focus on Black women, we unavoidably turn to their relationships with Black men.

In talking about catalysts in the building and takeoff of a Movement, we in The Organization Us say, "one spark in the right season and situation can set a whole forest on fire." By right season we mean the right time, a point at which the people are pushed to the edge of endurance, and by right situation we mean the right conditions, the point at which the masses always in motion form a critical mass, have a clear vision and strong organization, and develop an unbreakable will to struggle.

Family and Community

For Love and Struggle:
Beyond the Crash, Hustle and Floss

The wide sweep of history ultimately finds its foundation in the lives of the people who make it. At the heart of the history we make are men and women working in partnership to pursue, do and bring forth good in the world. And there is no greater good than the love and life they share and bring into being in the midst of the many and varied things they do with and for each other and the world. Thus, as we celebrate this second month of Black History with its focus on Black women, we unavoidably turn to their relationships with Black men.

Certainly, the dominant society has not given us any guidelines or good models we can work with. After all, a society that asserts that "a dog is man's best friend" and that "a diamond is a girl's best friend" can't offer useful information on how we as men and women can and must relate. Moreover, neither can we be informed by a society whose movies and other media regularly mutilate and misrepresent our image as men and women, posing us as deformed and humiliated men and molested and stereotypical women waiting for the molester and oppressor to return and recognize us with an Oscar or paid performance for surrendering, singing and dancing to our own degradation. Indeed, it's hard to be a real Black man and woman in a corporate-pimping and plundering society, which worships wealth and power, masters social and self-illusion and hides from itself the war and waste it imposes on the world. But we must be men among men and women among women in the world.

Our task, then, is to engage this historical moment from our own cultural vantage point, to identity truthfully and straight forwardly problems as well as strengths and possibilities and begin to imagine and build the relationships and world we want and deserve to live in. In a word, we must build and maintain rock-strong, profound and fulfilling male/female relationships in a context not conducive to them. Put another way, the challenge is to love freely in an unfree context, to be gentle and caring in a harsh and uncaring world, to practice equality in a sexist society, and to give meaningfully of oneself in a context of possessive and vulgar individualism which fosters selfishness and exploitation of others for one's own benefit. And in spite of the difficulties, real and imagined which we face in achieving this, there is no real sane or ultimately satisfying alternative to our loving fully and freely and together building and sustaining the good and meaningful relationships we want and deserve.

It is a common contention that the smallest example of the strength and health of the nation or people is the family. And at the heart of the family and the ground of its health and strength are quality male/female relations. It is important to realize, then, that there is no isolated solution to the problems and challenges we face. Whatever solutions we evolve must be seen and approached in the context of an interrelated web of relationships in family, community and society. For the problems of male/female relations are tied to the problems of the community and the problems of the community are tied to the problems of and with society, i.e., its racism, classism, sexism, etc. Nevertheless, there is no better place to start in our struggle to build family and community and to free ourselves as a people than to start with assessing and altering for the best our relations between male and female, man and woman.

To achieve this goal, we must first prepare ourselves by cultivating attitudes and approaches which are dignity-affirming, life-enhancing, and love-sustaining and move away from those which encourage the negative and negate the positive. This means, above all, that we base ourselves in and build on the best of our own cultural concepts and practices, that we develop the capacity for self-criticism, criticism and self-correction, that we avoid recrimination, be oh so sensitive to each other's needs and rush to repair any and all injuries immediately. And finally, this means we must recognize and respect the rightful attentiveness and care and the long and sometimes difficult struggle it takes to build solid foundations and flourishing relationships.

Although we can define love in various ways, I want to define it here as *ultimate attentiveness and appreciation that expresses itself in mutual investment in each other's happiness, well-being and development.* The stress here is on mutuality, equality, shared respect, shared

232

concern for each other, and a shared commitment to each other that is deep and enduring and every day and hour alert and active for the good. It is within this framework that we establish several guidelines for achieving and sustaining the shared good of love and life.

At a minimum we need: (1) shared dignity-affirming and life-enhancing views and values, especially the *Nguzo Saba*, the Seven Principles; (2) shared aspirations and interests that lead to complementary partnership in all things good and beautiful; (3) clear terms to establish, maintain and develop the relationship; and (4) a profound friendship in which we think good of each other, want and work for the good of each other, share good and do good for and with each other in endless ways.

Moreover, we need (5) support structures which strengthen us in the positive and guide us from the negative; (6) shared activities that reinforce the bonds between us; (7) means of continuous renewal and reinforcement; and (8) personal and collective struggle to bring good into the relationship and the world. For the call to love freely is at the same time a call to create the context in which we can do this. Thus, we must struggle against the negative in us and in society. And we must dare imagine and struggle with others to build and sustain the good relationships and world we want and deserve, a world of ever-increasing human freedom and flourishing. Indeed, as we in Us say, "If not this then what, and if we don't do it, who will?"

2006 March 9

Black Men Missing:
But Not Without A Trace

In the Sixties, we sat around tables talking about new times and the new world we were struggling to bring into being. We were men with a sacred and consuming mission—liberation and a higher level of human life. We had expected beautiful new beginnings and powerful ways to assert ourselves in the world. As Black men in motion, speaking a clear and cleansing truth to power and the people, and organizing and mobilizing our people for liberation, we had imagined a revolution, not only in society but in our own lives and in the way we understood and asserted ourselves in the community, society and the world.

Our women were there struggling as much and as ever beside us, although we know now we did not always give them the recognition and respect they deserved. We had mostly imagined that we would change all this after liberation. We had not fully realized we had to build relations and engage in practices that prefigure and make possible the good world we struggle for. It was a mistake that we would deeply regret and correct afterwards. Still, in spite of this and other mistakes of various kinds, we pushed forward, forging our identity and destiny in relentless opposition to the established order.

But then something happened to us and our people. The revolutionary struggle began to unravel, groups were dismantled prematurely and began to disappear, families fragmented, police and FBI suppression increased and proved to be disruptive, divisive and deadly, and the stress of it all broke the brittle and drove the frightened and less committed down various avenues of escape. And many Black men went missing, AWOL, absent without leave from both the battlefront and the homefront. Steadily, many started leaving home and hangin' out with the homies, droppin' out and dopin' up in dirty places, gangbanging, being locked down and let out on a short leash called probation or parole, bringing home a hidden history called down low, and trying to recover and rebuild unraveled relations and a new life in the midst of thick uncertainty and thin opportunity. And then there were those who were left behind without fathers or mentors and who made up their life as they went along. Now they and many among us, fear growing up and getting older, and thus play the role of perpetual teenagers, revering rap subculture as a mini-religion, and steadily learning and living the loose and lumpen life and lyrics it encourages.

And so now, we are reduced to talking about lost lives, dried-up dreams, ruined relations, fractured families, deadly diseases running rampant, low or absent educational achievement, unemployment, self-destructiveness, and underground predatory practices that disrupt and damage the community and deal death every day. Yet, somehow we must as Black men, stand up, step forward and with our women, rebuild our lives, families and community, and continue the liberation struggle so many of us walked or were carried away from under various conditions.

To do this, we must first know and respect the meaning of manhood and see it as a self-conscious personal and social achievement and practice. This means moving beyond the simple biological fact of maleness and increased age and engaging in a process of bringing ourselves into being in the most culturally and morally grounded ways. This is the meaning of the teachings of the *Odu Ifa* (245:1) which says "If we are given birth we must bring ourselves into being again." It, then, is not enough to be male; we must make ourselves into men, and having achieved the status, sustain and constantly refine the idea and the practice. This is why the ancestors established rites of passage (*majando*) for men as well as women, to begin at an early age to teach us how to become and be African men and women in the world. For we are males by birth, but we must learn and struggle to be men, especially African men in a European-dominated context.

Regardless of what they and others say about us, we must define ourselves, name ourselves, create for ourselves, speak for ourselves and carve out of this hard rock we call reality a place for us and our loved ones to stand in and flourish. And we cannot do this if we define ourselves as "n-'s", name ourselves dogs, create only harm and havoc, speak the vulgar and vicious language and lyrics of our own degradation and instead of making new and life-enhancing places, mindlessly participate in practices which destroy us, damage our people and delight our oppressor.

Next, if we are to heal ourselves and repair the world, we must do it in partnership with our women. We must take our stand here on the awesome and indispensable need of quality relationships between man and woman whatever other relationships we might treasure or find attractive. Our partnership in life, love and struggle is as necessary as sunlight, as indispensable as air, and as life-sustaining as water. It is also as stabilizing as earth, and as life-enhancing as love and learning. Thus, we must find a way back home to rebuild and reinforce the family, and forge a new relationship with this other half which makes us whole, a relationship of complementarity defined by equality, mutual respect, and shared responsibility in life, love and struggle.

Finally, we must heal, repair and transform ourselves in the midst of our ongoing struggle to repair and transform the world. Our health and wholeness depends on our taking responsibility for our own lives and breaking the hold of an oppressive, sick society. It is important here to note that in spite of the bleakness of the pictures painted, there still remains a majority of Black men who have weight and worth in the world. And even those who have fallen have left traces we can follow to find and raise them.

Thus, together we must free ourselves from all things and thoughts which enslave and oppress us. We must build brotherhood support groups like the Senu Brotherhood Society, mentor young boys, stop the therapeutic chest-thumping about how bad we be, and begin the long and difficult struggle to build a good world and be respected as men among men, and men among women anywhere we are in the world.

2006 March 3

Cosby Without Comedy:
On the Loose and Not Laughing

Bill Cosby, it seems, is on the road again, on the loose and not laughing, raging against the masses, raising issues he focused on last year in a speech to the NAACP, marking the 50th anniversary of *Brown v. Board of Education* that outlawed school segregation. It is about drug-dealing and dropouts, absent and irresponsible fathers, vulgar speech and misdirected sperm, poor parenting and teen pregnancy, and lack of adequate respect for the suffering and sacrifice of our ancestors for good in the world. It is not these problems at issue, but how he phrases and presents them. Some wrongfully question his character and his commitment, and even his family life and his right to speak on the issues. But others rightfully criticize his ideas and arguments for their inherent weakness and raise questions about how they are presented in a racialized context tailored for right-wing manipulation and misuse.

There is no need to question Cosby's motives or sincerity. He has come into consciousness late, but he has shown concern for education and family issues over a long period of time, earning his doctorate in education, donating millions to colleges and universities, and writing books on education and family. Nevertheless, there are issues of importance as well as flaws in his angry assertions that must be addressed.

Cosby's criticism of the masses with some barbs at the church, Black intellectuals and liberals-at-large are too often harsh, unbalanced, class-based, simplistic in indictment and proposed solutions, and leave society and its racist rulers an undeserved immunity from responsibility, critique and prosecution. Cosby is too harsh in his name-calling and calling out "knuckleheads" and "low-economic peoples." It degenerates into infantile rage, suggesting the world should respond immediately to his recently arrived at or announced position. It is unbalanced in that it fails to give due credit to the parents and young people who don't fit his formula of pathology—even in the poorest neighborhoods. He doesn't recognize and hold up as models the youth who refuse to sell or take drugs, dropout, join gangs, get pregnant or surrender to a life of crime, self-destruction and defeat. And he doesn't give adequate and rightful attention to the parents who work hard and sacrifice for their children's welfare and education and stress education as an indispensable path upward.

His criticism is also class-based, a bourgeois criticism of the so-called embarrassing, loud, lazy and dangerous lower classes. He probably does not notice the similarity of his views with those of the ruling race/class in its race and class indictment and hegemonic howls against the masses. Such discourse also avoids a necessary criticism of the Black middle class and its post-Movement brain and resource drain from the community, and the resultant loss of institutional capacity to address in a timely and effective manner the problems Cosby cites. His criticism of the Black church does not deal with its transformation from its emphasis on a gospel of social justice to a gospel of personal prosperity, nor the destructive effect of this on the Black community and its ongoing struggle for social justice.

Cosby's criticism is also too simplistic as are his solutions. His advice to the 2006 graduating class of Spellman College to which he and his wife donated $20 million was that women should "take charge" because "all men are in prisons (and) not there" is an example. Indeed, it sounds henny-pennyish both in its assessment of the situation and his all-women-no-men solution. Women *and* men must be in charge, and if women are told to write-off and disrespect the men, what happens to any real concept of marriage and family, joint parenting and shared responsibility in love, life and struggle? Indeed, in spite of the clear and present danger of many self-destructing men, it is not a sound argument to make about the whole community or even all the men in it. There are strengths and weaknesses everywhere. Our task, Amilcar Cabral tells us, is to struggle to turn our weaknesses into strengths. This transforming practice, he says, is the real meaning of struggle.

Cosby's failure to criticize society yields problems of analysis, solutions and presentation. The problems of analysis and solutions lay in his overemphasis on personal responsibility without adequate stress also on community and societal responsibility. As bearers of dignity and divinity, humans have moral agency, i.e., a capacity and will to choose and act. But choices take place in a context and that is why we must strengthen the primary context of the family and community, so that choice for good is part of one's character and supported morally and materially.

Cosby also lets society avoid its role in our oppression, its impositional, ideological and institutional racism, and plays into the racialization of social problems instead of recognizing a complex interaction of the personal, communal and societal. It's not just about hard work, good manners, excellent education, crime-free lives, and Huxtables in the house. In fact, the call to work requires the presence and possibilities of jobs. The call to excellent education requires early programs of advancement in quality schools and programs of recruitment, admission and retention in colleges. And the call for a criminal-free life requires not only restraint on anti-social behavior, but also restraint of criminal behavior of the police, and the end of unjust imprisonment and the unequal application of the law and justice.

The problems posed by Cosby are not new or startling, but rather standard for all socially-conscious, concerned and active people. The need, then, is for realistic solutions which we, as a community, take responsibility for and work out together. For although our oppressor is responsible for our oppression, we are responsible for our liberation. And part of that responsibility is holding our oppressor responsible. This means not simply lecturing, but rebuilding and strengthening institutions and rebuilding a Movement for social justice and good in this society as well as the world.

2006 June 8

Foundations for Black Fatherhood:
Principles and Righteous Practice

As we move this month towards Father's Day, let us pause and pay due homage to those fathers who have kept their commitment, honored their obligations, and sacrificed and struggled to take care of their families, and give them rightful guidance in the good and time-tested way of our ancestors. And let these fathers in the midst of their rightful praise, remember and raise in respect the names of all those who have made their achievements possible, especially the mothers of their children who in partnership with these fathers brought the children into being, loved, nurtured and raised them and set them on the path to a good and meaningful life.

And let us pay special homage to those fathers who stayed steadfast in spite of unfavorable circumstances and less money and means than the middle class, who have waded waist-deep in the murky and merciless waters of the surrounding society to save and support their sons, reinforce and redeem their daughters, and with their wives created a love-filled place of peace, harmony and hope they all could call home. But let us also show appropriate sensitivity and support to those who have tried and try, but have not been as successful, those who make good-faith efforts but for reasons complex and compelling cannot and do not always do as well.

And finally, let us, as the *Husia* teaches, "stretch forth our hands to those on the road to ruin" and to those who've already reached that unpleasant place. Let's criticize wrong and unrighteous behavior, laxity, laziness and the loss of will, triflingness, betrayal, dishonesty and destructive behavior. And let us work tirelessly to help them turn their lives around. For as the *Husia* teaches us, "the good we do for others we're actually doing for ourselves," for we are building the moral community we all want and deserve to live in.

There is no hard and fast formula for being a good father, no easy answers on the internet or at the barber shop or on radio and TV talk shows. And there is no simple solution available in self-help manuals made for those designated as "dummies". But there is a foundation and framework in our own culture, rooted in millennia of moral and spiritual teachings on being a good person and parent, living a good, caring and responsible life, and leaving a legacy for future generations worthy of the name and history African. Therefore, to talk of fatherhood or motherhood in the African sense of the word requires our understanding and approaching it in the context of our own culture as an ancient, ongoing and honorable tradition. It is a tradition rooted in and reflective of fundamental principles and corresponding practices, principles which orient and ground us and encourage and sustain rightful and righteous practice.

In the African tradition, a father is first and foremost a man in the most expansive sense of the word. This includes his recognition and respect for the process of becoming a man and the practice necessary to sustain it; respect for women, our species half which makes us and humanity whole; moral and mental maturity; and willing acceptance of obligations to family, friends, community, and humanity as a whole. A father is a man among men and a man among women. Rooted in his culture and community, he moves smoothly thru the seasons of his life, from teen to adult, young man to middle age and eldership, learning, teaching and serving appropriately at every stage.

Fatherhood also requires a mutually respectful and supportive relationship with the mother. The best fatherhood whether in marriage, divorce or separation is rooted in a complementary partnership with the mother that recognizes the cooperative character of creating and sustaining life and elicits respect from each partner. Indeed, the well-being of the children and their respect for each parent depends on the respect and support parents give to each other. And we know that parenting, like love and life, works better and is best as a shared commitment and practice of mother and father, male and female, bound and balanced together in righteousness and duly respectful of the awesome responsibility they share.

Thirdly, fatherhood requires that a man be a model of the life he wants his children to live. He will practice the Seven Cardinal Virtues of *Maat*—truth, justice, propriety, harmony, balance, reciprocity and order. He will speak truth, do justice, act properly and appropriately towards his children, wife and other women, as well as others, cherish and work for peaceful togetherness, avoid extremes in thought, emotion, speech and conduct, return good given and give goodness knowing it will return, and discipline himself so that his life is in order and everyone benefits from the rightful expectation of his doing good in his family and the world.

Fourthly, a father must realize and act on his shared right and responsibility with the mother of his children to guide and give direction and discipline to their children. Parents may humbly and properly sometimes doubt the rightness of their decisions and thus review and amend them. But they should never surrender or even doubt their right and responsibility to provide guidance, direction and discipline or their children's need for these.

Finally, a father and mother must wage constant struggle for the hearts and minds of their children, to cultivate in them a commitment to excellence and also the avoidance of evil. This translates as a struggle to keep the stranger and oppressor out of our house and minds, and keep them free from images, ideas, literature and language destructive of life-and-dignity-affirming African values which are as essential as breath and blood flow. Our task, then, is to intensify our struggle against our oppression on every level, overcome our own weaknesses and build a new and good world in which our families and people and the peoples of the world can be really free and flourish and walk in the world in a whole 'nother way.

2006 June 15

The Movement

Remembering the March: Rebuilding the Movement

In the midst of the struggles of the oppressed peoples of the world, we, of necessity, move in parallel practice and sustained solidarity with them to achieve human freedom, justice, and flourishing in the world. And thus, Min. Louis Farrakhan, leader of the Nation of Islam, has called us together again to stand at that pivotal point in the U.S. and the world, Washington, D.C., and reaffirm our right and responsibility of resistance to oppression and injustice and our intention to intensify and expand our struggle for freedom, justice, and good in the world.

And so we of Us and many more organizations, institutions and persons have joined the Nation of Islam again in a cooperative effort to organize another massive march in D.C. to mark the initiation of the Millions More Movement. Thus, it is a march dedicated not only to commemorate the tenth anniversary of the Million Man March/Day of Absence of October 16, 1995, but also to reaffirm policy and practice commitments we made then, and to lay the basis for rebuilding our movement for fundamental and far-reaching social change. Indeed, there is no greater homage we can pay to the MMM/DOA than to translate its social policy statements into practice and the March itself into a movement to achieve this. And we now, as then, reaffirm the best values and practices of our social justice tradition, which requires at a minimum, respect for the dignity and rights of the human person and all peoples, economic justice, shared power, cultural integrity, and relentless struggle to secure and sustain these.

Thus, we seek to rebuild a movement not just organize and conduct a march. By *movement* I mean *an ongoing collective struggle with a shared vision and shared values, interlocking structures, coordinated agendas and common goals, a far-reaching web of communications and interactions, and an interrelated common pool of resources from which to draw.* But the *movement, like our future, must be forged in the furnace and field of relentless struggle*, the ongoing struggle to bring good into the world. In our *MMM/DOA Mission Statement* of 1995, accepted by consensus, we put forth key areas of focus for our struggle which remain unfinished and ongoing tasks and which the Movement must address. First, we seek to build and practice an independent politics which is directed toward creating a free and empowered community, a just and good society, and a good and sustainable world.

Next, we seek to build a Black economic initiative "to enhance economic development, cultivate economic discipline and cooperative practices and achieve economic self-determination." Moreover, we seek to reaffirm and strengthen the Black family through quality male/female relations based on principles of equality, complementarity, mutual respect and shared responsibility in love, life and struggle.

Furthermore, we will continue the struggle for reparations in the fullest sense, that is to say a comprehensive initiative involving: public dialogue, public admission, public apology, public recognition of the Holocaust of African enslavement, appropriate compensation by the government, and corrective measures and structures to prevent its reoccurrence. Important also is the continuation of the "struggle against police abuse, government suppression, violations of civil and human rights and the industrialization of prisons; and in support of the freedom of all political prisoners, prisoners' rights . . ."

The *Mission Statement* also urges us to continue to struggle in the critical task of "organizing the community as a solid wall in the struggle against drugs, crime and violence in the community which we see as interrelated and which must be joined with the struggle to reduce and end poverty, increase employment, strengthen fatherhood, motherhood and family, support parents, provide education and prevention programs and expose and reject those who deal in death for the community." Moreover, we must intensify the struggle against homelessness and inadequate health care and the scourge of HIV/AIDS, seeking health and wholeness for our people.

We must continue to support African-centered independent schools and intensify and broaden the struggle for quality public education, as well as continue and reinforce our efforts to reduce and eliminate negative media approaches to and portrayals of Black life and culture. As a people in struggle, we must be about "strengthening and supporting organizations and institutions of the Black community concerned with the uplifting and liberation of our people." In addition, we must stand in solidarity with other African peoples and other Third World peoples in their struggles for liberation and ever higher levels of human life, and build appropriate alliances with other people of color and progressive people on the bases of common good and mutual benefit.

Finally, we seek to reaffirm the indispensability of the spiritual and ethical grounding of our people in accomplishing the historical tasks confronting us. And thus we embrace and seek to practice a common set of principles that reaffirm and strengthen family, community and culture, the *Nguzo Saba* (The Seven Principles): *Umoja* (Unity); *Kujichagulia* (Self-Determination); *Ujima* (Collective Work and Responsibility); *Ujamaa* (Cooperative Economics); *Nia* (Purpose); *Kuumba* (Creativity) and *Imani* (Faith).

And as we go forth to rebuild our movement and intensify our struggle for good in the world, let us remember the closing paragraph of the *Mission Statement* which calls on us to stand up and stand together as Black men and women in love, life and struggle for the good. For in doing this:

> "we honor our ancestors, enrich our lives and give promise to our descendants. Moreover, through this historic work and struggle we strive to always know and introduce ourselves to history and humanity as a people who are spiritually and ethically grounded; who speak truth, do justice, respect our ancestors and elders, cherish, support and challenge our children, care for the vulnerable, relate rightfully to the environment, struggle for what is right and resist what is wrong, honor our past, willingly engage our present and self-consciously plan for and welcome our future."

2005 August 18

Marchin' Towards A Movement:
Movin' Toward Liberation

We are on our way to Washington, marching towards a
Movement and moving towards liberation. But we know from the
hard and heavy-laden lessons of history, there is no quick and easy
walk or way to freedom and no magical or miraculous achievements
except those conjured up and called into being by the daily and
difficult struggle of the people to improve and expand their lives and
take hold of the history that confronts them. We know also that the
meaning of the March will be what we ourselves make of it; that the
course of the Movement will be determined by what we do with and
for it and thus, that it is on us to wage a relentless struggle to carve
out of the hard rock of reality a life worth living, a world and history
worth having and a legacy worth leaving for future generations.

But there are rumors among and around us that under the
constant and brutal burden of our oppression and the resultant
socially-generated and self-inflicted wounds, we have lost our way and
our will and no longer understand and assert ourselves in the
expansive and dignity-affirming ways that once made us a model
moral and social vanguard in the world. But the demands of history
and the designs of heaven call on us to be and do otherwise. And thus,
we must and do reject this self-serving assessment of our oppressor
and of those seduced or enslaved by the constant psychological war he
wages against us. For throughout our history we have chosen to rise
up in struggle determined to be free, establish justice and bring good
in the world, regardless of the odds and assessments against us.
Indeed, it is written in the sacred teachings of our ancestors, the *Odu
Ifa*, that we are divinely chosen to bring good in the world and are
morally obligated to develop the wisdom, character, capacity for
sacrifice, love of doing good, and willingness to struggle which this
awesome responsibility requires. And we know that although we are
all chosen by heaven and history, we must choose to be chosen, choose
to do good in and for the world and accept seriously this assignment as
the fundamental mission and meaning of human life.

It is clearly on us. Our oppressors cannot and will not do it.
Indeed, they had a chance to unite and work with the peoples of the
world, but decided instead to enslave and oppress them. We must

draw a clear line of demarcation between us and them. We must clearly distance ourselves from and oppose their White supremacist rampages in the world, their raw-meat racism, their high-tech terrorism, and their perverse peddling of domination as democracy, occupation as liberation, and conquest as legitimate corporate plunder. Again, it falls on us in alliance with other oppressed and progressive peoples and persons of the world, as Fanon says, to dare start a new history of humankind and set afoot a new man and woman in the world.   To achieve this, we must prefigure in thought and practice the world we want and deserve to live in. Thus in our daily lives and relations, we must think and care deeply about and put into practice principles that mould us into the new men, women and children reflective of the new world we struggle to bring into being, especially the *Nguzo Saba* (The Seven Principles): *Umoja* (Unity), *Kujichagulia* (Self-Determination), *Ujima* (Collective Work and Responsibility), *Ujamaa* (Cooperative Economics), *Nia* (Purpose), *Kuumba* (Creativity), and *Imani* (Faith).

We must and the *Odu Ifa* teaches, "Speak truth, do justice. Be kind and do not do evil." And we must also as the *Husia* teaches us, constantly heal and repair ourselves and the world making them better, more beneficial and beautiful than before. Indeed, this task and obligation called *serudj ta* calls on us to renew and rebuild the world and ourselves in the process. It is to raise up the ruined, repair the damaged, rejoin the severed, replenish the depleted, strengthen the weakened, set right the wrong, and make flourish the insecure and undeveloped.

Our task, then, is simultaneously personal, communal and world-encompassing reaching from New Orleans, Native America, and Biloxi to Port au Prince, Haiti, Africa, Palestine, Iraq, Afghanistan, and other sites of oppression and uncompromising struggle in the world. We must reaffirm our commitment in thought and practice to freedom for the oppressed; justice for the wronged and injured; power for the masses of people over their destiny and daily lives; and peace in and for the world. And to do this we must stand up and stand together as Black men and women, rebuild our Movement for liberation, reaffirm our role as a critical moral and social vanguard in this country and the world, and with other progressive forces dare build the world we all want and deserve to live in.

Again, our oppressor cannot be our teacher. As Fanon said, humanity is waiting for something from us other than an imitation or obscene caricature of our oppressor. And this means harnessing our own energies and activism, weathering the hurricanes of history and struggling constantly to bring, sustain and increase good in the world. The March is a site for the message; it will take a Movement of national and international reach and relevance to achieve our goals. And again, the March and Movement will be what we make them. The success we seek will depend on our own sacrifice and efforts and the liberation we long for will only come from waging a hard-won and decisive struggle. The time is now. There is no other. The answer is struggle. There is no alternative. We are the ones; there is no avoiding it.

2005 October 13

The Millions More March and Movement: Mission, Meaning and Struggle

This is a summary mission statement I presented at the Millions More March and Movement, October 16, as co-convener, member of the Executive Committee and co-chair of the Issues Committee of the MMM.

To our peoples, Africans everywhere; to our Native American, Latino and Asian brothers and sisters, and to all the freedom-loving and struggling peoples of the world: we give warm greetings in solidarity and struggle. And we bear witness as an African people that as our beginning was great and good so shall our development throughout eternity be if we dare struggle, speak truth, do justice and walk in the way of rightness.

We meet here in commemoration of the 10th anniversary of the Million Man March/Day of Absence and in recommitment to continue and intensify the struggle for freedom, justice, power for the people and peace in the world and to rebuild our Movement to achieve these goals.

We meet also in the shadow of the shattered lives of our people, an awesome catastrophe caused by the combined natural destructiveness of Hurricane Katrina and the criminal negligence and neglect of government officials at every level. Surely, we are obligated to insure that the living and dead are treated with the dignity due them, obligated to care for and support the survivors with commitment, compassion and loving kindness, and obligated to continue the struggle to end the racist and class conditions which caused this awesome catastrophe and gross injustice.

We meet too in the midst of the ongoing hurricanes of history which have wreaked havoc on our lives for centuries—the hurricanes of global oppression, injustice, domination and war. It is in this context that we declare our commitment and recommitment to the struggle for freedom for the oppressed, justice for the wronged and injured, power for the masses of people over their destiny and daily lives, and peace in and for the world.

Indeed, at this critical juncture and tragic moment in our history, we can offer no other advice for altering social conditions and human history except through struggle. For there is no real or lasting relief except through resistance, no freedom from oppression except that forged in the furnace and field of constant struggle and no justice, peace or possibility of liberation except that achieved and secured on the battlefield for a new and better world. In a word, we can only heal and repair ourselves by repairing and reordering the world through constant and continuous struggle.

Our charge and challenge, then, is to know the past and honor it; to engage the present and improve it and to imagine the future and forge it. In this effort and aspiration, we call for: (1) continuing and increased unity in the family, community and world African community, a principled and purposeful togetherness in love, life and struggle; (2) spiritual and moral grounding that reaffirms our commitment to good and urges us to turn our faith into the work of freedom, justice and peace in the world; (3) the reaffirmation and strength of the Black family through quality male/female relations based on principles of equality, complementarity, mutual respect and shared responsibility and through loving and responsible parenthood and mentorships; (4) quality and relevant education which is African-centered, culturally and ethically grounded, family and community supportive and world-encompassing; (5) policies and personal, family and social practice supportive of the health and wholeness of African people and which urge education, preventive medicine and avoidance of practices which are dangerous, disabling and deadly; (6) economic development aimed at economic justice, job creation, entrepreneurial parity, communal financial discipline, and investment within the community; (7) affordable and adequate housing for all, especially the homeless, the poor and the recently displaced, and structures and incentives to achieve this; (8) an independent politics based on an aware, organized and active community, conscious of the issues and its interests, insistent on quality and accountable leadership and open to coalitions and alliances with others for common good; (9) reparations in the fullest sense, a healing and repairing of the grave and gross injuries to a whole people as a result of the Holocaust of enslavement and its continuing effects as well as continuing oppression; (10) a massive challenge to and change of the justice system and prison industrial complex including the end of discriminatory sentencing, enslavement-like labor in the penal system, freedom for all political prisoners, prisoners' rights and an end to all forms of police abuse and brutality; (11) increased responsibility and accountability from our artists and entertainers; and (12) a just, genuine and enduring peace in and for the world including the practice of peace and non-injury in our own community so that peace truly embraces us and the whole world.

We have come marching towards a Movement and moving toward liberation. But we know from the hard and heavy-laden lessons of history, there is no quick and easy walk or way to freedom and no magical or miraculous achievements except those conjured up and called into being by the daily and difficult struggles of the people to improve and expand their lives and take hold of the history that confronts them.

We know also that the meaning of this March will be what we ourselves make it; and that the course of the Movement will depend on what we do for it. And we also know that it is on us as persons and a people to wage a relentless struggle to carve out of the hard rock of reality a life worth living, a world and history worth having, and a legacy worth leaving for future generations.

Thus, we must harness our own energies and activism, weather the hurricanes of history and create a counterforce for good in the world. For surely it is written in the sacred texts of our ancestors, we are divinely chosen to bring good in the world and this is the fundamental mission and meaning of human life. The March is a site for the message and our meeting. It will take a Movement of national and international reach and relevance to achieve our goals.

Let's get busy and rebuild our Movement, then, and with other oppressed and progressive people dare imagine and bring into being a new history of humankind. The time is now; there is no other. Struggle is the way; there is no alternative. We are the ones; there is no avoiding it.

2005 October 20

Making the Movement Real:
Principles, Process and Practice

From the outset, we had argued that for the Million Man March/Day of Absence to be more than an episodic public expression of pain and anger, we have to rebuild our Movement and approach it as part of our living tradition of struggle. It was a principle enshrined in the *MMM/DOA Mission Statement* 1995 which calls for "creating and sustaining a progressive independent political movement." And I repeated the call in an article titled "The March, the Day of Absence and the Movement" in the *Million Man March/Day of Absence: A Commemorative Anthology,* arguing that it must be transformed into a project of liberation, into the process and practice of "rebuilding the liberation movement."

In our discussions for the tenth anniversary March and Millions More Movement, I laid out the five fundamental things necessary to build the Movement which I had argued for in 1995: philosophy, structure, program, communications and resources. To build and sustain a Movement, a philosophy is indispensable. The people require, above all, a vision of a just and good society and a good and sustainable world, and a dignity-affirming concept of man and woman and the future of humanity.

And this vision must also point to possibilities inherent in the people and the struggle they wage for a new history of humankind. Certainly, the Mission Statement and recent additions offer a framework for such a vision. And it must be read, taught, studied and discussed not only in local organizing committees (LOC's), but also in the community as a whole. For it is the core of our common concerns and principles around which we organize and assert ourselves in society and the world.

The second challenge is to build and sustain a series of local, national and international structures which form a web of mutual support and enriching exchange, linked together to mobilize and organize the masses of our people on a vast scale in the awesome task of expanding the realm of human freedom and giving birth to a new history of humankind.

A third challenge is program. Again, we repeat: in the final analysis, practice proves and makes possible everything. The projects listed and laid out in the Mission Statement and its recent expansion must be pursued with vigor and a sense of impending victory. We have proposed programs which cultivate and call forth practices that enlighten and empower the people, satisfy human need and transform the people in the process. Clearly our programs speak to our ongoing struggle for freedom for the oppressed, justice for the wronged and injured, power of the masses of people over their destiny and daily lives, and peace in the world.

Building a communications network is the fourth challenge for a Movement. We must speak our own cultural truth, discuss, debate and decide critical issues and build a network of institutions and media to do this. We must use the internet in new and creative ways, create free space in public broadcasting, intervene in talk radio and established order venues, and put our agenda on the table. And we must also build and expand our own institutions and media.

The fifth major challenge of the Movement is to build and sustain a network of resources: money, material, skilled personnel and the masses, themselves. In terms of money, the challenge is to create a financing process which is responsive and responsible, responsive to the needs of the people and committed to accountability as an essential principle and practice. Also, a network of skilled personnel who volunteer and a network of sources for donation of materials are central requirements for a successful Movement.

Finally, the ultimate resource of any Movement is the masses of our people. Thus, as Nkrumah says, we must "go to the masses; start with what they know and build on what they have." In a word, we must organize, mobilize and politically educate them around their interests, learn from them, serve them and stand with them in the hard and heroic struggles we, as a people, wage for good in the world.

Indeed, a Movement, above all, is a coherent and collective process and practice involving four basic ongoing activities: education, mobilization, organization and confrontation. Education is always the first step. For in the beginning is the word that cultivates and calls for the enlightened and elevated consciousness of the whole people, a consciousness of their worth, weight and work in the world. It is a consciousness that comes naturally out of their self-determined participation at every level and in every area of struggle. Indeed, this is the path that opens up possibilities for them in coming to know and conduct themselves as men and women building the new world they want and deserve to live in as bearers of dignity and divinity.

To mobilize the masses is to constantly call them out on the battlefield for a better world, to raise before them urgent and ongoing issues which inspire them to reflect on and discuss the condition and future of their lives and the world, and to act righteously to end oppressions of all kinds and bring good into the world.

To organize the masses is to build with them structures that house and advance their interests and aspirations, institutions which provide space for collective decisions, leadership development and to establish permanent processes, practices and achievements they have brought into being with their own hands, hearts, minds, and efforts.

Finally, to confront the established order is to define, defend and fight for our interests and the interests of oppressed and struggling peoples everywhere. It is to know with Paul Robeson that "the battlefront is everywhere; there is no sheltered rear" and to act accordingly. It is to walk and work tirelessly with the masses as they discover the dawn, push their lives forward and even in the midst of battle begin to build the peace and good for which we struggle.

2005 October 27

Meditating on the March:
Achievements Made, Lessons Learned

Recently, we, the planners and organizers of the Millions More March returned to Washington to assess it and discuss the achievements, lessons and further course of our work to build the Movement, thinking deeply and with careful consideration about ways to understand, appreciate and carry out the tasks history has handed us. Min. Louis Farrakhan set the framework for our dialog, stressing the national and world historical nature of our work and struggle. He also stressed the need for us to reinforce our unity, not only to do our work and wage our struggle of liberation and give an inspirational model to the masses, but also to serve as an unbreachable wall against the sure and certain coming of the oppressor to undermine our efforts.

We talked too about the need to understand, appreciate and build on our achievement, about how it was important not to rush over praises to be given and lessons to be learned. Through the vision and initiative of Min. Farrakhan, the key role of the Nation of Islam, and the essential and varied work of all of us involved on every level, we had crafted and carried out a project of great importance. And it was important that we pause to understand and appreciate it.

Our achievement lies first in the diversity of our project. We had brought together in operational unity the largest and most diverse mass action in our history as a people in this country. Neither the March on Washington '63 nor the Million Man March/Day of Absence in '95 had such diversity. The diversity expressed itself in a wide range of ideologies, religions, politics and interests—Muslims, Christians, Maatians, Ifans, nationalists, integrationists, womanists, feminists, civil rights and human rights advocates, leftists, rightists, centralists, Black conscious gay rights advocates, and finally, the male/female balance on every level.

A second achievement, then, was reaffirmation of the centrality of male/female relations, not only to the Movement but the community as a whole. The essentiality of partnership in equality was always a key concern in both the conception and crafting of the project and women were in every capacity from executive committee members to co-MC. Even the Muslim women played key roles, not only in the executive committee, but at every level including security.

A third achievement was the level and quality of organization achieved to plan and carry out the project given its diverse participants and the magnitude of the event. This becomes clear in putting together the program for the day and balancing the collective interests of the project and the particular interests of the participants while maintaining and effective operational unity in the process.

Certainly, the massive turnout was also an achievement in itself. Estimates range from 500,000 to 800,000 plus. This is significant because of the need to overcome the usual declining interest and fervor in a follow-up event and also because the project lacked the mass media attention of the MMM/DOA in '95. The established order hoped it could disrupt the MMM/DOA by demonizing Min. Farrakhan and creating a gender rift. Having failed on both counts and actually inspiring Black defiance of this ploy, the media decided to give little or no coverage of the MMM 2005. But we prevail in spite of this.

Another important achievement is the transformation of former critics into participants and allies. This included preachers, civil rights leaders, feminists who joined the project early and played various roles in organizing and endorsement. It also is expressed in the fact that a gay rights organization that criticized the March has now accepted the primary Black focus of the Movement and joined it. It reminds one of a verse in the sacred *Husia* that says, "I kept my mouth free from attacking those who attacked me. My patient work turned my foes into friends and my enemies into allies."

Also important is that the project was clearly an act and practice of self-determination. It was conceived by Black people, planned, financed, organized and made successful by Black people. Again, the NOI as the key organization assumed the greatest share of responsibility for this, but it was also due to a wide range of African people who answered the call, stood up, stepped forward and helped bring it to success.

Moreover, an achievement of the project lies in its prefiguring in the community and society what we all want and deserve to live in and for which we work and struggle so hard. It is a community and society made up of men and women in equal partnership and shared responsibility to build an ethically grounded and empowered community, a just and good society, and a good and sustainable world. And it is a project respectful of diversity, self-determined and of necessity self-consciously committed not only to the health and wholeness of African people, but also with the well-being of the world in the social and natural sense.

Finally, the achievements of the MMM culminate in its offering a model of success and possibility. It is a model of leadership and organization, diversity, self-determination, operational unity, quality male/female partnership in repairing ourselves and the world, and the infinite resources and longing of the masses to enrich and expand their lives and forge a future worthy of our children, our people and the world.

The challenge now is to extract its best ideas and best practices and move from March to Movement. For in the final analysis, the March was the site of the message and our initial working together in preparation and practice for the larger project. And this project is none other than to build a social and ethical project and partnership with our people which not only aids them in satisfying their needs, but also raises their aspirations and makes them self-conscious agents of their own lives and liberation and the building of the new world we all work and struggle for.

2005 December 1

Striving and Struggling in Gary; Pimpin' and Hustlin' in Hollywood

It is a cold, clear and instructive contrast, one you can't miss or misread. Even if you have lost your eye-sight but still retain some of your in-sight, you can see it. There we were last week gathering in Gary, Indiana, the site of the historic Gary Convention of 1972, revisiting the Black Agenda forged there and recommitting ourselves to continue the striving and struggling for freedom, justice, power of our people, a just peace and a heavy good in the world. And there "they" were on Oscar night, seemingly a world away—the producers and performers, the puppeteers and puppets, locked in a lascivious embrace of common and corrupt cause, savoring the music, the moment and dreams of mo' money, pimpin', 'ho-in' and hustlin' in Hollywood.

And I thought about the sacrifice and struggles of Malcolm X and Fannie Lou Hamer, Ella Baker and Martin King, Frederick Douglass and Harriet Tubman, my parents and grandparents, and our people in general. I had been invited to give the luncheon address on Friday which was positioned between Harry Belafonte in the morning and Minister Louis Farrakhan in the afternoon. And I thought about them, their long-time commitment to the struggle and their recent international initiatives to reaffirm our role as a social and moral vanguard in the world and how they call constant attention to the countries and corporations that are the real and ruthless pimps and hustlers that prey on the world.

And then I turned again to the issue of hustlin' and pimpin' in Hollywood and thought how important it is to continue the struggle for political, economic and cultural liberation. There are many who wonder how could and why would Hollywood give an Oscar to Three 6 Mafia for its song, "*It's Hard Out Here for a Pimp*". But this is just another method the established order uses to normalize its racism. And they do this, not only by projecting deformed images of us, but also by encouraging us to see ourselves in the same way, so that we collaborate in our own oppression and degradation.

As I said at the Convention, one of the greatest powers on earth is the capacity to define reality and make others accept it, even when it's to their disadvantage. Thus, like Wal-Mart with Andy Young, the real hustlers of Hollywood team up with Black producers, actors and others to push their perverse products, sing their artificial praise and share their profits with them in a small, insignificant negro-kind-of-way. It's one of the problems of the Movement, that some members of the middle class, in their haste and hustle to "make it", sacrifice mass interests for class and personal interests, and torn from their roots among the people, often superficially embrace lumpen life like Whites, as the essence and most exciting aspect of Black life.

And so, it is said in some circles of Hollywood hustle that it's all about artistic freedom and creative excellence and that raw lumpen lyrics reflect the realness of Black life and deserve recognition, reward and even respect, not community censorship. But to suggest that the lowest form of Black life is its highest is to remake us into their own racist image and interests. It is to reduce the whole to a single part, to define the raw and vulgar as real, and to attempt to discredit the upright and virtuous as unreal and naive.

We all know that artistic freedom has both racial and political limits, as Ice-T discovered. Regardless of what can be and is said about peoples of color, there are some White ethnics you can't touch, signify or sing about if you want to stay in the flow of things. Nor can you say anything you want about the president or police. And in spite of claims of no censorship, the academy bleeped this so-called real Blackness when it came to White happy-home hour, or what they call in public, prime time. Before they even asked, J. Houston, the group leader of Three-6 Mafia, said "I started changing the lyrics as soon as we got nominated and I was happy to do it. I would have changed the whole song, every line, if the academy asked me to." So much for independent thug-thought and practice. Now contrast this to ducking behind the high bushes of hustle to claim artistic and personal freedom in raw resistance to community calls for even a modicum of dignity, decency and self-respect.

Hidden also in this sympathetic movie portrait of the hard-hustlin' pimp and his signature song, is the real-life brutalization and degradation of Black women, marketed as literally open to and for exploitation every day and way wanted. The Hon. C. Delores Tucker, a founder of the National Black Women's Political Caucus, spent the last years of her life leading the struggle, along with her husband Bill, to expose the corrosive effect of gangsta rap and to end corporate support for the racism, sexism and self-degradation that saturate its lumpen lyrics and deform the lives of its adherents. But it was and remains a hard struggle, for not only is gangsta rap wedded to music and married to money; it fits well within the racist and sexist character of society.

And this brings us back to Gary and our unfinished struggle. I began my lecture at Gary Convention II where we all must ultimately begin and end, stressing the need for striving and struggling for our common good and not letting ourselves be seduced by fantasies of false freedom and isolated advancement. As I told those gathered, "we are ever present at the crossroads of history with our foremother Harriet Tubman, who having freed herself, realized that whatever measure of freedom she had achieved on her own personal initiative, it was not meaningful or secure until the rest of her people were free. For she realized that Black freedom is indivisible and that as long as any Black person, any African, anywhere in the world is oppressed and denied dignity and freedom, all of us are somehow denied, damaged, and deformed. She realized that freedom was not simple flight nor individual advancement nor escape. Rather freedom, in its most substantive form, is the self-conscious practice of self-determination in and for community, and ultimately directed towards bringing good into the world."

2006 March 22

Concerning Seasons of Fire and Struggles for Freedom

In talking about catalysts in the building and takeoff of a Movement, we in The Organization Us say, "one spark in the right season and situation can set a whole forest on fire." By right season we mean the right time, a point at which the people are pushed to the edge of endurance, and by right situation we mean the right conditions, the point at which the masses always in motion form a critical mass, have a clear vision and strong organization, and develop an unbreakable will to struggle.

The widespread discussions of the passing, life and legacy of Mrs. Rosa Parks last week, rightfully raised questions about the making of history and the emergence and meaning of history makers. Without denying or diminishing the importance of Mrs. Parks to the Black Freedom Movement, we must give similar respect and a rightful reading of history to others whose life and struggle left legacies similar to her own. And we must always pay due homage and rightful respect to African American people and the process of struggle which made the Black Freedom Movement possible. Indeed, one of the greatest challenges in understanding and appreciating the Black Freedom Movement (1955-1975), both its Civil Rights and Black Power phases, is to recognize the continuity, comprehensiveness and complexity of the history out of which it emerges and in which it has its most definitive meaning.

We speak of continuity because we know that nothing comes into being by itself. All we do and are is shaped and often determined by that which comes before us. Thus, the Movement has a past, a past of relentless resistance and ongoing struggle. It is a struggle which reaches back to our fierce and heroic resistance to the European invasion, conquest, colonization and enslavement of Africa. And it continues during the Holocaust of enslavement in this country and during Reconstruction, culminating in the struggle against the savage system of segregation and the cave-like legalized and vigilante violence that accompanied it.

Secondly, we speak of comprehensiveness because a movement by definition is a broad based inclusive process and practice. It involves the masses and their many and various organizations, strategies for struggle, ideas and actions in pursuit of common goals.

Thus, a comprehensive focus on the Montgomery Movement's coming-into-being and growing stronger includes not only Rosa Parks, but also Jo Ann Robinson and the Women's Political Council, E.D. Nixon, of the Brotherhood of Pullman Porters and local NAACP, the Montgomery Improvement Association, the central organization for leading the Movement and Martin Luther King, Jr., leader of the MIA.

Likewise, in speaking of the larger national Black Freedom Movement and its origins in the struggles that immediately preceded it, we must include the NAACP, Charles Houston and the Brown Case, Ida B. Wells-Barnett and the campaign against lynching, and Messenger Elijah Muhammad and the Nation of Islam which stressed Black dignity and divinity, self-help and unity, and many other personal and collective initiatives of resistance and refusal to comply or remain quiet and inactive in our oppression.

Finally, we speak of complexity because so often we seek the simple solution, the single person and focus in situations where a more varied and elaborate understanding is required. We are taught to reduce the origins of the Movement to one person's sitting down. But it was the standing up in struggle of Mrs. Parks, others and the people that created the Movement in Montgomery and the U.S. as a whole. Moreover, we know that even as Ms. Parks and the MIA were standing up in Montgomery, other people elsewhere were also standing up and struggling. And all these struggles served as sparks which combined gave birth to our national Movement.

Certainly, the gruesome lynching of Emmett Till and the heroic struggle for justice waged by his mother, Ms. Mamie Till Mobley, stands also as a clear catalyst for the Civil Rights Movement and the Black Freedom Movement as whole, as Dr. Clenora Hudson-Weems has argued. Thus, it is important to understand both the Montgomery Boycott and the struggle for justice for Emmett Till as dual catalysts of the Movement, each a vital spark in the right season and situation which combined with other sites of struggle to set the whole forest of segregation and oppression on fire.

In Montgomery, it was the bus boycott around the arrest of Mrs. Rosa Parks, which offered a model and inspiration to African people as a whole. In the case of Emmett Till and the struggle waged by his mother, Ms. Till-Mobley for justice for him and the end of lynching, the consciousness and conscience of the people and the country were raised and challenged. And the country was exposed and put on trial for White supremacist savagery before the world. Black people all over the country felt a righteous anger and outrage at this barbaric act and were inspired by the courage of two Black men, Mose Wright and Willie Reed, who under threat of certain death, testified against Emmett Till's murderers. And people stood up, joined the struggle, made the Movement, and dared change themselves, society and the course of history.

Society, however, prefers to talk about sitting down in Montgomery rather than mutilation, murder and lynching in Mississippi. After all, how would cable and network news cover the savage and sadistic lynching of a 15-year old boy for an alleged transgression of White racist protocol? And how would corporations take out ads to honor Ms. Till-Mobley, righteously outraged, resisting calls for quiet and deferential ways to approach our oppression and the lynching of her son and instead, screaming and struggling for justice in loud and assertive ways?

The Hon. Marcus Garvey taught us that "our history is too important to be left in alien hands." Thus, we, ourselves, must write and speak the history we've made, an awesome history of struggle, sacrifice, achievement and eventual victory over our oppression, regardless of the odds against us.

2005 November 10

 VIII

Postscript

"We are the last revolutionaries in America. If we fail to leave a legacy of revolution for our children, we have failed our mission and should be dismissed as unimportant."

The Quotable Karenga (1967)
Maulana Karenga

Challenge and Task

Our challenge is to reaffirm our central identity in a vision and practice that not only improves and expands our lives as a community, but at the same time poses a central vision for a new public philosophy and policy for this country.

Our task then is to reestablish a *collective vocation* for our community which is not only the basis of our self-understanding and self-assertion but also contributes definitively to a new and expanded public philosophy and discourse on the just and good society in a global context. In a word, we must initiate and sustain a public discourse, which produces policies and practice with a substantive moral character as distinct from the current almost exclusive focus on procedures of right and justice.

Our central model is the Black Freedom Movement which from 1955 to 1975 was not only a struggle for rights and procedures but for the reaffirmation of human dignity, not only a means to achieve equal rights but a process of empowerment and expanding our self-understanding as agents of change, defenders of the good, and soldiers for the poor, vulnerable and marginal, in a word, a moral vanguard for the country and in a larger sense, the world. The need, then, is to recover this history and all that represents the best of what it means to be both African and human and to use it to shape a foundation for our present and future.

The public philosophy we propose then must be self-consciously *ethical* as distinct from the essentially *procedural*. For it is not simply laws we seek to be used to declare the end of racism or statistics, which show economic growth in spite of obvious human poverty. Rather, it is *access, opportunity* and *results* that emerge from reflection, discussion and action rooted in a profound belief in the Divine, a concern with achieving the good life and an ethical understanding of the conditions for human freedom and human flourishing in society and the world.

In the context of the best of African tradition, this means our initiation of a national discourse and practice, which are self-consciously rooted in and reflective of a profound and ongoing

267

commitment to: (1) the dignity and rights of the human person; (2) the well-being and flourishing of family and community; (3) the integrity and value of the environment; and (4) the reciprocal solidarity and cooperation for mutual benefit of humanity.

In this regard our central thrust should be to create a public philosophy and practice rooted in The Ethics of Sharing: (1) shared status; (2) shared knowledge; (3) shared space; (4) shared wealth; (5) shared power; (6) shared interests; and (7) shared responsibility (to build the good world we all want and deserve).

From *The Ethics of Sharing*

Maulana Karenga
(2002)

Commitment to Struggle

We come bringing the most central views and values of our faith communities, our deepest commitments to our social justice tradition and the struggle it requires, the most instructive lessons of our history, and a profoundly urgent sense of the need for positive and productive action. In standing up and assuming responsibility in a new, renewed and expanded sense, we honor our ancestors, enrich our lives and give promise to our descendants. Moreover, through this historic work and struggle we strive to always know and introduce ourselves to history and humanity as a people who are spiritually and ethically grounded; who speak truth, do justice, respect our ancestors and elders, cherish, support and challenge our children, care for the vulnerable, relate rightfully to the environment, struggle for what is right and resist what is wrong, honor our past, willingly engage our present and self-consciously plan for and welcome our future.

From *The Million Man March/Day of Absence*
Mission Statement

Maulana Karenga
(1995)

About the Author

Dr. Maulana Karenga is professor of Black Studies at California State University, Long Beach. He is also chair of the President's Task Force on Multicultural Education and Campus Diversity at California State University, Long Beach. Dr. Karenga holds two Ph.D.'s; his first in political science with focus on the theory and practice of nationalism (United States International University) and his second in social ethics with a focus on the classical African ethics of ancient Egypt (University of Southern California). He also holds an honorary doctorate of philosophy from the University of Durban-Westville, South Africa.

Moreover, he is the director of the Kawaida Institute of Pan-African Studies, Los Angeles, and national chairman of The Organization Us, a cultural and social change organization, so named to stress the communitarian focus of the organization. Dr. Karenga has had a profound and far-reaching effect on Black intellectual and political culture. Through his organization Us and his philosophy, *Kawaida*, he has played a vanguard role in shaping the Black Arts Movement, Black Studies, the Black Power Movement, Black Student Union Movement, Afrocentricity, rites of passage programs, the study of ancient Egyptian culture as an essential part of Black Studies, the independent Black school movement, African life-cycle ceremonies, the Simba Wachanga youth movement, and Black theological and ethical discourse.

Dr. Karenga is also widely known as the creator of *Kwanzaa*, an African American and Pan-African holiday celebrated throughout the world African community on every continent in the world. He is the author of the authoritative book on the subject: *Kwanzaa: A Celebration of Family, Community and Culture* and lectures regularly and extensively on the vision and values of Kwanzaa, especially the *Nguzo Saba* (The Seven Principles), in various national and international venues.

Dr. Karenga has also played a key role in national united front efforts, serving on the founding and executive committee of the Black

269

Power Conferences of the 60's, the National Black United Front, the National African American Leadership Summit, the Black Leadership Retreat, the National Association of Kawaida Organizations (NAKO) and on the national organizing committee of the Million Man March/Day of Absence as well as authored the *Mission Statement* for this joint project.

Dr. Karenga is author of numerous scholarly articles and books, including: *Introduction to Black Studies*, the most widely used intro text in Black Studies; *Selections From The Husia: Sacred Wisdom of Ancient Egypt; The Book of Coming Forth By Day: The Ethics of the Declarations of Innocence; Kawaida: A Communitarian African Philosophy;* and a translation and ethical commentary on the classical Yoruba text titled, *Odu Ifa: The Ethical Teachings.* His most recent publication is *Maat, The Moral Ideal in Ancient Egypt: A Study in Classical African Ethics.* An activist-scholar of national and international recognition, he has lectured on the life and struggle of African peoples on the major campuses of the U.S.A. and in Senegal, Nigeria, Egypt, South Africa, the People's Republic of China, Cuba, Trinidad, Britain and Canada.

He also served as chairman of the African American delegation to the Second World Black and African Festival of Arts and Culture, Lagos, Nigeria, 1977; the spokesman for a delegation of African American Educators of Independent Schools to the People's Republic of China; 1977; member of the Planning Committee for the Pan-African Festival of Arts and Culture, Dakar, Senegal, 1986; chairman of the delegation of educators/activists of the Organization Us to Cuba, 1986; co-planner and co-convener of the Annual Ancient Egyptian Studies Conference of the Association for the Study of Classical African Civilizations, Cairo, Egypt, 1987; Inaugural Lecturer for the initiation of Black History Month, London, England, 1987, Honorary Doctorate Recipient and Commencement Speaker, University of Durban--Westville, South Africa, 1998 and Official Guest and Lecturer, 160th Anniversary of Emancipation, Port-of-Spain, Trinidad and Tobago, 1998.

Moreover, he is the recipient of numerous awards for scholarship, leadership and community service including: the National Leadership Award for Outstanding Scholarly Achievements in Black Studies from the National Council for Black Studies; the Diop Exemplary Leadership Award from the Department of African American Studies-Temple University; the Richard Allen Living Legend Award from the

African Methodist Episcopal Church; the Pioneer Award from the Rainbow PUSH Coalition and Citizenship Education Fund; the Executive Committee Award for a Lifetime of Achievements, Department of Africology, University of Wisconsin-Milwaukee; the Outstanding Humanitarian Award, the Nigerian Community of Southern California and Associated Groups; the C.L.R. James Award for Outstanding Publication of Scholarly Works that Advance the Discipline of Africana and Black Studies, the National Council for Black Studies; and the Distinguished Africanist Award, the New York African Studies Association.

Index